324.2736 O31
Of the people :
33090003810548

P9-DNP-078

NO LONGER PROPERTY OF
THE LONG BEACH
PUBLIC LIBRARY

LONG BEACH PUBLIC LIBRARY
101 PACIFIC AVENUE
LONG BEACH, CA 90822

# Of The People...

"Sometimes it is said that man can not be trusted with the government of himself. Can he, then, be trusted with the government of others? Or have we found angels in the forms of kings to govern him? Let history answer that question."

—THOMAS JEFFERSON
In his inaugural address, March 4, 1801

# Of The People...

## THE 200-YEAR HISTORY
## OF THE DEMOCRATIC PARTY

329.3
O31o

NORTH

GENERAL PUBLISHING GROUP

*Los Angeles*

## DOROTHY BUSH
### IN MEMORIAM

Dorothy Bush was the memory of the institutional Democratic Party. As secretary of the Party for 46 years, she called the Roll of the States at 12 consecutive Democratic conventions. She was a living link between Franklin Roosevelt and Michael Dukakis, remembering our progressive roots and our fighting spirit, and demanding that the rest of us not forget.

Although influences as diverse as television, the McGovern Commission and the Mississippi Freedom Democratic Party transformed the way we selected our candidates, the way their nominations were announced to the nation never changed. While floor whips scrambled for delegates; while commentators added up and second-guessed; while delegates screamed and cheered for their states, their candidates, their favorite sons, Dorothy moved inexorably down the list.

But calling the roll was only the most glamorous of Dorothy's duties—a fitting reward for refereeing the fights and healing the wounds that every primary season brings. Forty years' experience distanced her from momentary rifts and enabled her to help the Party pull itself together.

The 1992 convention in New York will be the first in 48 years at which Dorothy Bush will not call the roll. We will miss her voice. We will remember her vision.

3 3090 00381 0548

Publisher: W. Quay Hays
Editor: Murray Fisher
Art Director: Deborah Daly, Daly Design
Assistant Editor: G. Colby Allerton
Assistant Art Director: Tanya Maiboroda
Production Director: Johann Tafertshofer
Typesetting and Color Separations: JT&A—Los Angeles, CA
Photo and Illustration Research: Diane Hamilton, Marilyn Wandrus
Research Assistant: Deborah Dickerson
Production Coordinator: Alan Sakato
Copy Editors: Nancy McKinley, Giovanni Pietanza

The publisher wishes to thank the following for their contributions to this book:
Special thanks to Joe Louis Barrow, Jr. and Eric London

The Democratic National Committee: Joan Baggett, Ronald H. Brown, Carol Darr, Brian Foucart, Charles Sweeney Ginny Terzano and Frank Williams

Contributors: Senator Bill Bradley, President Jimmy Carter, Governor Bill Clinton, Congresswoman Geraldine Ferraro, Senator Albert Gore, Reverend Jesse Jackson, Congresswoman Barbara Jordan, Senator Edward M. Kennedy, Senator George McGovern, Senator George J. Mitchell, Speaker Thomas P. "Tip" O'Neill, Governor Ann Richards

Very Special Thanks to: Jeff Butler, Stan Corwin, Kevin Eaton, John Emerson, Mark Hatfield, Jr., Sharon L. Hays, Sarah Fisher, Neal Levin, Sarah McMullen, Jean Paul Nataf, Deborah M. Nessett, Susan Ostrov, Robert Persson, Kelly Persson, Margo Romero, Johann Tafertshofer

Copyright © 1992 by General Publishing Group, Inc.
All rights reserved under International and Pan-American Copyright Conventions. This book, or any parts thereof, may not be reproduced in any fashion whatsoever without the prior written permission of the Publisher. For information address: General Publishing Group, Inc. 606 North Larchmont Boulevard, Los Angeles, California 90004

All views and opinions contained herein are solely those of the authors.

**Library of Congress Cataloging-in-Publication Data:**

Of the people—the 200 year history of the Democratic Party / [chronicled by America's foremost historians].
    p.  cm.
    Includes index.
    ISBN 1-881649-00-8 : $29.95
    1. Democratic Party (U.S.)—History.   I. General Publishing Group, Inc.
JK2316.034  1992
324.2736'09—dc20
                           92-72412
                              CIP

PRINTED IN THE USA BY CALIFORNIA OFFSET PRINTERS -9
10 9 8 7 6 5 4 3 2 1

# THE AUTHORS

RONALD H. BROWN, chairman of the Democratic National Committee, has had a long and distinguished career in Democratic politics, which includes serving as General Counsel and Staff Director for Senator Edward Kennedy and chairing the Task Force on Voting Rights and Voter Participation. He has been a political advisor to several presidential campaigns.

JOHN KENNETH GALBRAITH is the Paul M. Warburg Professor of Economics Emeritus at Harvard University. The award-winning author of over 20 books, he has served as John F. Kennedy's ambassador to India from 1961 to 1963.

ARTHUR SCHLESINGER, JR., a distinguished historian, is the author of many books, including *The Disuniting of America*. His long list of political posts includes a term as former special assistant to President Kennedy.

PAULINE MAIER, the William Rand Kenan, Jr., Professor of American History at MIT, received her Ph.D. from Harvard University. Her publications include *From Resistance to Revolution: Colonial Radicals and the Development of American Opposition to Britain, 1765–1776* and *The American People: A History*.

LANCE BANNING, an award-winning writer, is Assistant Professor of History at the University of Kentucky. His books have been nominated for Pulitzer and Bancroft Awards, among others, and he has numerous articles and essays in publication.

ROBERT V. REMINI is Professor Emeritus of History, and Research Professor Emeritus of Humanities at the University of Illinois at Chicago. He has authored seventeen books, including a three-volume biography of Andrew Jackson which won the National Book Award for nonfiction.

JEAN H. BAKER, a Professor of History at Goucher College in Baltimore, Maryland, is the author of a biography of Mary Todd Lincoln as well as several books on nineteenth century political history.

MICHAEL McGERR, Associate Professor of History at Indiana University, is the author of *The Decline of Popular Politics: The American North, 1865–1928*. A graduate of Yale University, he has also taught at the Massachusetts Institute of Technology.

JOHN MILTON COOPER, JR. is chairman of the Department of History at the University of Wisconsin. He has served as member or chairman of prestigious committees including the Advisory Committee for the White House Bicentennial Celebration.

ALAN BRINKLEY, Professor of History at Columbia University, is the author of *Voices of Protest: Huey Long, Father Coughlin, and the Great Depression* and the forthcoming *The Transformation of New Deal Liberalism, 1937–1946*.

ALONZO L. HAMBY is a Professor of History at Ohio University and the author of several books and numerous reviews and articles on the history of liberalism and the modern Democratic Party over the past 50 years.

STEVEN M. GILLON, Associate Professor of History at Yale University, is the author of *Politics and Vision: The ADA and American Liberalism* and *The Democrats' Dilemma: Walter F. Mondale and the Liberal Legacy*.

WILLIAM E. LEUCHTENBURG is the William Rand Kenan, Jr., Professor at the University of North Carolina. An award-winning historian, he has written, edited or contributed to over 40 books and has served as a consultant for studies and films including Ken Burns' monumental Civil War series on PBS.

GEORGE C. HERRING, Alumni Professor of History at the University of Kentucky, is a specialist in the history of U.S. foreign relations. His recent work, which has focused on the Vietnam War, includes *America's Longest War: The United States and Vietnam, 1950–1975*.

LARRY DUBOIS, a former staff writer for *Time* magazine, earned his masters degree from the Woodrow Wilson School of Public and International Affairs at Princeton University. His political articles have appeared in numerous publications including the *New York Times Magazine*.

DANICA KIRKA is a free-lance political writer whose work has appeared in the *Los Angeles Times*, the *Boston Globe*, the *San Francisco Chronicle* and the Associated Press.

ROBERT B. REICH teaches political economy at Harvard's John F. Kennedy School of Government. He served in the Carter administration as director of the Federal Trade Commission's policy planning staff, and has authored seven books, the most recent being *The Works of Nations*.

# CONTENTS

INTRODUCTION / 9
*A Legacy of Greatness*
BY RONALD H. BROWN

PREFACE / 11
*The Two-Party System: Retrospect, Prospect*
BY JOHN KENNETH GALBRAITH

FOREWORD / 13
*The Parties' Origins*
BY ARTHUR SCHLESINGER, JR.

CHAPTER ONE / 17
*The Struggle for Democracy*
1776–1800
BY PAULINE MAIER

CHAPTER TWO / 35
*The Jeffersonians in Power*
1801–1824
BY LANCE BANNING

CHAPTER THREE / 49
*Years of Triumph*
1825–1848
BY ROBERT V. REMINI

CHAPTER FOUR / 63
*In The Wilderness*
1849–1872
BY JEAN H. BAKER

CHAPTER FIVE / 81
*The Gilded Age*
1873–1896
BY MICHAEL McGERR

CHAPTER SIX / 95
*The Best...and Worst of Times*
1897–1920
BY JOHN MILTON COOPER, JR.

CHAPTER SEVEN / 113
*The Roosevelt Era*
1921–1944
BY ALAN BRINKLEY

CHAPTER EIGHT / 129
*New Frontiers*
1945–1968
BY ALONZO L. HAMBY

CHAPTER NINE / 145
*The Challenge Of Diversity*
1969–1992
BY STEVEN M. GILLON

CHAPTER TEN / 157
*Domestic Policy:*
*A Call for Compassion*
BY WILLIAM E. LEUCHTENBURG

CHAPTER ELEVEN / 167
*Foreign Policy:*
*A Beacon of Freedom*
BY GEORGE C. HERRING

CHAPTER TWELVE / 179
*Portraits of Ten Great Democrats*
BY LARRY DuBOIS

CHAPTER THIRTEEN / 201
*Why I'm A Democrat...*
INTERVIEWED BY DANICA KIRKA

AFTERWORD / 215
*Facing the Challenges Ahead*
BY ROBERT B. REICH

*Index* / 221
*Credits* / 224

# INTRODUCTION

# A LEGACY OF GREATNESS

## BY DEMOCRATIC NATIONAL COMMITTEE CHAIRMAN RONALD H. BROWN

In 1992 we Democrats are celebrating not only a political party but also a national vision. It is a vision of strength and power—our strength, America's power—flowing not from an isolated governing clique, but from millions of economically empowered, socially diverse and politically active Americans. Two hundred years ago, our Party's founders decided that wealth and social status were not an entitlement to rule. That wisdom and compassion could be found within every individual. That a stable government must be built upon a broad popular base.

The common thread of Democratic history, from Thomas Jefferson to Bill Clinton, has been an abiding faith in the judgment of hard-working American families, and a commitment to helping the excluded, the disenfranchised and the poor strengthen our nation by earning themselves a piece of the American Dream. We remember that this great land was sculpted by immigrants and slaves, their children and grandchildren.

The Democratic Party embraced the immigrants who flooded into cities and industrial centers, built a political base by bringing them into the American mainstream, and together we created the most powerful economic engine in history.

A generation later, Franklin Roosevelt pulled us out of the Depression by looking beyond the Democratic base and bringing water to California's Central Valley, electrifying Appalachia, saving farms across the Midwest. The Civilian Conservation Corps, the WPA, So-cial Security all brought Americans into the system, freeing us from fear, giving us a stake in the future, making the nation stronger. And with Harry Truman we began the fight to bring down the final barriers of race and gender. Though we have far to go, America has made tremendous progress.

My election as Party Chair is a testament to our success in breaking down walls. We must remember, however, that this chapter in our Party's history is the result of a 50-year Democratic commitment to civil rights and 200 years of reaching out to build a party of inclusion and diversity.

I truly believe that the Democratic Party is America's last, best hope to bridge the divisions of race, region, religion and ethnicity. As chairman, I see the history of our next hundred years in the mosaic of colors and ethnicities, of blue-collar workers and white-collar professionals, of the men and women who make up the Democratic Party.

As we hurtle toward a century of unknown challenges and immeasurable opportunity, the fundamental ideals of our Party have never been more critical. The government that leads us through these times must itself be governed by the same principles that have made America the greatest nation on Earth. The Democratic Party, the party "Of The People," has demonstrated for 200 years an unsurpassed devotion to the principles of strength, inclusion and opportunity. We led America to greatness.

We are ready to lead once more.

# PREFACE

# THE TWO-PARTY SYSTEM: RETROSPECT, PROSPECT

## BY JOHN KENNETH GALBRAITH

I t is now 52 years, slightly more than half a century, since I first became involved in the literary politics of a presidential campaign. My initiation was in 1940; in the autumn of that year I was asked to join a small group preparing speech drafts for FDR. We worked in a modest suite of offices at the Department of Commerce. In those relaxed and tolerant days, it did not call for comment or even thought that we were using official space, and for that matter, we were all on the public payroll. I trust that George Bush will not think this a precedent.

Only one of our contributions from that effort, alas not mine, remains in public memory. In speaking of the inevitable Republican opposition to the twentieth century, FDR made his deathless reference to the articulate advocacy of "Martin, Barton and Fish." The lovely sequence of names went over to the White House from us.

Later, with Stevenson, Kennedy, Johnson, Eugene McCarthy and George McGovern, I returned in some role, large or often quite small, to the presidential trail and trial.

Over these years I've never had occasion to doubt the deeper merits of two-party government. At its best it presents to the voter clear and understandable alternatives. The multiple choices in other countries of the democratic world and the ultimate coalitions, strong or weak, often leave me confused, as also they often do the citizens there.

However, if ours is a democracy based on simple, straightforward choice, there is one thing that is indispensable: There must be a choice. From this alone comes socially effective democracy. Only then does politics have purpose. And, on the record, only then for Democrats is there political success at the polls. Roosevelt, Truman, Kennedy, Johnson and, I think, Jimmy Carter in his first campaign offered such an alternative. And they won. When we did not offer an alternative, we lost.

The Republican Party is rightly the party of the economically comfortable, the self-regarding and the affluent. There is nothing wrong with that. Ronald Reagan's rich friends had their right to be heard and to urge, in this case with notable success, the political doctrine and the tax benefits that very specifically reflected their personal interest. It was natural that they should urge the now-famous doctrine that the rich were not working because they had too little money, the poor because they had too much.

The Democrats must be different: Our task is to speak unashamedly and clearly for those who, from need or aspiration, must have the support of compassionate, intelligent, effective and affirmative government. This is not a decision to be made in accordance with a controlling theoretical doctrine. There should be no surrender of thought to economic theology. No one denies the large and essential role of the market, of private enterprise in all its diverse forms. Equally we know that trade unions, minority rights, old-age security, unemployment compensation, support to public education, farm price supports, public health care, intelligent action to mitigate the sequence of boom and bust are what made capitalism tolerable. These are what calmed the angry and revolutionary attitudes that in the last century and early in this one threatened to destroy the system, a threat that instilled in one branch of the Republican Party its extreme, highly vocal and still continuing paranoia.

Only when the Democratic Party offers a socially effective alternative does it bring into its ranks—and to the polls—not alone the concerned and the compassionate but also the socially and economically excluded. That has been our strength in the past; that is where it will be in the future. We are the party of the middle class. We have also a deep commitment to the underclass. This commitment, I venture to suggest, we have not always seen.

In the heat of political campaigns, our candidates have more than occasionally become the victims of the current political strategist. This is an individual who is deeply versed in simple arithmetic, who believes that we win not by appealing to, motivating and enlarging our own constituency, but by subtracting votes from the Republicans. Relentlessly available to the media, the strategist tells in admiring detail of this design. The larger result is that the vital part of our natural constituency is persuaded that the difference in the two-party system is not sufficiently great to justify a trip to the polls. Turnout falls to a miserable half or less of the eligible electorate; in that half, alas, lies the Republican majority.

This was a mistake that Roosevelt, Truman, Kennedy and Johnson did not make. It is to Harry Truman we owe the enduring observation that when faced with a choice between a true conservative and an imitation conservative, the voters will always opt for the real thing.

So let us have no doubts as to the merits of the two-party system. But let us know that it works only when the voters are offered a clear choice. Such choice we must always offer.

This leads me to conclude with a favorable word on the Republicans. Not recently in our history have a party and its Presidents done so much to help clarify and make certain a choice. Mr. Reagan and Mr. Bush have their shortcomings, but no one can doubt the rich genius they have brought to articulating and giving practical effect to the kind of uncompassionate, wealth-favoring, expensively militarized, economically and socially negative government that, we may be sure, the majority of the American people do not want. Building on this help from the Republicans, our task is clear. It is to present an alternative, one that brings our potentially vast constituency with enthusiasm to the polls. Thus we win; no less, we validate the true worth of the two-party system.

# FOREWORD

# THE PARTIES' ORIGINS

## BY ARTHUR SCHLESINGER, JR.

We regard party competition today as the essence of democracy. Political parties, we assume, are the indispensable means by which citizens make the fateful decision who should govern them. Yet the rise of political parties was one of the last things the Founding Fathers intended or wanted; on the contrary, they regarded parties not as a means of democratic self-government but as a threat to it. Nevertheless, the decade after the adoption of the Constitution witnessed the beginnings of a party system. How to explain this swift emergence of parties in an ideologically anti-party Republic?

George Washington himself, offering his fellow citizens a political testament in his farewell address, had warned in the sternest language against "the baneful effects of the spirit of party." Parties, he said, were "potent engines by which cunning, ambitious and unprincipled men will . . . subvert the power of the people." The spirit of party was demagogic and for popular governments "truly their worst enemy." The "alternate domination of one faction over another" would lead, the Father of his Country solemnly told the American people, to "formal and permanent despotism."

Washington was expressing the philosophy historians term *classical republicanism*, which called for the subordination of private and local interests to the good of the commonwealth. In the classical republican view, the duty of the President was to stand above party and faction and to provide non-partisan leadership dedicated to the common good. *Faction,* the eighteenth century term for party, was abhorred as the vehicle of special interests and thus by definition the foe of the common good.

The fear of factionalism—and factionalism's product, the demagogue—pervaded that famed commentary on the Constitution, the *Federalist Papers.* Alexander Hamilton, in the last paragraph of the last *Federalist,* spoke ominously about "the military despotism of a victorious demagogue." His great rival agreed on the dangers of party strife. "If I could not go to heaven but with a party," said Thomas Jefferson, "I would not go there at all."

Hamilton expressed these thoughts in 1788, Jefferson in 1789. Yet by 1792 the same two men were themselves leaders of factions that in short order turned into parties. What had happened to override the Founders' anti-party philosophy? Human nature, it appeared, created problems for classical republicanism. The "mischiefs of factions," James Madison admitted in the tenth *Federalist*, were "sown in the nature of man." It was a human propensity "to fall into mutual animosities." And of all the many sources of factions, the most common and durable, Madison said, is "the various and unequal distribution of property." Rich and poor, creditors and debtors, "a landed interest, a manufacturing interest, a mercantile interest, a moneyed interest, with many lesser interests, grow up of necessity in civilized nations, and divided them into different classes."

The "violence of faction," Madison continued, could no doubt be cured by destroying liberty; "liberty is to faction what air is to fire"; but that cure would be worse than the disease. For better or worse, special interest existed and could not be wished away. "The regulation of these various and interfering interests," Madison concluded, "forms the principal task of modern legislation, and involves the spirit of party and faction in the necessary and ordinary operations of government."

If party spirit could not be totally suppressed, it must at least, Washington thought, be discouraged and restrained. With Jefferson as his secretary of state and Hamilton as his secretary of the treasury, Washington worried increasingly about incipient factionalism within his own administration. By May 1792 both Hamilton and Jefferson were prepared to justify their conflict. In what he described as a "picture of political parties," Hamilton charged that the views of Jefferson and Madison were "subversive of the principles of good government and dangerous to the Union, peace and happiness of the country." In a letter that same month to Washington himself, Jefferson charged that Hamilton's views were designed "to prepare the way for a change from the present republican form of government to that of a monarchy." He went on to speak of "the republican party, who wish to preserve the government in its present form" against "the monarchical federalists."

There is no precise moment when it can be said that the first American parties were founded. But 1792 can be plausibly claimed as the year when they began to emerge from the chrysalis. Jefferson's party was initially known as the Republican Party; Hamilton's as the Federalist Party. In the fall election, the two factions had a rudimentary party confrontation. Both Republicans and Federalists supported Washington for a second term; but the Republicans tried unsuccessfully to replace the Federalist John Adams as Vice President with the Republican George Clinton. (Under the original Constitution and until the 12th Amendment in 1803, the candidate winning the most electoral votes became President, the runner-up Vice President.)

The 1796 election saw a straight-out party contest for the presidency between Adams and Jefferson. Adams won, thereby preserving Federalist rule. The decisive test for party government came in 1800. This time Jefferson's victory raised the question of a change of regime.

Each party had hitherto seen itself as the true embodiment of the popular will and the other as a transient and illegitimate faction without rightful role in the nation's politics. Each had hoped to abolish the other and restore the classical republican concept of national unity. With Jefferson's victory, the young Republic raised the crucial question whether it would accept "alternate domination of one faction over another" as a premise of self-government. Despite the bitterness of the election and lurid Federalist apprehensions about the new President, the change of regime took place peacefully. The result was to give political opposition the definitive seal of legitimacy and to make party competition an organic part of the Republic's unwritten Constitution.

Thus parties emerged in spite of Washington and of the anti-party philosophy. They emerged because of honest disagreements among honorable men over the interpretation of the Constitution they had drafted together a few years before—disagreements over state rights versus the national government, over economic policy, over foreign policy; disagreements proceeding in large part from the deeper conflict of interests Madison had described in the tenth *Federalist*.

And parties emerged because, it soon appeared, they were necessary in order to make the Constitution work. The constitutional principle of the separation of powers tended to pit the executive and legislative branches against each other. Yet effective government required their collaboration. The party now arose to supply the connective tissue that would enable the President to win congressional support for his policies.

Parties, moreover, assisted—initially, at least—in the consolidation of the new nation. Even if they were for a long time essentially coalitions of state parties, they were in form national associations and, until slavery became the salient issue, influences against provincialism and separatism. Differences were argued out within the parties as well as between them, so parties reinforced the techniques of compromise essential to democratic government. Henry D. Thoreau had little use for politics, but he grasped the role of parties: "Politics is, as it were, the gizzard of society, full of grit and gravel, and the two political parties are its two oppositive halves, which grind on each other."

And party competition, it developed, became in addition a salient form of mass entertainment. Americans in the early nineteenth century had all too little in the way of diversion—no baseball or football, no tennis or golf, no movies or radio or television. "To take a hand in the regulation of society and to discuss it," Alexis de Tocqueville noted when he visited America during the age of Jackson, "is his biggest concern and, so to speak, the only pleasure an American knows. . . . Even the women frequently attend public meetings and listen to political harangues as a recreation from their household labors. Debating clubs are, to a certain extent, a substitute for theatrical entertainments."

The institutionalization of the party system took time. The Federalist Party crumbled away after the War of 1812, running its last presidential candidate in 1816. President James Monroe had no opponent at all when he sought re-election in 1820 , and during the so-called Era of Good Feelings, the United States was in effect a one-party country.

But human nature and the conflict of interests could not be escaped. In the 1820s the Republican Party began to divide into two factions—the National Republicans, who represented the mercantile, financial and soon the industrial interest, and the Democratic Republicans, who represented the agricultural, artisan and soon the workingmen's interests. The National Republicans elected John Quincy Adams in 1824; the Democratic Republicans, soon known as the Democrats, elected Andrew Jackson in 1828.

Jackson's victory brought a full-blown party system into existence. Martin Van Buren, Jackson's friend and successor, the first President born an American citizen, was the great champion of the organized party with party machinery, national conventions and national committees, all held together by party discipline and the cult of party loyalty. Van Buren had no doubt that parties were the destined instruments of American self-government. Party battles, Van Buren said, "rouse the sluggish to exertion, give increased energy to the most active intellect, excite a salutary vigilance over our public functionaries, and prevent that apathy which has proved the ruin of Republics."

The National Republicans became the Whigs in 1834, and in another 20 years the disintegration of the Whigs led on to the formation of the Republican Party, thereby setting the terms of party competition for at least the next century and a half. The Democratic Party, the first party, was the model—and, faithful through most of its life to its Jeffersonian and Jacksonian roots, it remains after two centuries the oldest political party in continuous existence anywhere in the world.

Thomas Jefferson and Benjamin Franklin were members of a five-man committee appointed by the Continental Congress to draw up America's Declaration of Independence from England. Because of his writing skills, it was Jefferson who drafted the document, an eloquent denunciation of British rule that laid the foundation for the first true republic in the modern world. After turning it in to the other delegates, he deplored the changes they demanded—and they argued among themselves—but it was finally signed after Franklin warned, "We must all hang together, or most assuredly we will all hang separately."

# CHAPTER ONE

# *THE STRUGGLE FOR DEMOCRACY*

## 1776–1800

### BY PAULINE MAIER

Americans did more than declare their independence in 1776. They also founded a republic, the first of the modern world, which transformed the Americans' struggle with Britain into a revolutionary event. The challenge of defining, establishing and defending that republic lay behind both its lasting accomplishments and the bitter disputes that divided the new nation in its first decades. Among those accomplishments was the momentous but unanticipated and largely undesired founding of the political parties.

What was a republic? On one level, the answer was obvious to everyone. The United States would have no king or nobles, no hereditary rulers of any kind. Instead, all power would come from the people. American government would therefore be representative, and so expand that "republican" part of the English constitution which was, as Thomas Paine said in *Common Sense* (1776), the glory of Englishmen, "viz., the liberty of choosing an House of Commons from out of their own body." In England, however, the Crown had used the offices, pensions and other rewards at its disposal to build a party of supporters in the Commons. Why was the English constitution "sickly," Paine had

asked, "but because monarchy hath poisoned the Republic; the Crown hath engrossed the Commons." To preserve their freedom, Americans understood that they would have to avoid such corruption. And parties, their observations of England suggested, were a sign of trouble.

The abolition of hereditary rule helped give meaning to the words that Thomas Jefferson, the father of what was to become the first National Democratic Party, had written into the Declaration of Independence. "All men" were "created equal" since no one was born with the right to rule another. They were, moreover, "endowed by their Creator with certain unalienable rights," among which were "life, liberty, and the pursuit of happiness." But who were included among "all men," and how far did equality extend? For the Founding Fathers, "all men" meant adult white males—certainly not women and children, who were "by nature" weak and dependent on others, and so could not assume the public responsibilities and related rights of "independent" republican citizens. And blacks? The irony of Jefferson, a slaveholder, asserting the doctrine of equality was difficult to deny, especially since he himself had referred to slaves as

The United States would have no king or nobles, no hereditary rulers of any kind. It had been written into the Declaration of Independence, "All men" were "created equal" and "endowed by their Creator with certain unalienable rights." At the time of the Revolution, however, the matter of equality—how far and to whom it extended—was open to debate.

men in a part of his draft of the Declaration that the Continental Congress deleted.

At the time of the Revolution, however, even the equality of adult white males was open to debate. Was the equality of "all men" at odds with the assumption that only men of talent, the members of a "natural aristocracy," would hold office in the American Republic? If not, how were such men to be identified? By wealth, perhaps, or education? Were extreme differences of wealth consistent with a republican government, which authorities such as Montesquieu, whose *Spirit of the Laws* Americans cited repeatedly, described as appropriate only for countries where property was equally distributed? Should the state redistribute

wealth, as with the "agrarian laws" of ancient Rome? And should education be made available to all children in a republic, so the state could draw on the talents of those born to the poor as well as the rich? Finally, did the authority of elected officials need to be enhanced by ceremonial distinctions? Or did such display suggest "artificial" social distinctions like those of Britain, which the Revolution had rejected? Did American equality imply a style of "republican simplicity"?

"Democratic" answers to these vexing questions were first offered in the 1780s by men such as William Findley and other members of Pennsylvania's "Constitutionalist" party, who rallied in defense of the radically democratic Pennsylvania constitution of 1776 against critics who sought to replace it. A Scotch-Irish immigrant who settled in the western parts of Pennsylvania, Findley was self-educated. By 1763, when he arrived in America at age 22, he had read so much about the country and was so knowledgeable that people took him for a native. Lean and wiry, of quick wit and ready with words, Findley demanded the respect even of more formally educated opponents, and obviously impressed his constituents, who elected him to a variety of state offices and to the United States House of Representatives for several terms between 1791 and 1817.

But Findley could never—would never—emulate men with the advantage of university educations or great wealth. Instead, he took joy in puncturing their pretenses and revealing their ignorance, always taking

**William Findley, an Irish Protestant immigrant, became a prominent member of Pennsylvania's "Constitutionalist" party in the 1780s. A man whose powerful mind and democratic sentiments won respect even from his opponents, Findley opposed ratification of the Federal Constitution. His was an early voice calling for the dissolution of the Bank of North America, the first major national bank.**

the side of the common people. For that reason he, like other vigilant Pennsylvania Democrats, attacked the charter Pennsylvania gave the Bank of North America—the country's first major bank—in 1782. In incorporating the bank, the legislature had given substantial privileges to rich men who had founded that institution, Findley charged, "for the sole purpose of increasing wealth." The charter therefore violated the state's bill of rights, which said government was created for the benefit of all men, not for the emolument of any particular man, family or set of men. Findley made no case for agrarian laws, which he, like most other Americans, considered an unjust violation of property rights. Yet the existence of "enormous wealth" in the hands of individuals was a "danger in free states" since such men, with the help of their dependents, easily acquired a corrupt "influence" over the state. "How absurd," then, "must it be for government to lend its special aid in so partial a manner," exacerbating inequality through an institution "inconsistent with our. . . customs, and circumstances, and even with the nature of our government." Essentially the same arguments would be raised five years later by Jeffersonian opponents of the first Bank of the United States, and 46 years later by the Democratic President Andrew Jackson in his own "bank war."

The popular politics that quickly emerged after independence in states such as Pennsylvania provoked fears for the future of the Republic. When the "Constitutionalists" won control of the Pennsylvania assembly, they repealed the charter of the Bank of North America. Elsewhere, similar elected legislative majorities made depreciated state paper money legal tender for the payment of old debts, or in other ways interfered with the rights of creditors. Such measures violated the rights of property owners, and so revealed a new threat to freedom—majoritarian tyranny. Nor was the danger confined to the wealthy: Religious minorities were equally vulnerable to hostile majorities. Somehow the extensive power Americans had entrusted to elected legislatures in their first state constitution had to be checked. That could be done in part by revising the state constitutions so that legislative power was balanced by that of the executive and judiciary branches. But an enhanced national government could also serve to check the wrongdoing of states—for example, by prohibiting interferences with the obligation of contracts or the making of anything but gold and silver legal tender.

In a sign of how wild partisan conflicts had become by 1798, Connecticut Federalist Roger Griswold and the Vermont representative Matthew Lyon battled it out on the floor of Congress. After Griswold cast aspersions on Lyon's revolutionary war record, Lyon spat in his face. A few days later, Griswold retaliated with a hickory stick.

There were also other reasons to replace the Articles of the Confederation, the first formal government of the United States, which had been drafted in 1777 and ratified in 1781. That document was a major step forward in the development of American national government, but it quickly showed signs of age. It by no means created a balanced government: All Federal power was entrusted to Congress. The Articles had also been ratified by states, not the people, as were state constitutions once Massachusetts inaugurated that practice in 1780. Moreover, in the first years of independence, the states had been unwilling to give Congress powers that they had denied Parliament to tax and regulate trade. Once the Revolutionary War ended, the states saw less need for Congress, and often failed to supply the funds it requested, or even to send delegates to its meetings. Congress' weakness was clear in its inability to keep the Spanish out of Kentucky and the British from courting Vermont, to enforce provisions on Loyalists in the peace treaty of 1783, to pay off its war debts, even to protect Federal property against the "Shaysite" insurgents in Massachusetts. Although the country was growing and prospering, Congress seemed at times in danger of disappearing altogether. What, then, would keep the states from warring with one another in their quests for land and trade?

For all these reasons, many delegates to the Constitutional Convention who gathered at Philadelphia in May 1787 believed that the United States, as Edmund Randolph of Virginia said in his opening speech, was in a crisis, one that threatened to fulfill predictions that the American Republic would disintegrate like all its historical predecessors. But if its proponents considered the Constitution to be the Republic's best hope, a last and desperate effort to salvage the Revolution, its critics saw it as a reversal of the Revolution of 1776. The Constitution, its "Anti-Federalist" opponents charged, would undermine the more representative and democratic authority of the states, entrust power to the rich and well born, and create a "consolidated" central government like that of Britain.

Despite deep divisions within several states, particularly Virginia and New York, the Constitution was ratified in 1788. Then, with the election of George Washington as the first President in 1789, the country seemed suddenly reunited. That tall, reserved Virginian had won the hearts of his countrymen by leading the Continental Army to victory in the Revolutionary War, then voluntarily retiring to the life of a Chesapeake planter. A man with so little apparent taste for power—and no son to succeed him—could safely be made President, and Washington was elected without opposition in 1789, then again in 1792. For lack of a better model, however, Washington thought of himself as a republican equivalent of a king and adopted a commensurate way of life. He would ride with dignity through New York City, the country's first capital, on a white horse with a saddle of leopard skin trimmed with gold, or in a coach pulled by a team of white horses, and lived in a mansion with uniformed guards in powdered wigs. Some ardent republicans found this style inappropriate and worrisome.

Like many other Americans of his time, William Maclay considered George Washington "the greatest man in the world." A western Pennsylvanian like Findley, Maclay had—unlike Findley—supported ratification of the Constitution, and then been elected to the United States Senate for a two-year term, with which his senatorial career ended. In his brief time in Congress, Maclay witnessed with disdain and growing anxiety the pomp and ceremony, the explicit efforts to follow British precedents in establishing the first Federal Government. He regretfully recorded in his diary the bows, proclamations and cheers that accompanied Washington's nervous and awkward inaugural address before the Senate on April 30, 1789. But he fairly exploded when the Vice President, John Adams, later referred to the President's "most gracious speech." Those words were used for the addresses of "his Britannic Majesty" and were therefore "improper" in the United States, Maclay said; indeed, "they will give offense" to a people who had just emerged from a "hard struggle for our liberty against kingly authority," and found "everything related to that species of government...odious."

Moreover, Maclay was beside himself when, after long deliberations, a Senate committee proposed that the President be referred to as "His Highness the President of the United States of America and Protector of the Rights of Same." The Constitution, after all, prohibited titles of nobility. Instead of "adding respect to government," as the proposers claimed, titles would "bring the personages who assume them into contempt and ridicule." Soon such proposals came to seem not just "silly," but proof that a "party" existed that sought not to promote the cause of the American Revolution by an amelioration of government for the better service of mankind, but to establish "a new monarchy in America, and to form niches for themselves in the temple of royalty."

Maclay resisted affiliating himself with a party, but he shared the hostility toward Alexander Hamilton's financial program that first brought together members of what Jefferson would soon refer to as the "republican interest." Throughout the first decade of its existence, in fact, that emergent party coalesced in opposition to the policies and influence of Hamilton. Born in the West Indies in 1755, the illegitimate son of a ne'er-do-well Scotsman of noble family who later abandoned his family, Alexander Hamilton came to America in 1773 under the patronage of wealthy persons who had recognized his great abilities and sent him to King's College (later Columbia). Before long, Hamilton was caught up in the revolutionary cause and, af-

Overleaf:
**Presided over by George Washington in 1787, the 55 delegates to the Constitutional Convention in Philadelphia— most of them wealthy northern merchants and slave-holding southern planters—were an unlikely group to draw up the constitution of a republic in which "all men are created equal." But in a marriage of political convenience and ideological idealism, they managed to hammer together a document that has stood the test of time as a blueprint for freedom and justice throughout the world.**

ter the outbreak of war, joined the American army, in which he served as General Washington's private secretary and aide-de-camp. Lacking close attachment to a particular state, like native-born Americans, Hamilton's loyalties were from the first to the United States, which he hoped would become an empire as great as that of Britain. To do so it would need a strong central government supported by men of wealth and power, whose interests had to be firmly bound with that of the nation. And it would need to develop commerce and manufacturing to balance the already established agricultural segment of its economy. After Washington became President, and appointed him the first secre-

tary of the treasury, Hamilton wasted no time in attempting to realize his vision.

He first proposed that the Federal Government assume the remaining revolutionary debts of the states as well as those of the United States—exchanging old certificates of indebtedness for new notes of obligation backed by the Federal Government—and fund them at face value, although they had often been bought by speculators for far less. That would firmly establish the credit of the United States and promote the interests of creditors, whose assets could fund economic development, binding them to the nation. Hamilton assumed he could count on the support of his old ally in the

**George Washington, America's first President, considered himself to be above politics, like the English king. The Federalists who most supported him were, for Washington, not a political party but a group of right-thinking men who supported the government against its anarchical opponents. He abhorred political parties, and warned of their dangers in his "Farewell Address."**

fight for ratification of the Constitution, James Madison, who by 1790 had become a leader in the House of Representatives, and who had long bemoaned the financial weakness of the old Confederation government. Madison, however, hesitated to endorse all of Hamilton's plan. He proposed that the United States repay speculators at a lower value, and also compensate the original holders, many of whom were veterans of the Continental Army. In the end, the House rejected Madison's plan, which was beyond the administrative capacity of the government at that time. Some Southerners opposed the Federal assumption of state debts because their states had already repaid many of their bonds and were unwilling to help retire those of states that had not, many of which were in the North. Others hesitated to reward speculators so richly, fearing that speculation would corrupt the people, pulling them from more productive work in a mad search for quick profits. But compromise remained possible. Hamilton turned for help to his cabinet colleague Thomas Jefferson, who in March 1790 had become Washington's secretary of state. Jefferson

The illegitimate son of a ne'er-do-well Scotsman in the West Indies, Alexander Hamilton came to America under the patronage of wealthy benefactors and went to King's College. Caught up in the revolutionary cause, he joined the army and served as secretary to General Washington. Appointed secretary of the treasury in 1789, he proceeded to promote his vision of America as a far-flung empire like Britain with a government supported by men of wealth and power.

James Madison was at the helm of the effort to secure ratification of the Federal Constitution. With Hamilton and John Jay, he went on to publish *The Federalist*, designed to explain and codify the Constitution. Having been in the United States during the 1780s, Madison was more experienced at democratic politics than his close friend and political ally, Thomas Jefferson, who had spent many of those critical years in France.

**The first Bank of the United States, proposed by Washington's Secretary of the Treasury Alexander Hamilton, was chartered in 1791 over the opposition of Secretary of State Jefferson and the Republicans in Congress, who argued that it would undermine the Union by granting unconstitutional power and political leverage to the men of wealth and privilege who founded it.**

obligingly arranged a dinner party at which Hamilton and Madison agreed to establish the new national government on the Potomac in return for two critical Virginia votes in favor of assumption. He later considered that concession one of the greatest errors of his life.

Suspicions hardened after December 1790, when Hamilton proposed that Congress charter a Bank of the United States. The Constitutional Convention, Madison recalled, had explicitly decided against giving Congress the power to incorporate. Hamilton argued that the incorporation of a national bank was constitutional as a "necessary and proper" means of fulfilling other functions entrusted to Congress. On that basis, opponents countered, Federal power could expand indefinitely. The bank, like funding and assumption, would bring greater advantages to the commercial North than to the agricultural South, and so, far from strengthening the Union, Jefferson charged, would weaken it by exacerbating sectional divisions and confirming the fears of the Constitution's anti-Federalist critics. Its financial benefits, moreover, would accrue to men of wealth, who would be even more closely tied not just to the nation but to Hamilton. Since the Treasury already controlled thousands of jobs in the customs service and post office, it could become a powerful agent of corruption—like its British counterpart.

By 1792, Jefferson concluded that Hamilton's program was designed to create "an influence of his department over the members of the legislature," and then to use that "corrupt squadron" of legislators "to get rid of the limitations imposed by the Constitution" and "prepare the way for a change, from the present republican form of government, to that of a monarchy, of which the English constitution is to be a model." Those with Jefferson in the opposition took the name "Republicans" because they believed they were defending not a partisan cause but the Republic, which is to say the Revolution, against subversion by what Jefferson called the "Monarchist Federalists." The Republican Party of the 1790s was not simply a continuation of the anti-Federalist "party" that had opposed ratification of the Federal Constitution, as its opponents tried to imply when they assumed the name of Federalist. In fact, one of the Republicans' leaders, James Madison, was a major architect of the Constitution and a man who helped orchestrate its enactment. The fears of the Republicans did, however, echo those of the anti-Federalists. Those fears increased and, with them, the consistency of partisan voting patterns in Congress, as a result of the French Revolution and the consequent outbreak of war in Europe.

Members of both emergent political parties agreed that the United States should stay out of that war. Hamilton's sympathies, however, lay with Britain, and Jefferson's with France, which had supported the Americans in their Revolutionary War against the British and had now become an embattled sister republic. Washington's proclamation of American neutrality in the spring of 1793 seemed to many Re-

After serving for two years as governor of Virginia, Thomas Jefferson retired briefly from public life—mourning the death of his wife—but returned in 1783 to win a seat in Congress. A year later he left for France, where he remained until the French Revolution, which his own Declaration of Independence had helped inspire. Appointed secretary of state by Washington, he became disenchanted with Hamilton's "monarchist" influence within the Federal Government and helped found a new party: the democratic Republicans.

publicans a violation of the French Alliance and a concession to Britain fully in keeping with the subversive schemes of Treasury Secretary Hamilton. "A dissolution of the honorable and beneficial connection between the United States and France," as a meeting in Caroline County, Virginia, declared, was part of an attempt to establish "a more intimate union" between the United States and Britain, and to take "a leading step toward assimilating the American government to the form and spirit of the British monarchy." And so, as Jefferson observed, the European war "kindled and brought forward the two parties with an ardor which our own interests merely could never excite."

In 1794, the development of parties took another leap forward after the Washington administration endorsed a treaty negotiated with Britain by John Jay. Though it settled several outstanding American grievances—the British agreed, for example, to finally vacate its posts in the American Northwest territory—it did so only by imposing humiliating concessions on the United States, and left unresolved issues of particular interest to the South, such as compensation for slaves "stolen" by the British at the end of the Revolutionary War. In its efforts to block Senate ratification and then implementation of the treaty, Republican congressmen caucused formally for the first time.

Meanwhile, divisions in the populace emerged and took an organized form. Foremost among them were the local "Democratic" and "Republican" societies that began in 1793, when the Democratic Society of Pennsylvania sent out circulars calling for their establishment throughout the nation. Informed of political events by newspapers, which increased in number from 100 to 230 and became increasingly partisan during the 1790s, the people readily organized, debated the issues of the day and passed spirited resolutions that expressed their "Republican" sympathies. They had, however, no overt connection with the congressional Republican Party, and assumed no "partisan" responsibilities such as nominating candidates or sponsoring election campaigns. At times the societies functioned as pressure groups—the Democratic Society of Kentucky, for example, supported free navigation of the Mississippi—but more often they modeled themselves on the old Sons of Liberty, who organized resistance to Britain's Stamp Act in 1766. Their commitment to the "dissemination of political information" similarly recalled the revolutionary era's

committees of correspondence. The Democratic-Republican societies also resembled many earlier political organizations in being short-lived. Most disappeared as increasing violence in France undermined Americans' enthusiasm for the French Revolution and, above all, after President Washington denounced them in November 1794 as "self-created societies" and associated them with those rebels in western Pennsylvania who had risen up that year against the Federal excise tax on whiskey.

President Washington's discomfort with organized political opposition was, in fact, widely shared, which necessarily retarded the development of parties. In the eighteenth century, "party" was generally condemned along with "faction," which James Madison had defined in his tenth "Federalist Paper" as a group united by some passion or interest against the rights of others or the "permanent and aggregate interests of the community." Madison argued there that the Federal Constitution would serve to break the "violence of faction" that marked state politics in the 1780s, and which was especially dangerous in a republic, whose survival depended on the public-mindedness of the people. Writers and speakers were quick to recall that faction and internal divisions had caused the fall of the ancient republics—of Athens and Rome—and, as a New York lawyer put it in 1794, would have the same effect in America "unless the spirit of party be repressed." Two years later, in his farewell address, Washington also warned against "the baneful effects of the spirit of party" as "truly the worst enemy" of popular governments. In monarchies, party might provide a check on government and "keep alive the spirit of liberty," but in governments "purely elective," that spirit tended always to run to excess. The consequent "disorders and miseries" led men "to seek security and repose in the absolute power of an individual" to the ruin of public liberty.

Washington's address, which had been drafted by Hamilton, was itself a partisan document, meant to discredit the Republican opposition. But it said little that the Republicans had not at one time or another themselves affirmed. Republicans might argue, as Madison had in 1792, that parties provided a way to check power in republics as well as monarchies; they might suggest, as Thomas Jefferson did after Washington condemned the Democratic-Republican societies, that parties were an exercise of free speech. But the

Elected President in 1796 after Washington retired, Federalist John Adams presided over his party's declining years of power, stirring outrage among Jefferson and his anti-Federalists with the Alien and Sedition Acts, a series of repressive measures aimed at silencing political opposition.

only justification readily at hand for organized opposition to the policies of an established government lay in the right of revolution, and its implementation required, as the Declaration of Independence said, "a long train of abuses and usurpations, pursuing invariably the same Object" and demonstrating "a design to reduce" the people "under absolute Despotism." No one was ready to level that charge against the administration of George Washington.

And so party development remained primitive and tenuous—as the election of 1796 revealed. The Republicans had been led by James Madison since December 1793 when Jefferson left the State Department and retired to private life. By common consent they supported Jefferson for President against the Federalist John Adams, but could agree on no one vice presidential candidate. Nor did they apparently seek Jefferson's consent to run, for fear he would refuse. And in fact their standard bearer, deeply involved in agricultural experiments and the long-term rebuilding of his home, Monticello, made no effort to win the election; that work fell to party stalwarts such as John Beckley of Pennsylvania and Aaron Burr of New York. Republican publications recalled that Jefferson had drafted the Declaration of Independence and "framed the sacred political sentence that all men are born equal," claimed that Adams considered that assertion "a farce and falsehood," and hailed Jefferson as the only man who could "reconcile contending parties"—as if a Republican victory would end party divisions.

A greater opportunity for the reconciliation of partisan differences lay in a deep bond of friendship that had once bound Jefferson and Adams. The two men were, on the face of it, strikingly different. Jefferson, whose mother was from the prestigious Randolph family of Virginia and who inherited a plantation acquired by his father, was tall, thin and reticent in social encounters. Adams, eight years older than Jefferson, came from a less privileged background. Literally a country cousin of the better-known Boston revolutionary Samuel Adams, he had fought his way to prominence. Of "middling height," as his grandson described him, with a "stout, well-knit frame," he was warm and outgoing, though he had a quick temper and remained acutely sensitive to insults. The two men had, however, served together in the second Continental Congress, where they were allies in the fight for independence. Indeed, both were appointed to the committee charged with drafting the Declaration of Independence, and Jefferson later recalled that Adams was the "ablest advocate" in Congress of Jefferson's draft declaration "against the multifarious assaults it encountered." Later, in the mid-1780s, when Adams and Jefferson served together as American diplomats in Europe, their friendship tightened, in part due to Abigail Adams' solicitude for the recently widowed Jefferson and her kindness to his youngest daughter. The two men also shared a profound love of books, which each collected beyond the limits of their own consciences.

Jefferson knew Adams' faults as well as any man— he was vain, irritable and unskilled at calculating the motives that governed men, Jefferson noted—but also recognized his integrity, profundity and good judgment, and found Adams "so amiable" that in 1787 Jefferson had written James Madison that "you will love him if ever you become acquainted with him." Jefferson had supported Adams' diplomatic appointments and congratulated him on his election as Washington's Vice President. Their friendship waned in the early 1790s after Jefferson publicly suggested that Adams admired the British constitution more than what became a good republican. But on December 28, 1796, before he knew for certain the outcome of the presidential election, Jefferson wrote Adams an extraordinary letter. Never for "one single moment" had he doubted that Adams would win the presidency, he said, while explicitly disavowing any personal desire for that office. "I have no ambition to govern men," Jefferson insisted. "It is a painful and thankless office." He hoped Adams' administration would be "filled with glory and happiness," and reaffirmed the "solid esteem of the moments when we were working for our independence, and sentiments of respect and affectionate attachment."

The letter was never delivered due to the intercession of James Madison, who had been in the United States and deeply involved in the political struggles of the 1780s, and whose understanding of democratic politics was in 1796 far more developed than Jefferson's. But when Federalist Adams won the election and Republican Jefferson, who came in second, became Vice President, each made an effort to work harmoniously with the other. Adams once referred to Jefferson as "an old Friend... with whom I have often had occasion to labour at many a knotty Problem." Now he noted that Hamilton's departure from the Treasury had removed the "cause of the irritation upon [Jefferson's] Nerves" of "a few years ago." Meanwhile, Jefferson recognized in Adams "perhaps the only sure barrier" against Hamilton's returning to power. Adams, in fact, had his own reasons to resent Hamilton, who had attempted to manipulate the electoral vote to prevent Adams' election. On several issues, moreover, Adams was nearer the Republicans than Hamilton and his "High Federalist" followers. He shared the Republicans' fear of armies, and once described the bank as a "system of national injustice" that sacrificed "public and private interest to a few aristocratic friends and favorites." In the interest of

The Sedition Law, passed by Federalist congressmen despite Republicans' objections, in effect, outlawed political opposition to the Adams administration. The nation had to be saved from "absolute Despotism" and the only way to do it was at the ballot box. With Jefferson as its nominee, the Republicans acted as a national party organization and won the crucial election of 1800.

harmony he was prepared to reaffirm his hostility to monarchy and aristocracy and his respect for the French nation.

But dreams of political harmony were fated to failure at a time when partisan feelings had become so intense that, as Jefferson observed, "men who have been intimate all their lives, cross the streets to avoid meeting, and turn their heads another way, lest they should be obliged to touch their hats." The new Vice President was soon at work devising ways to strengthen the "republican body" in Congress, where he could work with Albert Gallatin, an intense and disciplined political taskmaster who inherited Madison's congressional

leadership after he retired from the House in 1796.

Party divisions, already tightly drawn, became more so after France began an undeclared war on American ships and in late 1796 refused to receive the new American minister to France, Charles Cotesworth Pinckney. Adams' effort to negotiate a solution through a special diplomatic commission failed when three French agents—later designated X, Y and Z—demanded a loan and a substantial bribe before opening talks. The American commissioners refused, and, after the news broke, the "XYZ Affair" provoked a wave of anti-French sentiment in 1798. With their control of Congress confirmed and enhanced, Federalists

A wily and ambitious power broker, New York's Aaron Burr came close to being elected President when the democratic Republicans chose him as their nominee for Vice President in 1800. Tied with Thomas Jefferson in electoral votes, he lost when the issue was settled in the House of Representatives, where Alexander Hamilton had lobbied against him as "a most unfit and dangerous man." Their feud ended tragically in 1804 when Burr killed Hamilton in a duel.

called for war. They suspended the Anglo-American treaties of 1778, organized a Navy Department, authorized attacks on French armed ships, tripled the size of the army—which would be led by Washington with Hamilton as his second-in-command—and levied new taxes to pay for these measures. Republicans feared that force was in fact to be used against the Federalists' domestic enemies, much as the British had attempted to suppress opposition by sending troops to Boston back in 1774. And in 1799 armed force was in fact used against the anti-tax "Fries Rebellion" in western Pennsylvania.

Finally, over unanimous Republican opposition, Federalist congressmen passed the Alien and Sedition Acts, which were a blatant attempt to suppress the Republicans. They required that immigrants—who were suspected of having Republican sympathies—be resident fourteen years rather than the previous five before voting, gave the President greater power to deport aliens, prohibited all associations "to oppose any measure or measures of the government of the United States," and imposed severe punishments for writing, publishing or saying anything against the government or President of the United States "with intent to defame...or to bring them...into contempt or disrepute." The Sedition Law, in effect, outlawed political opposition to the Adams administration. Its political purpose was clear in its expiration date, which coincided with the inauguration of the President to be elected in 1800. If the Federalists lost that election, they would then be free to criticize the new administration. In the meantime, Republicans could not expect the courts to protect their civil liberties. After a decade of one-party rule, all Federal judges were Federalists.

These measures confirmed the Republicans' worst fears: The nation had to be saved from what the intrepid John Taylor of Caroline called "an anglo-monarchic-aristocratic-military government." So unmistakable an effort to reduce the people to "absolute Despotism" justified revolution, but Anglo-American revolutionary tradition had long taught that the peaceful means of redress had to be exhausted before an injured people could turn to force. The calls of the Virginia and Kentucky legislatures, drafted by Madison and Jefferson, for state "interposition" against the "unconstitutional" Alien and Sedition Acts were rejected by other states. But a powerful "peaceful means of redress" remained at the ballot box and in what a later age would call politics.

In the election of 1800, the Republican congressional caucus nominated both Jefferson for President and Aaron Burr for Vice President, and clearly acted as a national party organization. Well-developed networks of local corresponding committees that nominated candidates and conducted campaigns were already established in Pennsylvania and New York. Now similar party mechanisms were organized in other states, such as Virginia and New Jersey. Even where no such organization existed, voters chose between party tickets, and candidates affiliated with one of the two major parties were most likely to win. Even county officials sometimes ran as Republicans or Federalists in 1800. Through such means, the Republicans won control of the presidency and both houses of Congress, but not without high drama.

Republican members of the electoral college were so united in 1800 that they cast the same number of votes, 73, for Jefferson and for his running mate Aaron Burr. That gave their party victory over John Adams with 65 and Charles Cotesworth Pinckney with 64. But since electoral votes were not yet cast separately for President and Vice President—a practice established in 1804 with the enactment of the 12th Amendment—Jefferson and Burr were formally tied. The election therefore had to be decided in the House of Representatives, where each state had one vote. The Federalists held a numerical majority in the Senate—prompting Jefferson to state that he had been delivered to his enemies—but they controlled only six of the sixteen state delegations. Since two others were divided, the Federalists were able, by casting their votes for Burr, to prevent the election of Jefferson through some 35 ballots. Finally, on February 17, ten states cast their votes for Jefferson. Only then was it clear that there would be a President to inaugurate on the fourth of March.

In the midst of these events, even Hamilton demonstrated his loyalty to the Republic. Federalists, he counseled, should prefer Jefferson to Burr, whose lack of principle, extraordinary ambition and penchant for demagoguery made him "the most unfit and dangerous man of the community." Jefferson at least had "pretensions to character," integrity and a commitment to principle. "If there be a man in the world I ought to hate," Hamilton noted, "it is Jefferson. With Burr I have always been personally well. But the public good must be paramount to every private consideration." Three years later he would die at Burr's hand, shot in a duel called by Burr to vindicate his honor against Hamilton's well-founded aspersions on his character.

Jefferson referred to the Democratic-Republican electoral victory as "the revolution of 1800" because it ended the threat to freedom manifest in the Alien and Sedition Acts and in the Federalists' use of armed force to suppress domestic political opposition. He assumed office with a calmness that was striking against the high tension of his election, and with remarkably little ceremony. He walked to the Senate from the boardinghouse where he lived, casually greeting friends along the way. His was the first inauguration to be held in the new capital of Washington, where most streets were mud paths and many buildings remained half built. Jefferson's informality fit so frontier-like a city, and it also distinguished his presidential style from that of his predecessors. He seems, however, to have assumed that the era of party conflict ended with his victory. "We are all Republicans," he said in his inaugural address. "We are all Federalists." With the "monarchist" threat put down, the justification for opposition also lapsed. Now onetime partisans were free to discover, as Pennsylvania's Dr. Benjamin Rush observed, that "they had differed in opinion only, about the best means of promoting the interest of their common identity."

In these volatile opening years of partisan conflict, the Republicans and Federalists began a tradition of two-party politics that would prove a formidable means of promoting political moderation and stability and would be an enduring monument to freedom of speech. The existence of a legitimate opposition party has, for good reason, come to distinguish free from unfree states. The party warriors of the 1790s, therefore, served their country well—better perhaps than any others in the history of the United States who had so little understanding of what they were doing.

When Thomas Jefferson was elected President in 1800, he considered his party's triumph "a revolution in the principles of our government" and began a dramatic program of reform designed to restore democratic rule and "republican" simplicity. Unimpressed with the trappings of presidential prestige, he wore what some called shoddy attire and often rode to work on his horse.

# CHAPTER TWO

# THE JEFFERSONIANS IN POWER

## 1801–1824

### BY LANCE BANNING

R eflecting on the victory of 1800, Thomas Jefferson described his party's triumph "as real a revolution in the principles of our government as that of 1776 was in its form." Jefferson exaggerated, as was frequently his bent, and yet his statement also captured two important truths: The party battle of the first few years of the Republic was as fierce as any in our annals, flowing as it did from radically contrasting visions of the sort of nation the United States should be; and Jefferson's inauguration did initiate as sharp a change in governmental attitudes and policies as almost any party triumph we might name.

For twelve years after the adoption of the Constitution, the infant Federal Government had been guided by a Federalist design for national greatness, which was probably complete in its essentials when Alexander Hamilton, the first secretary of the treasury, introduced his plan for managing the revolutionary debt. Hamilton's concerns were Hobbesian and European in their flavor. He faced toward the Atlantic and envisioned an arena of competing empires into which America must enter much like any other state. In time, as he conceived it, the United States could take a

brilliant part in this arena. But to have this kind of future, it must first possess the economic, governmental and financial preconditions for successful competition. Meanwhile, the United States must conscientiously maintain a good relationship with Britain, the single nation, with its naval power, which could threaten it most dangerously in war or, through investments in the new Republic's economic growth, assist it most impressively toward greatness. Taking British institutions as a model and realizing that his goals demanded careful central guidance, Hamilton had set out to build a modern state, a nation able to compete with European empires on the Europeans' terms.

The project started with the plan for managing the public debt. Hamilton assumed that Federal funding of the state as well as national obligations would accomplish much besides the reestablishment of public credit. It would tie the economic interests of a vital segment of America's elite to the success of national institutions and create a counterbalance to the state institutions that had always seemed the greatest danger to the Union. Even as it bound the monied interests to the central government's success, it would erect a framework for the nation's future role in global competition, transforming governmental obligations into liquid capital that could be multiplied again by using the certificates of debt to back a national bank. The bonds and banknotes could be used, in turn, to foster manufacturing and commerce, whose rapid growth would lay the groundwork for the nation's economic independence. It was a brilliant scheme, in service to a grand ambition, and it worked in much the way that Hamilton expected. A clash with Britain was avoided during the 1790s, though only at the cost of a demeaning treaty and a naval war with France. The funding program and the national bank provided capital for economic growth. As revolutionary France embarked on twenty years of war with most of Europe, the new Republic prospered.

But nearly every aspect of the Federalist design was deeply incompatible with other founders' concepts of the nature of a sound republic. Within three years of Washington's inauguration, Jefferson, James Madison and others had concluded that the economic program was intended to "administer" the new Republic toward a government and social order that would undermine the Constitution and subvert the democratic Revolution. From the first, the funding program stirred anxieties about corrupting links between the Federal Government and special-interest factions. In addition, critics saw, it would entail a major shift of

**The Seventh Congress, voting on party lines with its new Jeffersonian majority, enacted everything their new President recommended: removal of restrictions on free speech, international neutrality, reduction in the size of the armed forces, tax repeal and payment of the national debt. Instead of collapsing into disorder, as the Federalists predicted, the nation prospered.**

wealth from south to north, from west to east, and from the body of the people to a few rich men whose fortunes would expand dramatically as a result of Federal largesse—all of which seemed inconsistent with republican morality, with harmony between the nation's sections and with the relatively modest distances between the rich and poor that seemed essential to a representative regime. Federal encouragement of manufacturing and commerce would compound these problems, while the broad construction of the Constitution urged in their defense would bring about a major shift of power from the states to the central government and from the House of Representatives to the Federal executive. The economic program and the disregard of constitutional restraints both seemed to center power at a level and in governmental branches least responsive to the people, while creating in the congressmen and private citizens who were enriched by governmental payments an interest fundamentally at odds with that of the majority of people, whose direct involvement in the nation's daily politics most Federalists obviously seemed to dread. In this direction, Jeffersonians insisted, lay a deadly danger to the Union, oppression of the most productive portion of the people, destruction of the necessary sympathy between the rulers and the ruled and even the reintroduction of hereditary rule. After 1798, when war hysteria and Federalist distrust of popular opinion culminated in a naval war with revolutionary France, enlargement of the army and repressive legislation that was meant to put an end to the domestic opposition, many Jeffersonians believed that Federalists were ready for a final blow at liberty and even for political reunion with the English fountainhead of Federalist ideas.

The victory of 1800, as the Jeffersonians conceived it, rescued the Republic from a counterrevolutionary plot. Still, a change of men was not enough without a change of measures; and the Jeffersonian conception of a nation's needs was vastly different from the vision that had guided it throughout its first twelve years. Where Hamilton had faced toward the Atlantic and envisioned rapid economic change, the Jeffersonians preferred a democratic distribution of the nation's wealth. Though Jefferson and his lieutenants—Madison at State and Albert Gallatin at Treasury—were very much concerned with freeing oceanic commerce and providing open markets for the country's agricul-

Thomas Jefferson's chief financial advisor and congressional leader during the 1790s, Pennsylvania's Albert Gallatin rose to serve as secretary of the treasury during the eight-year Jefferson administration, a post he filled again during the presidency of his friend James Madison, third of the triumvirate that had led the Jeffersonians during their early years.

tural producers, their ambitions for the nation focused on the West, where a republic resting on the sturdy stock of independent farmer-owners could be constantly revitalized as it expanded over space. Where Hamilton had wanted to create a potent state, they were determined to confine the Federal Government to the responsibilities the Constitution had intended, trusting that America would revolutionize the world by force of sheer example of its democratic institutions. Where Hamilton had seen the national debt as an advantage (because it could be used to back a stable currency supply), the Jeffersonians despised it. To their minds, the interest payments on the debt enriched the monied few at popular expense and forged a dangerous, corrupting link between a few rich men and governmental leaders. They would not repudiate it, to be sure, but they were willing to subordinate much else to paying it as quickly as existing contracts would allow—and yet without resorting to internal taxes, which were better left, in peacetime, to

In 1790, Madison agreed to talk four congressmen into supporting Hamilton's plan for an assumption of state debts if Hamilton would help him win a permanent location for the Federal Government on the banks of the Potomac, a cherished object for Virginians since the middle 1780s. The physical layout of the capital reinforced the constitutional separation of powers but also contributed to the inefficiency of the government during the administrations of James Monroe and John Quincy Adams.

the states.

The Jeffersonians did not immediately dismantle all their predecessors' work. With sound Republicans in power, they assumed, the country could be eased toward change; and it would change more certainly that way. But Thomas Jefferson proclaimed their dedication to a fundamental change of course in his inaugural address, announcing their commitment to "a wise and frugal government which shall restrain men from injuring one another, shall leave them otherwise free to regulate their own pursuits of industry and improvement, and shall not take from the mouth of labor the bread it has earned." This kind of government, he hinted, would be guided by a set of policies profoundly different from the Federalist design: genuine neutrality, not national subservience to Britain; rapid payment of the national debt; and the withdrawal of the Federal Government from its involvement with the nation's economic life.

Reform began in 1801 while Jefferson awaited the December meeting of the Seventh Congress, where the Jeffersonians would have majorities in both the Senate and the House. Presidential pardons went to the remaining victims of the Federalists' Sedition Act. A handful of the most committed Federalists were purged from Federal office, and the President appointed only sound Republicans to fill these public trusts. Then, when Congress met, Jefferson suggested the repeal of all internal taxes. "The remaining sources of revenue will be sufficient," he insisted, "to provide for the support of government, to pay the interest on the public debts, and to discharge the principals in shorter periods than the laws or the general expectations had contemplated. . . . Sound principles will not justify our taxing the industry of our fellow citizens to accumulate treasure for wars we know not when, and which might not perhaps happen but from temptations offered by that treasure."

Public burdens, Jefferson admitted, could be lifted only if expenditures fell, too. But there was room to wonder "whether offices or officers have not been multiplied unnecessarily." The army, for example, had been swollen far beyond the nation's needs. "For defense against foreign invasion, their number is as nothing; nor is it conceived needful or safe that a standing army should be kept up in time of peace." The judiciary system, packed and altered by the Federalists at the conclusion of their reign, would naturally "present itself to the contemplation of Congress." And the laws concerning naturalization might again be liberalized.

The Seventh Congress, voting usually on party lines, enacted everything that Jefferson had recommended. It also gave approval to a plan by Gallatin for the complete retirement of the public debt by 1817, despite the abolition of internal taxes. Indeed, the session seemed to Jefferson so good a start toward introducing proper principles that there was little left to recommend in 1802. The effort of the next few years would be to keep the course already set.

"The Revolution of 1800" was amazingly successful. To the Federalists' surprise, America did not collapse into disorder. Instead, the country prospered and expanded as it never had before. In 1804, the people showed their general approval, reelecting Jefferson by a margin of 162 electoral votes to just 14 for C. C. Pinckney and increasing the Jeffersonian majority in Congress. By that time, the President had even shown that he would not permit fine points of principle to stand between his conduct and the public good. In 1803, he authorized the purchase of Louisiana from the French despite his doubts that strict construction of the Constitution authorized the act. The Louisiana Purchase doubled the size of the United States and seemed to promise that the Republic of the Jeffersonian vision—the Republic of independent, landowning farmers who seemed to Jeffersonians ideally fitted for self-governance and freedom—could continue to expand for generations yet to come.

Unhappily, there was a weakness in the Jeffersonian ideal, and it was far from minor. Alexander Hamilton had always argued that a ruthless world would not permit republican idealists to hold their course in peace. Other powers would prevent it. And, indeed, in 1803, France and Britain resumed their ti-

**Meriwether Lewis, Jefferson's private secretary, and William Clark, brother of Revolutionary soldier George Rogers Clark, were chosen to lead an expedition into the far northwest before the purchase of Louisiana was completed in 1803. Leaving St. Charles, Missouri, in the spring of 1804, their party of 23 soldiers, three interpreters and a single slave traveled up the Missouri River and down the Columbia River, reaching the Pacific on November 15, 1805. They had explored much of the modern American northwest.**

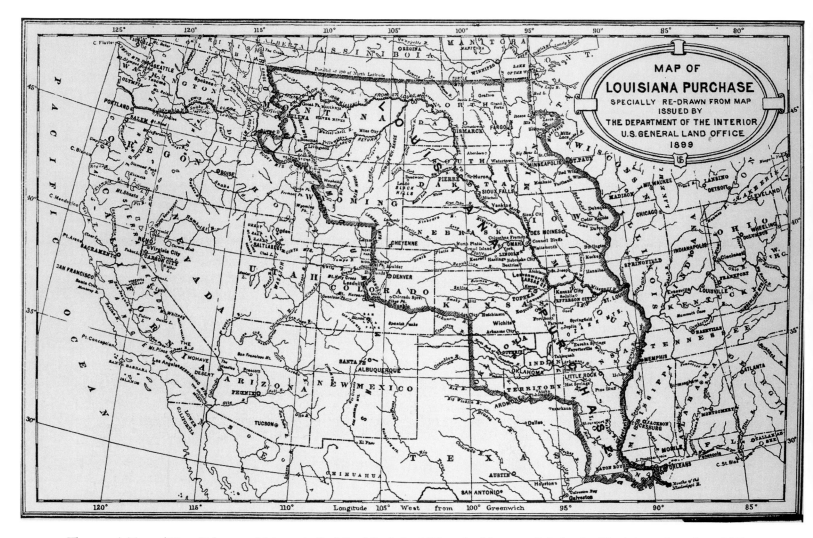

The acquisition of New Orleans, which controlled the Mississippi River, had been a vital aim for Virginians since the middle 1780s. On January 12, 1803, Jefferson named James Monroe to join Robert R. Livingston, the minister to France, in an effort to secure a tract of land or navigation rights on the lower Mississippi. Facing a resumption of his war with Britain, Napoleon offered to sell the whole of Louisiana, 828,000 square miles, for some $15,000,000, or four cents an acre. Concluded on May 2, 1803, the Louisiana Purchase treaty doubled the size of the United States and promised an enormous expansion of Thomas Jefferson's "empire for liberty."

tanic war. By 1805, these two great powers, the tiger and the shark, were each attempting to deny the other the advantages of neutral commerce. As the greatest trading neutral of the age, although a very minor military power, the United States was caught between these giants. By 1807, they had seized some 1500 U.S. ships, and there were few remaining ports to which Americans could sail without the threat of seizure by one or the other of the two warring powers. Moreover, in the summer of 1807, near the mouth of the Chesapeake Bay, the British frigate *Leopard* fired upon the American warship *Chesapeake*, forced it to submit to search, and impressed four sailors into British service. For years, the British had been stopping merchant ships to search them for deserters, impressing naturalized Americans of British birth, and sometimes taking native-born Americans by mistake. The "Chesapeake" affair, however, was an act of war.

War was what the people called for in a fury reminiscent of the XYZ Affair ten years before. Especially along the frontier—in Indiana, Michigan and Illinois, where British officials in Canada soon began to give assistance and encouragement to Tecumseh and the Prophet, Shawnee brothers who were trying to unite the western tribes against the advance of American settlement—the demand for war rose steadily from this point on. Yet Jefferson's administration was determined to confront the troubles in the way in which their principles required. Both war itself and all the normal preparations for a war—high taxes, swollen military forces, rising debts and larger governmental powers—had always seemed to them a deadly peril for republics. Any of these measures would require a radical reversal of the course they had been following since 1801.

In addition, Jefferson and Madison had always reasoned that America possessed a weapon that provided an alternative to war, a weapon that had proven its effectiveness during the long struggle preceding American independence. That weapon was her trade. Most American exports, as they saw it, were necessities of life: raw materials and food on which the Europeans

In 1800, less than a million Americans lived west of the Appalachian Mountains, mostly in the two new states of Kentucky and Tennessee. By 1819, when Missouri applied for statehood, more than a fourth of the population lived west of the Appalachians, and the Union had expanded from the original 13 colonies to 22 states that included Ohio, Louisiana, Indiana, Mississippi, Illinois and Alabama. Some immigrants came directly from Europe, but most poured westward from the seaboard states.

and their colonies were vitally dependent. Most American imports, on the other hand, were "niceties" or "luxuries" that the United States could either do without or manufacture on its own, at a shop or household level. Thus, in any confrontation with the Europeans, especially the British, the United States could force the enemy to terms by a denial of its commerce and without the dangers to its government or social order that a war would pose.

In 1807, Jefferson's administration answered French and British measures by placing a complete embargo on foreign trade. The Jeffersonian embargo did impose some hardships on the British. Unhappily, its consequences for America were even worse; it called for more self-sacrificing virtue than Americans were willing to display. Under the embargo, all American sailings for foreign ports were halted for more than a year. The result was a depression which affected every section of the country, but was most severe in Federalist New England, whose economy was heavily dependent on its shipping. Resistance by New Englanders was fierce; non-cooperation and illegal sailing could be countered only with enforcement measures so draconian that they endangered the Jeffersonians' reputation as defenders of civil rights. The Federalists enjoyed a brief revival.

In short, the great embargo broke America before it broke the Europeans. To maintain the peace within America, the Jeffersonians, whose party principles were unaffected when James Madison succeeded Jef-

As President in 1808, James Madison soon found himself caught between both sides in the Napoleonic Wars, with Hamilton's "High Federalists" favoring Britain and Jefferson's Democratic Republicans supporting France. Bowing to political pressure, he declared hostilities against Britain and launched America into the War of 1812. It was a struggle that tested Madison's resolve, but it galvanized the nation and got him elected to a second term.

With his brother Tenskwatawa (called the Prophet), the Shawnee chief Tecumseh led a native American revitalization movement and worked to unite the western Indian nations against the advance of white settlement in the early years of the Republic. Tecumseh blundered by allying himself with the British in the War of 1812 and was killed at the Battle of the Thames.

ferson in 1809, were forced to settle for less stringent measures. The embargo was replaced in 1809 with a measure confining non-intercourse to trade between America and France or Britain. In 1810, non-intercourse gave way to a provision that restrictions would be reimposed on either European power if the other would respect the country's neutral rights. Realizing that the end of the American restrictions could only aid the British, Napoleon delivered an ambiguous announcement which suggested that he would exempt American vessels from his Berlin and Milan decrees. Madison chose to interpret the announcement as fulfilling the American demands and called upon the British to repeal their Orders in Council. When the British government refused, he reimposed non-intercourse with Britain.

By the winter of 1811–1812, commercial warfare had been pressed, in one form or another, for a full four years. It had enraged New England and encouraged the resurgence of a party that the Jeffersonians regarded as a danger to democracy itself. The people were becoming restless under policies that damaged their own prosperity without compelling any change by Britain. The choice now seemed to lie between war and submission to the British, and neither the people's sense of national honor nor the survival of the Jeffersonian party—a party which still believed that American liberty depended on its guidance—would permit submission. Thus, before the new Twelfth Congress met, Madison reluctantly decided on a war. In what was basically a party vote, a declaration passed the Congress on June 18, 1812.

What followed was a tragedy of errors: eighteen months of warfare during which it was a constant question whether the United States would manage to survive intact, followed by a peace that settled none of the essential issues over which the fighting had begun. After years of stubborn dedication to an anti-preparation ideology, America embarked on war with Britain with sixteen warships and a regular army of less than

7000 men. The War of 1812 brought little glory, other than some striking victories by U.S. frigates in single-ship engagements with the British and, of course, the smashing triumph at New Orleans, where Andrew Jackson crushed the enemy before receiving news that peace had been agreed upon two weeks before (at Ghent in Belgium on December 24, 1814). But then, the War of 1812 had not been fought for glory. And if little had been gained, nothing had been lost in a collision with the greatest imperial power on earth. National honor had been satisfied. The Union had endured. The Jeffersonians had learned important lessons.

The war had major consequences for the nation. In December 1814, as Jackson was preparing to defend New Orleans, a convention met at Hartford, Connecticut to consider New England's grievances against the nation, which had crippled the administration's effort to conduct the war. The delegates demanded radical amendments to the Constitution to protect the section from the national majority in Washington, D.C., and threatened stronger actions if the changes were refused. Their manifesto reached the capital in close con-

junction with the news of Jackson's triumph. In consequence, New England's effort to extort concessions in the face of war appeared both foolish and disloyal. Lifted by the people's pride, the Madison administration rose to unexampled heights of national prestige. Simultaneously, the reputation of the Federalists was damaged beyond repair. Within four years of Madison's retirement, the triumph of the Jeffersonians was practically complete. The nation entered into a period of one-party rule.

As it did, the Party readjusted to the lessons of the war and to the economic transformation it had fostered. Early in 1815, President Madison recommended a peacetime army of 20,000 men. In his last annual message, on December 5, 1815, the great co-architect of Jeffersonian ideals called also for a Federal program of internal improvements, tariff protection for the infant industries that had sprung up during the war and the creation of a new national bank (Congress having refused in 1811 to recharter the old institution). All these measures were enacted by the Congress early in 1816, although the President refused to sign the bill for inter-

The War of 1812 began with the surrender of a 2000-man American army at Detroit on August 16 of that year, but the victory of "Old Ironsides" over *HMS Guerriere* off Nova Scotia three days later was a stunning success against the finest navy in the world and a sorely needed boost for American morale.

Control of the Great Lakes was vital in the border warfare that marked the War of 1812. On the most decisive engagement between the British and American fleets, U.S. Captain Oliver Perry saw his flagship destroyed beneath him but refused to surrender and went on to win a great victory in the battle of Lake Erie on September 10, 1813.

Commanded by Sir Edward Pakenham, 7500 veterans of the Napoleonic Wars descended on New Orleans in the last of three British invasions in 1814. Andrew Jackson, commanding 4500 American troops, established a defensive bulwark between the Mississippi and a swamp, forcing the invaders to assault across bare ground. In the battle on January 8, 1815, Jackson suffered 21 casualties, but the British lost over 2000 men in the greatest American victory of the war.

nal improvements until a constitutional amendment clearly authorized the Federal Government to act. Once again, the country shifted course.

Madison's proposals, to be sure, were not an unconditional surrender to the Federalists' ideas. the President still hoped that education, an enormous reservoir of western lands and the continued leadership of the legitimate defenders of the people's Constitution would indefinitely postpone the civic evils he and Jefferson still feared. Like Jefferson, however, Madison had learned that "there exists both profligacy and power enough to exclude us from the field of interchange with other nations": that Americans must either manufacture more of the necessities and niceties of life, accept "dependence on that foreign nation or. . . be clothed in skins and. . . live like wild beasts in dens and caverns." Accordingly, he hinted that the party's old ideas might be successfully combined with fragments of the Hamiltonian design—although without the Hamiltonian monopolies or Federalist contempt for popular political participation. In the process, Madison legitimized the other side of a debate that had embroiled the nation since adoption of the Constitution.

The old debate did not abruptly stop. In 1819, a serious financial panic and a sectional collision over the admission of Missouri to the Union provoked new

Riding a tide of postwar prosperity and good will, James Monroe was swept into the presidency in the one-sided election of 1816, and re-elected unopposed in 1820. He presided over an era of rapid geographic and economic expansion in these early days of the Industrial Revolution. And in his historic Monroe Doctrine, he laid the cornerstone for a new foreign policy by declaring that the U.S. would not tolerate intervention in the Americas by any European nation.

Son of the Federalist second President, John Quincy Adams joined the Democratic Republicans and won election as a senator from Massachusetts in 1803. Appointed secretary of state under Monroe, he negotiated the Treaty of Ghent, which ended the War of 1812, then ran for President in 1824. Elected in a controversial vote by the House—which chose him over war hero Andrew Jackson, who had outpolled him by almost 50,000 votes—Adams served out his single term without popular or Congressional support and was defeated by a vengeful Jackson in the landslide election of 1828.

arguments about the country's transformation and the legislation of 1816. In the guise of Henry Clay's "American System," a Hamiltonian conception of a self-sufficient nation, where industrial development would build domestic markets for the farmers' surplus and Federal programs like the tariff and the national bank would tie the country's sections into a harmonious whole, would soon revitalize the old disputes. Moreover, the United States has seldom seen a less effective central government than during the years between 1820 and 1828, not least because the last of the Jeffersonian Presidents, James Monroe and John Quincy Adams, did not believe in leading Congress, while the Jeffersonians in Congress did not believe in being led. Monroe, the third of the Virginia dynasty of Presidents, a close associate of Jefferson and Madison throughout the party battle, and the last of the revolutionary veterans to hold the presidential office, presided grandly over the "Era of Good Feelings" that

began with his essentially unanimous culminating in the proclamation of the Monroe Doctrine in the annual message of 1823. John Quincy Adams, whose conversion from the party of his father to the Jeffersonian alliance was a vivid symbol of its triumph, recommended Federal measures going well beyond the modest readjustment made in Madison's last months. But Adams' ambitious program died at birth, in part because he would not use the powers of his office to promote his program or even to defend himself against the fragmentation of the Party. Presidential leadership and presidential patronage still smelled of influence and corruption, while the disappearance of the Federalists had freed the Jeffersonians to fight among themselves. But even as they did, the fundamental principles enunciated at the Party's founding would endure as a foundation for the views of both the Democrats and Whigs, revitalized and reconstructed for the age of Andrew Jackson.

Andrew Jackson won the presidential election of 1824 by 50,000 votes, but his opponent John Quincy Adams was voted in by the House when a rumored deal was struck with Senator Henry Clay to trade his support for an appointment as secretary of state. Adams kept the bargain, and Jackson inveighed against "corruption and intrigues" in Washington, rallying support behind a new coalition of southern planters and reformist northern republicans: the Democratic Party.

# CHAPTER THREE

# *YEARS OF TRIUMPH*

## 1825–1848

### BY ROBERT V. REMINI

Getters Andrew Jackson, the hero of the Battle of New Orleans, sat in his carriage seething with rage as he headed from Washington to his home outside Nashville, Tennessee. Along the way at various towns where he stopped, irate citizens surrounded his carriage to express their indignation over his betrayal by the "corrupt politicians" in the House of Representatives who had robbed him of the presidency. Old Hickory had won a plurality of popular and electoral votes in the presidential election of 1824 and clearly appeared to be the choice of the American people. But he did not have the constitutionally required majority of electoral votes and so the election was thrown to the House, where on February 9, 1825, the members chose John Quincy Adams to be the next President, a candidate who had won 15 fewer electoral votes and 30,000 fewer popular votes than Jackson in the fall election.

"We did all we could for you here," shouted one man to the general when he stopped off at a small town in Pennsylvania, "but the rascals at Washington cheated you out of it."

Old Hickory reacted instantly. He drew himself up to his full height of six feet. His gray-white hair bris-

tled with electricity; his sharp lantern jaw, jutting forward, accentuated the fierceness of his agitation; and his intensely blue eyes flashed anger as he roared out the words: "Indeed, my friend, there was cheating, and corruption and bribery, too." At every stop on his way home, Jackson repeated his outrage. "The people [have] been cheated," he thundered. "Corruption and intrigues at Washington...defeated the will of the people."

Jackson was referring to a rumor, widely circulated and believed in Washington, that a "corrupt bargain" had been struck between John Quincy Adams and the Speaker of the House of Representatives, Henry Clay of Kentucky, who had agreed to deliver enough votes to Adams in the House election to win the presidency—in return for which Adams would appoint Clay his secretary of state. And when Adams did win the presidency and then appointed Clay to head the State Department, a great many people, including Jackson, convinced themselves that the two men had indeed bargained "to steal the presidency" from the legitimate winner. "Was there ever witnessed such a bare-faced corruption in any country before?" raged Jackson.

Not long after he returned home, political leaders

Affectionately nicknamed the "Little Magician" in recognition of his superb political skills, New York's Martin Van Buren was among those calling for a rededication of the old Jeffersonian party to its founding principles. One of the moving forces behind Jackson's second presidential campaign, he ran as his vice presidential running mate in the election of 1832.

At various times secretary of war, secretary of state, senator from South Carolina and Vice President, John C. Calhoun spent most of his political career in search of a constitutional means of protecting slavery from Northern demands for abolition. His belief in the right of a state to nullify Federal law almost led to a civil war under the Jackson administration.

from every section of the country began to unite behind him in order to defeat the "monstrous union" of Adams and Clay in the next presidential election. These included, among many others, Senator Martin Van Buren of New York—short, balding, elegantly dressed, with the "most fascinating manners," called the Little Magician in recognition of his superb managerial and political skills; John C. Calhoun of South Carolina, secretary of war under President Monroe, fiercely intelligent and intense, with dark piercing eyes, who spoke in staccato fashion in a voice that was sharp and reedy; and Senator Thomas Hart Benton of Missouri, big and blustery, with a booming voice that rocked the Senate chamber whenever he spoke. Together, they organized the 1828 campaign on Jackson's behalf.

Van Buren called for a restructuring of the old

Jeffersonian Republican Party through an alliance between what he called "the planters of the South and the plain Republicans of the North," a party rededicated to the principles of Thomas Jefferson, but better organized in order to safeguard the liberties of the American people against the "corrupt intriguers in Washington." Calhoun agreed. "I believe," he wrote to Jackson, ". . . that the liberties of the country are in danger." The question was whether "power and patronage of the Executive or the voice of the people" will be "the real governing principle of our political system."

The organizational efforts of these men produced a new coalition that called itself the Democratic-Republican Party, or simply the Democratic Party. On the whole, Democrats opposed elitism and centralized government and, like Jackson, believed in the people and their right to self-rule. "The people are the Government," Jackson repeated over and over. "The people are sovereign. Their will is absolute." The opposition party of Clay and Adams came to be known as the National Republican Party. It adopted Clay's "American System," which called for a vigorous central government that would legislate a program of protective tariffs, a national bank and Federally funded public works.

The election of 1828 demonstrated how expertly the Democrats could campaign with a popular hero as their candidate. General Jackson was beloved by the people and the Democrats did not let them forget how much they owed him for his smashing victory over the British in New Orleans during the War of 1812. They established a chain of newspapers across the country to extol the virtues of Old Hickory and excoriate his opposition as the party of aristocrats brought to power by corruption and fraud.

Thus, the revitalized Democratic-Republican Party came into existence with a great shout of moral outrage against unscrupulous politicians in Washington who showed nothing but contempt for the "will of the people." Banners emblazoned with the words "JACKSON AND REFORM" appeared everywhere—north, south, east and west. In brief, declared the Democratic press, "the parties are Jackson and Adams, democracy and aristocracy."

Local and state committees were formed, frequently called Hickory Clubs, which organized and conducted rallies, parades, barbecues, dinners, street demonstrations and all manner of hoopla to attract the ever-increasing number of voters. Thus, the election of 1828 became a campaign of songs and slogans. Men wearing hickory leaves in their hats threw small coins among the crowds that watched them; they carried hickory canes as they marched in parade, and they

**Known as "Old Bullion" for his passionate advocacy of "specie"—gold and silver coin—and his opposition to paper money, Missouri's Thomas Hart Benton was Andrew Jackson's most potent voice in Congress during the political struggles that marked the oratorical golden age of the Senate.**

**Second only to Jackson, Henry Clay was the most popular man in America. Recognized as a statesman who could find solutions to seemingly intractable problems—particularly regional differences over slavery—he is regarded by many historians as perhaps the greatest senator in American history.**

**In one of the great dramatic events in American history, some 20,000 people congregated around the east portico of the Capitol to watch Andrew Jackson take his oath of office from Chief Justice John Marshall at the presidential inauguration of 1812. Afterward, thousands of admirers jammed into the White House for a raucus victory celebration for the President of the people.**

erected hickory poles in town squares, at crossroads, on steeples and steamboats. "Many of these poles were standing as late as 1845," wrote one contemporary, "rotten momentoes [sic] of the delirium of 1828." Although Democrats did not originate these campaigning methods, they brought them to a new level of inventiveness.

"Planting hickory trees!" snorted the opposition press. "Odds nuts and drumsticks! What have hickory trees to do with republicanism and the great contest?" To their great chagrin, they soon found out. Jackson won a tremendous victory in the election of 1828, with

56 percent of the total popular votes cast. And in the electoral college, he carried everything south of the Potomac River and west of New Jersey.

At his inauguration on March 4, 1829, some 20,000 people jammed their way into the vicinity of the Capitol to witness the triumph of their hero. "Persons have come five hundred miles to see General Jackson," exclaimed the astonished Daniel Webster, "and they really seem to think that the country is rescued from some dreadful danger!" At the conclusion of the inaugurating ceremonies, the crowd followed Jackson back to the White House and swarmed through the mansion, "scrambling, fighting, romping." The President, wrote the wife of a Maryland senator, was "nearly pressed to death and almost suffocated and torn to pieces by the people in their eagerness to shake hands with Old Hickory." Liquor was spilled on the floor, cut glass and china smashed, and men were seen standing with muddy boots on chairs and sofas to get a glimpse of the new leader. "It was a proud day for the people," reported one Democratic newspaper. "General Jackson is their own President."

Jackson proceeded to inaugurate a program of "reform, retrenchment and economy." He dismissed from office those guilty of fraud and incompetence and those "appointed against the manifest will of the people." He also called for a policy of "rotation" in filling government offices, a policy the National Republicans sneeringly referred to as a "spoils system." They also denounced his success in winning passage of the Indian Removal Act in 1830, by which the "Five Civilized Nations"—Creeks, Cherokees, Chickasaws, Choctaws and Seminoles—were transported to the Indian Territory west of the Mississippi River. Also, by adhering to a policy of strict economy, he wiped out the national debt. When he took office the debt stood at $60 million; by 1835 it had been completely extinguished.

"This month of January 1835," boomed Thomas Hart Benton at a Democratic celebration, "in the 58th year of the Republic, Andrew Jackson being President, the national Debt is paid! And the apparition, so long unseen on earth, a great nation without a national debt stands revealed to the astonished vision of a wondering world!"

Jackson also declared war against the Second National Bank of the United States because, among other things, it had dared to use its money to influence the outcome of national elections. The bank, Jackson contended, was a "hydra-headed monster" that subverted the electoral process, impaired "the morals of the people," bought Congressmen and sought "to destroy our

**Along with Henry Clay and John C. Calhoun, legendary orator Daniel Webster was one of the Great Triumvirate during the U.S. Senate's golden age. An intense nationalist, Webster concluded his famous debate with Senator Robert Y. Hayne of South Carolina over the nature of the Union with the ringing words: "Liberty and Union, now and forever, one and inseparable."**

**Andrew Jackson called the Bank of the United States a "hydra-headed monster" because it subverted the electoral process, impaired the "morals of the people," bought congressmen and sought to "destroy our republican institutions" by concentrating power in the hands of an elite few. "The Bank," he told Martin Van Buren, "is trying to kill me, but I will kill it." And he did.**

republican institutions" by concentrating power not among the people but in the hands of an elite few. When the President vetoed the bank's recharter bill, the wily Henry Clay believed he had an issue by which he could defeat Old Hickory in the presidential election of 1832. He was wrong.

During the 1832 campaign, the Democrats once again demonstrated their organizational skills. They programmed parades and barbecues and other forms of ballyhoo to get their message across. One parade in New York City stretched a mile long. The route was lighted by torches, and the marching faithful carried hundreds of banners depicting Jackson with Jefferson and Washington. Among the banners fluttered a live eagle, tied by the legs and perched on a pole surrounded by a wreath of leaves. The marchers halted periodically in front of the homes of well-known Democrats, where they let out a series of lusty "huzzas." They also stopped before the homes of National Republicans and razzed them with syncopated groans. Then they sang:

*"Hurra for the Hickory Tree!*
*Hurra for the Hickory Tree!*
*Its branches will wave o'er tyranny's grave.*
*And bloom for the brave and the free."*

Cartoons were used extensively in this campaign, especially by the National Republicans, who denounced "King Andrew I" as a tyrant and dictator. But the people did not believe these attacks on their President. Jackson was loved and trusted by the masses of people who recognized and appreciated his deep commitment to democracy, and they overwhelmingly supported him. Henry Clay was trounced in the election. Jackson received 219 electoral votes against 49 for Clay. The popular vote gave Jackson 688,242 and Clay 473,462.

As he returned to Washington following his victory, Jackson focused his thoughts almost entirely on events transpiring in South Carolina, where dissatisfaction over a new tariff had provoked the passage of an ordinance of tariff nullification which might have

Although the donkey later became the symbol of the Democratic Party, its first association with a Democrat was to criticize Jackson's veto of the rechartering of the Bank of the United States.

led to secession and civil war. Jackson threatened to lead an army into South Carolina, but the crisis was averted when Congress passed a compromise tariff in 1833.

At the conclusion of his second term, Jackson retired to his home outside Nashville and was suc-

ceeded by his Vice President, Martin Van Buren, who intended to continue Jackson's policies. Unfortunately, within a month of his inauguration, a dreadful economic depression struck the nation. It was part of a worldwide depression, although the opposition party, now called the Whigs, blamed the nation's fiscal woes

A Democratic editor wrote derisively in the presidential election year of 1840 that William Henry Harrison would be content to live in a log cabin with a barrel of cider. The privileged, wealthy Harrison and his fellow Whigs knew a good image when they saw one, seized upon the remark and conducted the so-called Log Cabin Campaign that won the election for Harrison.

on Jackson's financial policies, especially his war against the bank and his issuance of a "Specie Circular" on July 11, 1836, which forbade anything but gold and silver for the purchase of public lands. Some 600 banks failed, most eastern factories closed, the building of roads, bridges and canals was suspended, thousands lost their jobs and hungry laborers rioted in the cities to obtain food. As a result of this depression, known as the Panic of 1837, which lasted several

**Running on his war record, Old Tippecanoe—as William Henry Harrison had been known ever since his defeat of the Shawnee Indians at Tippecanoe, Indiana—was the beneficiary of a dreadful economic depression that alienated the voters and swept Martin Van Buren out of office. But after delivering the longest inaugural speech in history on a cold March day in 1841, he took ill of pneumonia and passed away a month later, the first President to die in office.**

years, Van Buren was a crippled President by the election of 1840.

The Whigs adopted Democratic techniques and methods of conducting a presidential campaign and nominated General William Henry Harrison, known as Old Tippecanoe, on account of his defeat of the Shawnee Indians at Tippecanoe, Indiana, in 1811. John Tyler of Virginia, a former Democrat, was nominated for the vice presidency, and throughout the campaign the Whigs chanted:

> *"Tippecanoe and Tyler Too,*
> *Van, Van is a used up man."*

Quipped one Whig: "There was rhyme, but no reason in it."

Americans flocked to the polls in unprecedented

**Called "His Accidency," because he was the first Vice President to succeed to the presidency on the death of his predecessor, John Tyler insisted that he had all the powers of a duly elected President, even though some disputed it. He soon won recognition for his claim, settling the Maine boundary dispute with Britain and—though he was a recent convert to the Whigs—campaigned for acquisition of Texas with the help of the Democrats in Congress.**

Manifest Destiny was the catchphrase coined to embody the spirit of territorial expansionism, the belief that Providence had bestowed on America the right to expand from ocean to ocean. True believers championed the cause of acquiring Texas and even Oregon, an area from the 42nd parallel to 54°40', then jointly occupied by the U.S. and Britain. The Democrats wanted it all.

numbers in 1840, a large percentage of them undoubtedly Democrats, but they turned their backs on Van Buren and swept Harrison into office.

While delivering the longest inaugural address in American history, President Harrison caught cold, and after only one month in office he succumbed to pneumonia—the first President to die in office. He was succeeded by the former Democrat, John Tyler; and although Tyler had switched parties, he had not renounced his Democratic principles. When Clay sought to enact the Whig program of economic measures, President Tyler vetoed them, including a bill to establish a new national bank. "Egad," laughed one Democrat, "Tyler has found one of old Jackson's pens

and it wouldn't write any way but plain and straitforward."

With the help of the Democrats in Congress, Tyler then sought to engineer the acquisition of Texas, which had already won its independence from Mexico. The Whigs, under Clay's direction, opposed the acquisition, fearing a war with Mexico, and they nominated Clay once again to run for the presidency in 1844. As their standard bearer, the Democrats chose the first dark horse in American history: James Knox Polk of Tennessee, or Young Hickory, as he was called.

Like many Americans at the time, Democrats were imbued with the spirit of what John L. O'Sullivan, editor of the *Democratic Review*, called "Manifest Destiny."

This was a belief that "Providence" had given the nation a right to possess the entire continent in order to extend the blessings of liberty and self-government on all who resided within this land. They not only championed the acquisition of Texas but of Oregon as well. Oregon, lying roughly from the Rocky Mountains to the Pacific Ocean and from the 42nd parallel to 54°40', was jointly occupied at this time by the United States and Great Britain. Democrats wanted it all. "Fifty-Four Forty or Fight," they cried. The possibility of concurrently fighting Mexico to acquire Texas, and Great Britain to acquire Oregon bordered on madness, but the nation seemed determined to stretch its boundaries from ocean to ocean.

During the campaign, Clay wrote two letters to Alabama editors that were published around the nation in which he seemed to waffle on the issue of expansion. Democrats jeered him, and then put it into rhyme:

> "He wires in and wires out,
> And leaves the people still in doubt,
> Whether the snake that made the track,
> Was going South, or coming back."

Democrat James Knox Polk, a protégé of Andrew Jackson known as "Young Hickory," was elected America's first dark horse President in 1844. Calling for the annexation of Texas and acquiring Oregon from the British, he then provoked a confrontation on Texas' southern border to justify declaring war on Mexico, which was shattered in a series of devastating battles with the American army. Among the fruits of victory were New Mexico and California.

The presidential election of 1844 was close. Although he was not well known and faced an opposition candidate who was regarded as one of the nation's great statesmen, Polk won—but only by a whisker. What helped him enormously, especially in the large northern cities, was the influx of many Irish and German Catholics who swelled the ranks of the Democratic Party. With good reason, they feared the Whigs as religious bigots and voted almost to a man for the dark horse. Out of the 2,698,605 popular votes cast in this election, only 38,181 votes separated the two candidates. Had Clay won New York, he would have captured the presidency.

With what some called a mandate from the American people, in the final months of Tyler's administration, Congress now passed a joint resolution annexing Texas to the United States. "Texas is ours!" shouted the Democrats. And the dying former President, Andrew Jackson, added his feeble voice to the tumult: "I not only rejoice but congratulate my beloved country."

In his inaugural address, President Polk seemed dissatisfied with acquiring only Texas. He went on to declare in his message that the United States had a "clear and unquestionable" title to Oregon, a state-

ment that some feared would surely provoke a war with Great Britain. But both Polk and Britain chose to negotiate the issue and ultimately settled on the 49th parallel as the line separating Canada from the United States. The treaty was signed in 1846.

Mexico proved more troublesome. Polk had his eye on California, and when Mexico refused to sell it, he deliberately provoked an incident along the Texas-Mexico border that resulted in a military action in which sixteen American soldiers were killed or wounded. Informed of this action, Polk asked Congress for a declaration of war and both Houses immediately complied. Polk signed the declaration on May 13, 1846.

Leader of the Whigs, Henry Clay implored the Senate to oppose acquisition of Texas in order to avert a war with Mexico. Condemning the Democrats' vision of Manifest Destiny, he ran for President against Polk—and nearly won.

Americans were encouraged to settle in Texas with promises of home rule and generous land grants in return for which they agreed to become Mexican citizens. But when their attempts to win annexation by the United States prompted the Mexicans to centralize control of Texas, General Santa Anna led an army into Texas and wiped out a garrison of 180 Texans at the Alamo.

The war shattered Mexico. In one battle after another, United States troops, even when they were outnumbered, defeated the Mexican forces sent against them. General Zachary Taylor won several battles in northern Mexico, while General Stephen Kearney marched from Fort Leavenworth to San Diego, seizing Santa Fe along the way. And General Winfield Scott, landing at Vera Cruz, marched to Mexico City, defeated an army attempting to block his path and captured the city. All resistance to American arms collapsed, and the Treaty of Guadalupe Hidalgo was signed on February 2, 1848. Mexico recognized the Rio Grande as its northern border and ceded New Mexico and California to the United States. In return, the United States agreed to pay Mexico $15 million and assume claims by American citizens against Mexico of up to $3.25 million.

When Polk kept his promise not to run for re-elec-

Enduring deprivation, hardship and Indian attacks, wagon trains of settlers spread out across the continent during the early decades of the nineteenth century. Traveling trails that the first explorers had blazed west—the Santa Fe, the Oregon, the Mormon, the Old Spanish and the Oxbow—they populated lands from the Mississippi to the Pacific and Canada to the Rio Grande.

During his last 25 years, Jackson suffered from rheumatism, dysentery and the effects of other diseases contracted during his military career in fighting Indians, the British and the Spanish, and he experienced intense physical pain because of a bullet he carried in his chest. Just before his death on June 8, 1845, a saddened Jackson was preoccupied not with his ailments but with forebodings about the tragic consequences of deepening divisions within the Union over slavery.

tion in 1848, the Democrats nominated Lewis Cass, a former secretary of war in Jackson's cabinet. Seizing their opportunity, the Whigs chose a Mexican war hero, General Zachary Taylor, as their candidate, and he won the election largely because Martin Van Buren, now the candidate of the third party, the Free Soil Party, which advocated the abolition of slavery, took enough votes away from Cass in New York to cost him the election.

The United States now stretched from ocean to ocean, occupying a vast continent that guaranteed its future greatness. But a quarrel over the extension of slavery into these newly acquired lands seemed in-evitable after Pennsylvania Congressman David Wilmot in 1846 offered an amendment to an appropriations bill that forbade the introduction of slavery into any territory to be acquired in the future. Southerners swore they would leave the Union if the benefits of the Mexican War were denied to them. Just before his death on June 8, 1845, Andrew Jackson foresaw the consequences of this looming quarrel. If the Union cracked apart, he warned, it would take "oceans of blood and hundreds of millions" to put it back together. It was a warning, tragically, that went unheeded.

The guns began firing in April of 1861. One million Confederate soldiers went into combat against 2.3 million Union troops. By the time Grant and Lee signed the armistice that ended the Civil War four bloody years later, over 620,000 men had been killed, the South lay in ruins along with the shameful institution of slavery, and the course of American history was changed forever.

# CHAPTER FOUR

# *IN THE WILDERNESS*

## 1849–1872

### BY JEAN H. BAKER

During the quarter century from 1849–1872, the Democratic Party faced the gravest challenges in its history. In the end, these years would carry no great leader's name. Nor would they be celebrated for any party-inspired public policy. Even devoted followers recognized "the most disastrous epoch in party annals." "Our condemnation to hell," wrote another in the spiritual language partisans often used. "And when is salvation?" Fragmented before the Civil War, separated into southern and northern halves during the war, removed from national power into the thickets of opposition and condemned as traitors in the aftermath of Reconstruction, the Party displayed its durability. Simply to survive such adversity was to triumph and to become, henceforth, like the post–Civil War Union, secure.

Yet no one, not even the Party's Whig opponents, predicted such misfortune in the late 1840s. With the assurance of a powerful majority party that had elected nine of the thirteen Presidents after George Washington's two terms and that had controlled one or both houses of Congress five times after Andrew Jackson's second term, the Democrats dismissed their presiden-

tial loss in 1848 to General Zachary Taylor as a temporary setback. Explanations came easily. Divisions in the New York party had led some Democrats to vote for the Free-Soilers, who opposed any extension of slavery into new territories. But this third party was destined to fade away.

Next time the faithful would organize more effectively and "do their duty," using the party structure that reached from state conventions into local districts. And by 1850 a new compromise, with its careful balancing of southern and northern interests, seemed to have ended sectional tensions. At least the optimists in the Party thought so.

Centrally organized after the formation of a national committee in 1848 to oversee party concerns between presidential elections, the Democrats looked forward to the election of 1852. To win, "the Democracy"—in the affectionate party label that linked partisanship to a national ideal—must mobilize the faithful. Most were as loyal to the Party as to their church. Having learned their politics at home, some remembered a Democratic ancestry that reached back to a grandfather's vote for Thomas Jefferson or a father's reverence for Andrew Jackson. "It has been the pride

Silk banners were often carried during campaigns in Democratic torchlight parades. But this didn't help in 1848 when Michigan's Lewis Cass and Kentucky's William Butler lost to a Whig presidential ticket led by General Zachary Taylor.

of my life to rank myself as a Democrat," wrote one Ohioan.

Such men never "scratched a ticket" to substitute the name of another party's candidate. Nor did they stay at home in an era in which turnouts for presidential elections ran over 70 percent and in 1856 reached over 80 percent. Such zeal was not limited to presidential elections. Nearly as many voters in the highly competitive two-party politics of mid-century America cast ballots for lesser offices like sheriff, state delegate and town alderman as for those at the top of the ticket like congressman and President.

With party politics serving not only as a habit but as ceremony and boisterous entertainment as well, this generation's partisans marched in torchlight parades, erected huge poles that soared into the sky with the name of their Democratic favorite on top and listened avidly to long stump speeches often lost in the wind of an age before microphones. Then they cast their

Democratic ballots, many decorated with a drawing of their hero Andrew Jackson or sometimes the rooster that signified their party had much "to crow about."

In 1852, as they prepared to do battle with the Whigs, the Democrats had to first nominate a presidential ticket at their national convention. There was excitement and novelty as nearly 300 delegates chosen at county conventions gathered in Baltimore. It was only the sixth such assembly in their history. Few delegates had a deep commitment to any candidate, awaiting instead the decision of a state or local leader to go for perhaps Lewis Cass of Michigan, an acknowledged "Northern man with Southern principles." Others preferred a younger man such as Senator Stephen Douglas, the popular five-foot, four-inch "Little Giant" from Illinois. And a third segment hoped that James Buchanan, the rich bachelor with the wandering eye from Pennsylvania's Lancaster County, would be chosen.

Delegates, leaders and presidential aspirants held intense bonds to their party and believed the convention a means of achieving unity. To this end they formed a committee of organization to select permanent officers and report rules. Next they created a committee of credentials to determine who was eligible, along with a committee of resolutions to provide a party creed. All these committees were arranged on the Federal principle of one delegate from each state. When the voting began, the unit rule assured consensus within most state delegations. Likewise, the two-thirds rule required for the nomination, which Northerners considered a sop to the South, depended on the the harmony that Democrats felt was one of their cardinal principles.

Forty-nine ballots later, the Democrats nominated the dark horse Franklin Pierce, a former senator from New Hampshire whose unknown convictions made him attractive to an increasingly divided party. The

Diminutive Illinois Senator Stephen A. Douglas began in county politics and rose to become a well-known Democratic leader in the 1850s, struggling to negotiate peacefully the differences between abolitionists and secessionists. He supported the Union when the nation divided and war broke out in 1861, but in June, broken in spirit, the "Little Giant" died.

Attractive to a divided party because of his unknown political convictions, former New Hampshire Senator Franklin Pierce was nominated as the Democrats' dark horse candidate for President and defeated Whig Winfield Scott in 1852. Hoping to defuse regional divisions over slavery, Pierce backed the Kansas-Nebraska Act but failed to win renomination.

STEPHEN FINDING "HIS MOTHER".

In this newspaper cartoon, Uncle Sam and Columbia chastise Democrat Senator Stephen Douglas for promoting the Kansas-Nebraska Act, which allowed settlers to decide for themselves whether or not to have slavery in these territories. Angry opponents of the Act denounced it for contributing to regional unrest and united in 1854 to form a new faction that called itself the Republican Party.

Democratic platform also demonstrated the growing disagreement over the slavery issue that now seemed to reach into every aspect of public affairs. True to "the distinctive features of our political creed," the Party's resolutions were mostly a series of prohibitions on congressional powers. These included a denial of Federal authority over the "domestic institutions" of states, this era's cue phrase for slavery, a word nineteenth century Democrats avoided in their official documents.

Pierce won easily over Winfield Scott in the fall elections, carrying all but four states. Some said his victory came because he was a truer friend to compromise than Scott was. But Democrats—north and south—who looked beyond this temporary settlement and the immediate satisfaction of a return to power

and control over national patronage worried about "the feverish pulse" threatening the health of the Republic. Not only was the disagreement apparent in Congress, where the election of a Speaker of the House became more difficult in the 1850s, but sectional loyalties were rapidly corroding party discipline on national issues relating to slavery. On these roll calls, northern and southern Democrats increasingly voted with members of their region.

Everywhere northern Democrats were abandoning their previous "shrine of party," especially after the passage of Stephen Douglas' Kansas-Nebraska Act, which granted settlers in those territories the right to decide for themselves whether to have slavery. Northern Democrats of free-soil complexion were outraged at a piece of legislation that undid the Missouri Com-

The presidency was a prize Buchanan had long coveted, but he became enmeshed in the secessionist crisis of 1860 and declined to run for re-election. He had tried to remain conciliatory toward the dissident southern states, but abandoned that strategy before he left office and denied them the right to secede from the Union, though many of them did.

promise. Since 1820, the Compromise had prohibited slavery north of the 36°30' parallel running through southern Missouri. Meanwhile, in the South, former Whigs were joining the Democrats.

What Senator Douglas was after in the Kansas-Nebraska Act, among other intentions, was the characteristic democratic solution of letting the people of each territory decide for themselves. Popular sovereignty, it was called in the newspapers and by Douglas, who held as his strongest conviction the authority of local communities to serve as a check on the centralization of power. But in the streets and towns and especially in Kansas, where Americans were already fighting over slavery, the Kansas-Nebraska Act was known as "squatter sovereignty." Whatever its name in the politically overheated 1850s, Douglas' formula for ending controversy only increased the divisions among Democrats.

In fact, the whole party system was in turmoil. A former Whig from Maryland was only one of thou-

James Buchanan, Polk's secretary of state, won the nomination over President Pierce and Senator Douglas in 1856, then won the tumultuous fall election against candidates from two parties, both splintered from the defunct Whigs: Republican John C. Freemont and former President Fillmore, nominee of the xenophobic, anti-Catholic "Know-Nothing" Party.

DEMOCRATIC CANDIDATES

FOR PRESIDENT,

JAMES BUCHANAN.

Vice-President, J. C. Breckinridge.

69

In "The Verdict of the People," a boisterous street scene that typified the hurley-burley of American politics in the mid-nineteenth century, Caleb Bingham portrayed an election day marked by uninhibited political arguments and electioneering at the polling place, with voters filling out their ballots not only in full view but after open consultation with their neighbors.

sands who announced that he was forced into the Democratic Party after twenty years in opposition because "that party has become the bulwark of Southern rights." In Ohio a Democrat announced that he was leaving a party that had been the pride of his life because "the lion of Democracy has become the jackal of Slavery." Still others held to their allegiance because they considered their party one of the few remaining national organizations in the period of sectional tension. "Our whole country, the Democracy and the Constitution" became their slogan.

Amidst these partisan shifts, in 1856 Democrat James Buchanan won the presidency he had long coveted. Ominously for the Democrats, he had been challenged by candidates representing two new parties— the Republicans and the American (or Know Nothing) Party, the latter opposed to the growing influence of immigrants and Catholics. Gone were the Whigs, the Free-Soilers, the Free Democrats (a free-soil faction of the Democrats organized mainly in New York) and the

ephemeral Liberty Party, an antislavery movement. Gone were the local issues that had often served to cut across more dangerous regional differences. The oldest and now the only political organization binding North and South together, the proud Democracy had survived one of those rare occurrences: a realignment of political parties and voting behavior. But for how long?

The answer came in the spring of 1860 in the exotic surroundings of Charleston, South Carolina, with its elegant architecture, its radical pro-secessionist attitudes and its views of the unfinished Fort Sumter, a Federal installation. Here, in 100-degree heat, Democratic delegates convened to nominate a President and to write a platform. But the Party that had cautiously treaded its way through the explosive issues of the 1850s proceeded to shatter in physical confrontations between Northerners and Southerners whose devotion to the Party now buckled. First, the platform committee splintered over the South's demand for con-

**Stephen Douglas defeated him for a Senate seat after a series of celebrated debates in 1858, but in their 1860 rematch, Abraham Lincoln prevailed over his eloquent adversary. Their views on slavery were similar, but Douglas tried to portray him as an abolitionist radical and Lincoln denounced Douglas for defending the Dred Scott decision. Lincoln won the debate and the election.**

gressional protection of slavery in the territories. Then seven Southern delegations walked out. At one point during a torrential rainstorm, when Douglas supporters attempted to get a vote, the galleries emptied onto the floor. A riot began; small groups of delegates grappled with one another, "surging about like waves of the sea and urged on by the audience." Soon, angry delegates were leaving Charleston to reconvene—and perhaps reunite elsewhere.

Instead, after three other conventions, by November of 1860 voters confronted the results of this schism in not one but two Democratic presidential tickets, one led by Stephen Douglas' Northern Democrats and the other by Kentucky's John Breckinridge of the National Democratic Party, a faction committed to the protection of slavery by the Federal Government in the territories. Party history had become a bitter preview of the nation's fate.

In November, the Republican Abraham Lincoln was elected President by a plurality of votes. Lincoln had carried only the North in an election that displayed the extent to which the United States was already two nations. Unknown to many Americans and already condemned in the South, Lincoln was familiar to his fellow Illinoisan Douglas, who had come to respect him during their debates in 1858. As they contended for the Illinois Senate seat, Douglas and Lincoln offered the voters a compelling discussion of the implications of the extension of slavery and the Dred Scott decision, which would permit slaveholders to take their slaves into Western territory. Neither man opposed slavery in the southern states; the argument was not about its past, but its future.

The two men's differences in size and personality highlighted their conflicts over policy. Lincoln was tall, calm and melancholic. Douglas was short, fat and mercurial. But they shared intense ambition, enthusiasm for parties as an instrument of national importance and of personal prestige, and an abiding commitment to the Union.

Lincoln had lost the senatorship to Douglas, but not their rematch in 1860. Within weeks of Lincoln's election as President, South Carolina led a parade of southern states out of the Union. In every case, the leaders of this revolution were southern Democrats, determined to create a new Confederate States of America. At first most northern Democrats cautioned against coercing the South. "Let them go in peace"

John C. Breckinridge, who had served as Vice President under James Buchanan, ran again in 1860, this time for President. Nominated by the "National Democrats," a faction committed to the protection of territorial slavery, he campaigned against not only the Republicans' Abraham Lincoln but "Northern Democrat" Stephen Douglas, winning nine southern states but losing the election.

was their cry of conciliation, for at this point they would appease their "erring sisters." "War," insisted a Democratic congressman from Ohio, "is no remedy."

Then the guns of April 1861 began as South Carolinian batteries shelled Fort Sumter in Charleston Harbor. Lincoln immediately called up 75,000 militia and began the organization of an army, most of whom were on duty in the West. At first all was quiet along the Potomac, though there were skirmishes near Washington. Only in July were both sides ready for the slaughter that followed.

When Lincoln's call came, thousands of northern Democrats volunteered. Following Stephen Douglas' impassioned plea to be "patriots not traitors," they followed the Union. Even Fernando Wood, a former New York mayor notorious for his southern sympathies,

Encamped outside Washington to protect the capital, the 96th Pennsylvania Infantry awaits the call to action. It came in the spring of 1862 when General George McClellan ordered them to join the rest of his vast Army of the Potomac in a march southward to flank enemy lines and capture the Confederate capital at Richmond. It was a bloody campaign, and it failed.

called upon Democrats in his organization to "form a Phalanx" and support their country now under attack. By July his Mozart Hall regiment was training in Yonkers, and soon they were fighting in Virginia as members of the Union army. New Jersey's Third Congressional District (one of the Democrats' safe seats during the Civil War) sent hundreds of volunteers officered by the district's Democratic leaders to serve the Union. Even those who did not fight remembered the symbolic act of Douglas, who had reached out to hold

Lincoln's hat as the new President delivered his first inaugural address in March of 1861.

Not every Democrat was so loyal to the Union. Individual Democrats (probably more often than Republicans) did desert, did oppose Lincoln's preliminary Emancipation Proclamation in 1862 and throughout the war did encourage negotiations before the unconditional surrender of the South. Congressman Clement C. Vallandigham of Ohio was the most notorious. Arrested for criticizing the war, he was exiled to the Confederacy and later ran unsuccessfully from Canada for Ohio governor in 1863. His platform was "I am a Democrat, for Constitution, for law, for Union, for liberty."

True to their understanding of loyal opposition—which as the party of government they had rarely been—Union Democrats opposed what they believed to be Lincoln's tyrannies. They protested the closing of newspapers; they fulminated against the arrests and trials of civilians in military courts; they called attention to the government's suspension of the ancient protection of habeas corpus. They were for the freedoms and liberties of Americans even during Civil War.

Though a distinct minority in the wartime con-gresses, an organized band of Democrats voted against the Republicans' legislative program of emancipation, confiscation (by which the government took the property of Confederates in rebellion against it), high tariffs and a national banking system. Convinced that blacks were inferior even in their biblical origins and that therefore African-Americans could never be citizens, they opposed a bill that permitted blacks to serve in the Union army. Throughout, Democrats adhered to their pre-war principles that the primary function of their party was to stand for, and implement, their convictions that the best government was the least government. Just as the state should do nothing that the country could properly do, so the national

Frustrated by McClellan's reluctance to take the initiative in combat, Lincoln visited his commanding general in the field to prod him into action, but despite his numerical advantage over the Confederates, the overcautious McClellan continued to await replacements rather than press the offensive, even in pursuit of Lee's retreating army. "If you do not want to use the army," Lincoln wrote him, "I would like to borrow it for a few days." Finally, he removed McClellan from command.

government must not interfere with state business. But in time of war, when government naturally expands its power, the Democratic message often seemed little more than obstructionist.

For generations, Democrats had believed themselves watchmen guarding the Republic from too many laws and too much government interference. Now they held to the slogan that one Democratic editor used on the masthead of his newspaper: "The Sovereignty of the People, the Rights of the States, and a Light and Simple Government." Removed from power and the spoils of office that tightened the bonds of the Party among their followers, practical Democrats of the war period reaffirmed the importance of patronage to their organization.

As a result of the Democrats' continuing partisan opposition, the now-powerful Republicans converted them into traitors and held them to be at the heart of every subversion. There were in fact few instances of

sabotage during the Civil War, but in the Republican imagination every Democrat became a copperhead—a traitorous snake in the grass like Vallandigham.

Still, the Democratic Party endured, in part because the local nature of American politics always provided an election victory somewhere. Success in carrying a state legislature like the one in New Jersey or electing a congressman in New York boosted party morale. Then, in the 1862 elections, the Party gained 35 seats in Congress, elected governors in New Jersey and New York, and carried statewide contests in Illinois, Pennsylvania and Indiana. Although divided about their proper response to the war, the Democrats resisted the encouragement of Lincoln to join his hastily created Union Party. This, according to protesting Democrats, was no more than a Trojan horse for the Republicans. Meanwhile, in the Confederacy, where Democrats had been strong before the war, President Jefferson Davis discouraged all partisan opposition. To his disadvan-

**Democrats regarded George McClellan as a wartime hero. After his removal from the military in 1862, he ran for President as a Democrat in 1864 on a platform that criticized the war and sought reconciliation with the South. Though he carried 44 percent of the votes, McClellan lost to Lincoln.**

**Democrats powwowed at the 1864 national convention in Chicago in a giant wigwam, nominating McClellan as their standard bearer. The very fact that an election could be held during a civil war affirmed the deep attachment of all Americans to the electoral process. But there was no denying that the Party's divided loyalties on the issue of slavery during the war put it out of touch not only with the people but with its own tradition of equal justice, ceding the moral high ground to the Republicans.**

tage, he operated without the loyal opposition the wartime Democratic Party provided for the Lincoln government.

Lacking a powerful national voice after Stephen Douglas died a few weeks after Fort Sumter fell—a death mourned by Democrats as symbolizing their shattered party—the Democrats still faced the presidential elections in 1864 with confidence. They remembered the gathering tradition of one-term presidencies after Andrew Jackson's two terms. They remembered "the partisan imperative" that had made them active seekers of power and position before the war. Democrats also observed the divisive factions

within the Republicans. They drew attention to the continuation of war that was draining the blood of young Americans. Union General Ulysses Grant might stand before Richmond, but he had stalled there. "We are coming, Abraham Lincoln," went one Democratic song, "with the ghosts of murdered men."

Nominating a popular symbol of their patriotism, Union General George McClellan, on the first ballot, delegates at the Democratic National Convention in 1864 included a "peace before reunion" plank in a platform that criticized the Republicans' "four years of failure." Clearly the Union remained the centerpiece of their ideals. While McClellan accepted his party's

**After the war, the Republican majority passed a program of legislative reform during the years of Reconstruction. In this wood-cut, former slaves celebrate the passage of a civil rights bill designed to outlaw various forms of discrimination. But the old ways ran deep. Even the Emancipation Proclamation, signed in 1863, didn't really begin to take hold until the turn of the century.**

complaints against Republican "tyrannies," he later explained that he supported the surrender of the Confederacy before any negotiations began. Although Lincoln was easily re-elected, the tenacious Democrats received 44 percent of the vote. Closed into minority status with the South out of the Union, they had still remained competitive. As significant as the returns was the assumption by members of both parties that even during a destructive civil war, the Republic was best served by a competitive election between two contesting political organizations.

To Democrats it seemed that the war would never end, though in fact by the presidential election of 1864, Lee's army was cornered in Virginia. Barefoot and hungry, its soldiers fought on with only the possibility

of a negotiated peace as a realistic goal to save the Confederacy. Finally, in April of 1865, with Sherman on the march in North Carolina, the Army of Northern Virginia surrendered to its powerful antagonist, Grant's Army of the Potomac. Eleven days later, Abraham Lincoln was assassinated, and the nation went into mourning as thousands lined the tracks from Washington to watch the funeral train bearing his body to its final resting place in Springfield, Illinois. In life, Lincoln had been a divisive and partisan figure throughout the war. In death, he was transfigured into a unifying symbol of reconciliation.

The Vice President, Democrat Andrew Johnson of Tennessee, a tailor's son, was sworn into the presidency and served out the remainder of Lincoln's second term. Democrats hoped to ride Johnson's coattails back into power in the next election, but he became the center of a movement to create a new party of conservatives called the National Unionists that could attract Democrats and Republicans alike. Their standard bearer, however, was not only a proud and obstinate political maverick but also, some said, an immoderate drinker, and after a few months in office had alienated not only the Republicans but many of his own party as well. When he refused to act on congressional Reconstructionist legislation even after it was passed over his veto, he was finally brought up on charges of impeachment and driven from office in 1868.

The ensuing political vacuum was filled by New York's Samuel Tilden, leader of the Democrats' swallow-tail faction, named for their elegant dress and deep pockets. Tilden had a talent for organization, and in 1868 he formed speakers' bureaus, gathered lists of Democrats and mailed pamphlets throughout the land emblazoned with the Democratic message that the "Republican radicals would make white men slaves to their arbitrary laws." In the summer, the Democratic National Convention nominated the former New York Governor Horatio Seymour, who only reluctantly took the stump. With most of the South still controlled by the Republicans, Seymour carried 47 percent of the vote but lost to the popular Ulysses Grant.

A hero on the battlefield, Grant proved an ineffectual President. His regime was marked by scandals that included his close associate's selling of offices, an effort by his brother-in-law to corner the gold market and the selling of stock as bribes to highly placed government officials. But in Congress, meanwhile, the process of "reconstructing" the Union was under way. Democrats supported a policy of "restoration" whereby white Southerners (who could be expected to support their party) were pardoned and permitted to return to Washington as representatives of their states. Opposing the wartime amendments intended to give freed male slaves the rights of citizenship and voting, Democrats instead held to "the Constitution as it is, the Union as it was, and the Negroes where they were."

Two years later, President Grant's corruption split the Republicans. Hungry for victory, the Democrats accepted perhaps the strangest bedmate of their history in Horace Greeley, the crusty editor of the *New York Tribune*. But Greeley was no Democrat; the South was still controlled by the Republicans and the

New York's Horatio Seymour was one of the few Democrats to serve as a governor during the Civil War. In the wake of his inflammatory speech attacking the Lincoln government on July 4, 1863, New York City erupted in a bloody riot. Nominated for President in 1868, he ran against Grant and lost.

Democrats remained in the wilderness. Still the Party had learned that fusion was no solution. To return to power they must be Democrats—true followers of the Jeffersonian and Jacksonian faith who opposed the flood of Reconstruction legislation with their ancient battle cry: financial retrenchment, equal rights before the law and justice in serving every white man. "We are Democrats, and we must stay Democrats," concluded one state leader.

Meanwhile, on the local level as well as in Congress, the Democrats fought the Republicans over Republican-designed procedures for the return of the former Confederate states to the Union. Democrats supported amnesty and pardon for white Southerners

An impossible scene even to imagine before the war, Currier and Ives portrayed a gathering that dramatized how far the nation had come down the road to equality in the years of Reconstruction: a group of former slaves, most of them southern Democrats—one Senator and six Representatives—who had won election to the 41st and 42nd Congress.

who had fought for the Confederacy. They opposed the Freedman's Bureau, which was designed to aid the newly freed slaves, and the 15th Amendment, which established black male voting. Out of step with twentieth century principles, they stood for reunification under the traditions of the past. Briefly in a so-called "New Departure," southern Democrats flirted with disaffected Republicans and sought black votes in the South. But by the 1870s they returned to a harsh "white line" policy that depended on the mobilization of white voters and the persistent opposition to Federal power that had marked their policies since Douglas' Kansas-Nebraska Act. In time this strategy would create a dependable source of Democratic electoral votes.

At the beginning of Reconstruction, white Democrats who had fought against the Union were disenfranchised, making the former Confederacy a Republican stronghold. In time the coalition of newly freed African-Americans, former Whigs and new Southerners was displaced. So-called Bourbon Democratic leaders of wealth and stature returned to run the Party as they had before the war. As Democrats solidified their hold and continued to recover a region that had been the strength of their Party on the eve of the Civil War, their possibilities for victory increased. Meanwhile, their popularity grew in the North. In northern cities the opportunities for urban political machines based on patronage and effective administration of city affairs developed. William Tweed and John Kelly's Tammany organization became models of a mature machine that influenced voters by catering to special needs with vital urban services.

By the 1870s, the Democratic Party had been buffeted by nearly twenty years of challenging events. Then, in the early 1870s, a brief post-war depression

**It was a sign of how far the Democrats had fallen during the years of the Civil War that the Party actually nominated a Republican for President in 1872. Facing the popular Republican incumbent, Ulysses Grant, they turned to Horace Greeley, an ardent pacifist-abolitionist who had protested the war and excoriated slavery as editor of his newspaper, the *New York Tribune*. Focusing his campaign attacks less on the Republicans than on the party that nominated him, he lost badly in November.**

swept across the United States, and Democrats countered their opponents' Waving of the Bloody Shirt of wartime memories with their own Showing an Empty Purse, emptied by Republican fiscal policies. But it wasn't until 1874 that the Democrats achieved their first national victory since the election of Buchanan in 1856. Aided by hard times throughout the nation, the Party won over two-thirds of the seats in Congress, erasing Republican voting margins. "This election," crowed one Democrat, "is not a victory but a revolution." It was not that, for it would be five years before the Party controlled both the Senate and the House, and another ten before Grover Cleveland would be elected. But 1874 did inaugurate a return from the wilderness by a party that had survived the worst.

The experience of the Democratic Party during the

quarter-century from 1849–1872 displayed, if nothing else, the loyalty of their members during a catastrophic period in Party affairs. In its efforts to save the Union, the Party had played both sides of the slavery issue. It had opposed the policy revolution of the Republicans in the wartime congresses, and after the war it had reached out a welcoming hand to returning Confederates, not to blacks. Democrats had survived by remembering the ideals of their past as a community of believers led by Jefferson, Jackson and Douglas. They had also endured because of their grass-roots organization and because of the importance of parties during this era. Although the political landscape changed after the war, they still held to the same ideals and the sense of brotherhood. Now they looked forward to the presidential election of 1876.

Grover Cleveland, a former mayor of Buffalo known for his aversion to wasteful expenditure and political patronage, ran with Thomas A. Hendricks and won on a reform ticket for the Democrats in 1884. Known as the "Buxom Buffalonian"—"Uncle Jumbo" by his nephews—he seemed to embody not only Democratic values but the expansiveness of the Gilded Age itself.

# CHAPTER FIVE

# *THE GILDED AGE*

## 1873–1896

### BY MICHAEL MCGERR

I n 1872, the Democratic Party actually nominated a Republican for President—that was how far the Democracy had fallen since the start of the Civil War. Facing the popular Republican incumbent, Ulysses Grant, the Democrats had no obvious candidate of their own, so they endorsed Horace Greeley, the outspoken, sometimes erratic editor of the *New York Tribune*, who had already been nominated by a motley group of Grant's opponents, the Liberal Republicans. Greeley lost badly to the quiet hero of the Union in November. Already in the minority in the United States Senate, the Democrats also lost control of the House of Representatives that year. Saddled with a record of hostility to the Union war effort and to the Reconstruction of the South, the Party had reached a sad nadir at the start of America's Gilded Age.

By the mid-1880s, however, Democrats were back in power in Washington. In 1884, the country put a Democrat, Grover Cleveland, in the White House. Defeated for re-election four years later, Cleveland reclaimed the presidency in 1892. With majorities in the House and Senate, the Democratic Party was finally ready to govern the nation. But by 1896, the Democrats were in disarray again, deeply divided by

the traumatic events of the decade. This political roller-coaster ride was a result of turbulent times. The Gilded Age, which got its name from a novel by Mark Twain and Charles Dudley Warner, would be stereotyped as an epoch of new wealth, raw energy, gaudy display and shaky public morals. It saw rapid industrialization of the nation, the rise of large-scale corporations, the battle between labor and capital, the relative decline of rural America, and the continuing immigration of millions. Confronting such tumultuous change, both Democrats and Republicans alike had trouble figuring out how to hold on to power and to lead the country.

Despite all these difficulties, the Gilded Age was still a golden age for America's major political parties. The Democrats and Republicans would never again command so much material and cultural power. In the late nineteenth century, American men considered unswerving loyalty to one party or another as a basic element of being a man. To be an independent, rather than a committed partisan, was supposedly to be less than a real man. The parties could count on male voters to join political clubs, to march in great torchlight parades and to vote a straight party ticket almost without fail. Moreover, the Republicans and Democrats

The powerful boss of New York's Tammany Hall, William Tweed, once offered half a million dollars to political cartoonist Thomas Nast not to publish a particular caricature of him. It ran anyway, fueling the public cry for "Reform" in the Gilded Age. This one depicts the "ruins" of his corrupt machine after an election setback in 1871, but it wasn't until 1872 that Tweed was finally convicted and imprisoned. He died behind bars.

controlled the major medium of communication: Most of the nation's thousands of daily and weekly newspapers pledged allegiance to one party or the other. In their passionate editorials and their often biased news stories, these papers preached the virtues of rabid partisanship. The parties also controlled the machinery of elections: Local Democratic and Republican Party organizations ran nominating primaries and printed paper election ballots with relatively little governmental supervision. Last, and certainly not least, the major parties controlled the distribution of government jobs at the local, state and national levels. With so much patronage at their disposal, the Democracy and the Grand Old Party could call on thousands of workers, ready to donate money and time to election campaigns. All in all, it was a fine time to be a party politician.

Still, politicians needed victory at the polls. Democrats may have despaired of winning after the sorry spectacle of 1872. But the Party soon demonstrated surprising strength. Despite the defeats of the 1860s and early 1870s, the Democrats had a strong political base. In a famous, unguarded moment in 1884, a Republican preacher excoriated Democrats as the party of "rum, Romanism and rebellion." That controversial remark, which may have cost the Republicans the presidency, told a certain truth. Deeply committed to the idea that government should leave people free to live their lives, the Democrats were indeed the party of "rum," of staunch opposition to the prohibition of alcohol and saloons. Believing that government should not go too far in enforcing morality for the churches, the Democracy was also the party of "Romanism," of Roman Catholics and many non-evangelical Protestants, who favored a strict separation of church and state. Dubious about strong central government, the Democracy was also the party of "Rebellion," of Southerners who had fled the Union in 1861 in the name of state's rights. Across the nation, the Democratic ideology of personal freedom, minimal government and laissez-faire drew together a diverse coalition of workers and rich men, immigrants and native-born, farmers and city dwellers.

At the same time, the Republicans, for all their victories, were vulnerable in the 1880s. The second Grant administration was shaken by depressing revelations of corruption. With the end of Reconstruction, with the sometimes violent repression of the southern black vote, the Republicans lost control of the old Confederacy. In 1873, a financial panic inaugurated economic hard times. And the Democrats gradually began to emerge as the party of limited, responsible government and "reform." In the mid-term elections of 1874, they won back the House of Representatives. Sam Randall, the Speaker who had risen from the rough waterfront of Philadelphia, became known as "The Brakeman" for the way he slowed Federal spending. In the Empire State of New York, Governor Samuel Tilden earned a reforming reputation for his prosecution of Democratic corruption—the peculation of Tammany Hall's Tweed Ring.

Seemingly poised for a comeback in the nation's centennial year of 1876, the Democrats nominated Tilden for President against the Republicans' choice, Governor Rutherford B. Hayes of Ohio. A cold, elegant, quietly calculating corporate lawyer who had

**A generation of Republican domination had entrenched the special interests in Washington, and though it wasn't until 1884 that the Democrats returned to power, they began to cry out for lower taxes, smaller government and political reform in the 1880s. With the Civil War long over, the taxes wrung out of the American people were supposedly benefitting only the lobbyists.**

made a fortune in railroad and other investments, Tilden was condemned as "Whispering Sammy" and "the Great Forecloser." Whatever his defects, Tilden was a brilliant political innovator. At the time, the Democratic Party, like the GOP, had little national organization. Despite, or perhaps because of, strong state and local organizations, the national committee had little power. Tilden ran a more centralized campaign, in which the national committee sent out "literature"—pamphlets and fliers—to lists of carefully targeted voters. Local Democrats had little interest in Tilden's "Literary Bureau" back in New York, but the campaign marked an important departure in American politics. It also appeared to mark a narrow victory for Tilden on election night. But then Republicans seized on reports of fraud, intimidation and other irregularities in Louisiana, South Carolina, Florida and Oregon. Suddenly the issue was in doubt. Amid talk of rebellion, of "Tilden or Blood," an unprecedented special Federal commission awarded the presidency to Rutherford B. Hayes by a single electoral vote, and Democrats were left bemoaning the "Crime of '76."

Nevertheless, the Party groped toward recovery. In the mid-term elections of 1878, Democrats won control

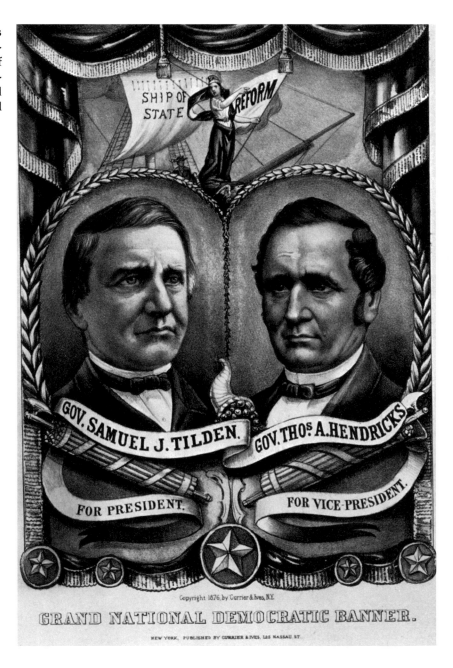

**Samuel J. Tilden and Thomas A. Hendricks headed the Democratic ticket of 1876 promising to pilot the "Ship of State" in the name of "Reform." Tilden, who had championed prosecution of Boss Tweed, outpolled Rutherford B. Hayes but lost the election in a controversial Congressional power play.**

In a typical political cartoon of the time, 1880 Democratic presidential nominee General Winfield Scott Hancock—ridiculed as "General Went Off Half-Cocked" by the Republicans—confronts GOP "Philistines" jubilant over their victory in Vermont's October state elections. They had even more cause for jubilation a month later when Hancock lost the national election.

of both houses of Congress for the first time since before the Civil War. In 1880, the Party turned to another "reform" candidate for the presidency. A hero of the Mexican War, as well as the Civil War battles of Gettysburg, Spotsylvania and the Wilderness, General Winfield Scott Hancock of New York had a reputation for rectitude. "Hancock the Superb" also had the apparent advantage of an almost barren political record. His Republican opponent, Congressman James A. Garfield of Ohio, was another Civil War general and another cautious politician. Not surprisingly, the campaign never brought the issues into sharp focus. Perhaps as a result, the man the Republicans called "General Went Off Half-Cocked" lost narrowly in November.

The campaign of 1880 made it clear that a vague commitment to the idea of "reform" would not carry the Democratic Party back into the White House. Gradually, with difficulty, public attention began to focus on a set of issues. Angry over corruption, a growing number of voters, particularly educated, genteel

Northeasterners, demanded "civil service reform" that would loosen the hold of parties on patronage jobs. Awarding government posts on the basis of merit rather than party loyalty obviously threatened the power of the parties. But, increasingly, there were votes to be found in civil service reform.

Meanwhile, the tariff—the taxes levied on imported goods—took on renewed importance as the centerpiece of Federal economic policy. The issue may seem dull or narrow now, but to many Gilded-Age Americans, an increase or decrease in import duties was the best way to stimulate dynamic and equitable economic growth. Yet the tariff, like civil service reform, was a dangerous issue for the parties. Republicans generally favored higher "protective" tariffs in order to preserve and build up the home market for domestic producers; Democrats generally preferred minimal tariffs "for revenue only" in order to safeguard minimal government, "natural" economic laws, low consumer prices and overseas mar-

**In the Gilded Age, opponents portrayed the Republicans as the anti-labor party of big-business "monopolists" who were benefitting from high protective tariffs. And indeed many leading politicians were known to be "friends" of an emerging group of industrialists who were amassing great fortunes.**

kets for farm products. But each party divided over the issue. Many Democrats favored protection, at least for goods produced in their own districts. In Congress, a group of Democrats—"Sam Randall and his Forty Thieves"—blocked any serious reduction of the tariff.

In the early Eighties, Democrats fought out these and other issues of policy. The results of the battle became clear at the national convention in Chicago in 1884, where the Party nominated another reforming governor of New York for President. In his ponderous way, Grover Cleveland, the former mayor of Buffalo, represented concessions to the spirit of civil service reform and tariff reduction. The "Buxom Buffalonian," known as "Uncle Jumbo" to his nieces and nephews, was the incarnation of Democratic values. He believed fervently in laissez-faire and limited government: In Buffalo, he had been the "Veto Mayor." The fact that some New York party bosses despised Cleveland only endeared him further to many Democrats. "They love him most," a supporter told the convention, "for the enemies he has made."

Cleveland faced a remarkable Republican opponent in the election. James G. Blaine of Maine, former Speaker of the House and secretary of state, was the prototype for the charismatic politician of the twentieth century. A captivating figure, Blaine impressed contemporaries as the "Plumed Knight" and the "Magnetic Man." His private life was unquestioned, but his public life was stained by scandal. As Speaker of the House, Blaine had clearly tried to cover up corrupt ties to railroad corporations. "Blaine, Blaine, James G. Blaine," sang Democrats. "Continental Liar From the State of Maine!" But then came the story that Cleveland, during a boisterous early manhood back in Buffalo, had fathered an illegitimate child with a woman named Maria Halpin. Now the public misbehavior of the "Magnetic Man" was counterpoised with the private scandal of "Uncle Jumbo," and the election became a vicious exercise in mudslinging as voters debated the merits of two men who, by today's standards, could never have been nominated. "Ma, Ma, where's my Pa?" Republicans asked derisively. "Going to the White House. Ha! Ha! Ha!" the Democrats answered nervously. He was indeed: Cleveland won narrowly in November. "Hurrah for Maria! Hurrah for the kid!" Democrats chanted. "I voted for Cleveland, and damned glad I did!"

If the Democrats had a close victory, they had an even more uncertain mandate. They did not have control of the Senate, but finally they had the White House. The first Democratic President since James Buchanan, Cleveland seemed to have a great opportunity. Certainly, he labored to create his own kind of government: The "Veto Mayor" became the "Veto President," vigilant against unneeded expenditure. "Public office is a public trust," he liked to say. But Cleveland, impatient with the demands of patronage

**The first Democratic President in a quarter century, Grover Cleveland delivered his inaugural address in 1884 without notes, dwelling piously on his favorite theme that "Public office is a public trust." Vetoing special-interest bills, he imposed Federal controls on business in 1887 and presided over four of the most prosperous years in American history.**

THE HERALD

*Harrison carries the State by 12000.*

**In 1888, President Cleveland took a big political risk in an election year by devoting his annual message to Congress to a dramatic demand for a lowering of the tariff. The election turned into a "campaign of education" on the tariff, and the Republicans did a better job of selling their policies in the press. On election day, Cleveland was soundly defeated by Benjamin Harrison.**

politics, alienated many party faithful. And in December 1887, he risked all by devoting his entire annual message to Congress to a dramatic demand for downward revision of the tariff. The Republicans, nominating Benjamin Harrison for President in 1888, took up the challenge. The election became a "campaign of education" on the tariff. Building on Tilden's methods, both parties relied more than ever on the "literature" and newspaper stories generated by the national committees. The Republicans did a better job: Harrison won a clear victory.

Power was hard to maintain in the Gilded Age,

however. In office, Benjamin Harrison soon had his own troubles. There were the inevitable party squabbles over patronage. In some states, Republican support for Prohibition and the exclusive use of the English language in the public schools further alienated many voters. Across the nation, a new protective tariff alienated many more. In the mid-term elections of 1890, the Democrats won back the House of Representatives. In the presidential elections of 1892, Cleveland had a rematch with Harrison. This time, the "Buxom Buffalonian" won a close victory to become the only President to serve two nonconsecutive terms in office.

Having won the Senate as well as the House, the Democrats were perfectly positioned to remake American government in their own image. But then the tide of change caught up with the Party, washed over Cleveland and nearly drowned the Democrats. While politicians debated the tariff and civil service, the problems of industrialization had multiplied. Everywhere in the Gilded Age, business and labor confronted each other: The workplace became a battleground as laboring men and women fought for higher wages, control over working conditions and the right to organize. There was 1877, when railroad workers staged an unprecedented walkout; there was 1886, when the Knights of Labor struck around the country and a bombing in Chicago's Haymarket Square stirred fears of anarchism; there was 1892, when labor and capital battled over the mines of Coeur d'Alene, Idaho, and the mills of Homestead, Pennsylvania.

At the same time, many of the nation's farmers were suffering. In the South, they lived with the exploitation of sharecropping and the crop lien; in the West, they lived with mortgages and high marketing costs. And everywhere, farmers lived with low prices on their crops. Understandably, rural Americans asked many questions about economics and politics, and especially about the nation's monetary system. Many people believed that if the national currency were based on silver as well as gold, then an increased money supply would lead to higher prices. But conservatives, Democratic and Republican alike, stoutly insisted that only gold should provide the basis of currency.

The anger of farmers and workers flowed into a broad nationwide fear about the growth of big business, the giant "trusts" and corporations like Standard Oil and the Pennsylvania Railroad. Many Americans

**The Gilded Age of the 1880s was a golden age for America's major political parties: Never again would they command so much material and cultural power. The Democrats or Republicans could count on male voters to join political clubs, to vote a straight party ticket, and to attend great rallies—like this victory parade for Cleveland after his re-election in 1892.**

In the Gilded Age, the work-place became a battleground be-tween business and labor as working men and women fought for higher wages, the right to or-ganize and improved conditions on the job. In July 1892, the steel workers' union was broken and sixteen people were killed when state troops were called in to put down a strike at Carnegie Steel in Homestead, Pennsylvania.

of all classes wanted the states and even the Federal Government to regulate the railroads. And many Americans wanted Washington to prevent the rise of giant corporations that would monopolize trade.

The upheaval over business, labor and agriculture put enormous strain on the political system. Third parties appeared—above all, the agrarian People's Party, called the "Populists," who ran a ticket for President in 1892. Some Republicans and Democrats had tried to respond to demands for change. In the Democracy, such politicians as Congressman Richard "Silver Dick" Bland of Missouri worked for legislation allowing the coinage of silver as well as gold. Southern Democrats, like Ben Tillman, the "One-Eyed Plowboy" of South Carolina, tried to speak the language of farmers. "I am simply a clodhopper, like you are," Tillman told his audiences. In the industrial states, some Democrats spoke to the concerns of working- and middle-class Americans. In Illinois, Governor John Peter Altgeld, a German immigrant, pardoned three men wrongly con-victed for their alleged role in the bombing at Haymar-ket Square. In Washington, Democrats and Republi-

cans combined in the late 1880s and early 1890s to pass economic legislation with at least symbolic value: The Inter-State Commerce Act of 1887 promised the regu-lation of railroads; the Sherman Anti-Trust Act of 1890 portended the limitation of big business; the Sherman Silver Purchase Act of 1890 prescribed the coinage of at least some silver.

Even these modest steps were too much for some conservatives. Returned to office, Grover Cleveland was determined to repeal the Sherman Silver Pur-chase Act and to lower the tariff. Then disaster struck. The Panic of 1893 turned into what was then the worst economic depression in American history; even today, it stands second only to the Great Depression of the 1930s. Amid unemployment and upheaval, Cleveland's policy misfired: The tariff revi-sion, badly bungled, pleased almost no one. At one point Cleveland himself declared that the bill meant "party perfidy and party dishonor." Condemning "the communism of self," the President allowed the measure to become law without his signature. Repeal of the Silver Purchase Act alienated agrarians and failed to revive the economy. Over the objections of Governor Altgeld, Cleveland sent Federal troops to keep the railroads running during the great Pullman Strike of 1894. The move heartened conservatives but alienated labor. Worst of all, perhaps, Cleveland's belief in limited government began to make him seem callous and uncaring, like Herbert Hoover in the Thirties. Soup kitchens became known as "Cleveland Cafes." The President, according to one tale, found a poor man eating grass in front of the White House. "I'm hungry and have to eat grass," the man explained to Cleveland. "Why don't you go around to

**Pitchfork Ben Tillman, the self-proclaimed farmers' spokesman from South Carolina, was hostile to Cleveland's conservatism in the depression of the 1890s. His populist reputation enjoyed a boost when he promised to go to Washington and "tickle Cleveland's fat ribs with my pitchfork!"**

**Sympathetic to the problems of workers, Illinois' German-born Governor John Peter Altgeld opposed Cleveland's use of Federal troops during the Pullman Strike of 1894 and risked political suicide by pardoning three men he felt had been wrongly convicted for killing seven police officers with a bomb during Chicago's Haymarket Square riot.**

the back yard?" Cleveland responded. "The grass is longer there."

Cleveland's record tore the Democratic Party apart. "Send me to Washington," Ben Tillman declared, "and I'll tickle Cleveland's fat ribs with my pitchfork!" Cleveland escaped "Pitchfork Ben," but the President and his conservative followers were done for. At the national convention in Chicago in 1896, the conservatives watched their power slip away. Congressman William Jennings Bryan of Nebraska, a handsome, dynamic advocate of silver, delivered an extraordinary speech to the delegates. Defending a "cause as holy as the cause of liberty—the cause of humanity," Bryan assailed the enemies of the people. His arms raised like a crucified Christ, Bryan finished: "You shall not press down upon the brow of labor this crown of thorns, you shall not crucify mankind upon a cross of gold."

**William Jennings Bryan, the "Boy Orator of the Platte," was the greatest political speaker of the 1890s. On the kind of grass-roots "stump" tour he helped to popularize, Bryan took his greatest political asset directly to the people.**

Only 36 years old, the "Boy Orator of the Platte" was nominated by acclamation on the fifth ballot.

Defeating Cleveland's followers was one thing; winning the presidency was another. Bryan earned the endorsement of the Populists, but he could not hold the votes of many Democrats, particularly the wealthy conservatives. Some would vote for the Republican candidate, William McKinley of Ohio; others supported a "Gold Democratic" presidential ticket. Without much money or newspaper support, Bryan traveled thousands of miles by rail to speak to audiences in big cities and small towns. His opponent, typically cautious, delivered speeches from his home in Ohio. But for the first time, both major candidates campaigned openly for the presidency. This epic, innovative contest testified to the great sense of crisis in the nation. The "Battle of the Standards" in 1896 was not just about the merits of the gold standard or the proper proportion of silver in the money supply. The two metals had come to stand for much more—for how much America must change, for which groups would wield power for generations to come.

For a time, it seemed as if Bryan might actually win. But the millions of dollars pouring into Republican coffers began to tell. On election day, Bryan lost by more than half a million votes. Something fundamental had been decided about the shape of the American future. The Democratic future was less clear. Torn apart, the Democrats would not claim national power again for years. But many Democrats—the Altgelds and the Bryans—were forcing the Party to confront the issues of industrializing America with a more activist philosophy of government. As a result, the Party was at least not confronted with the same dilemma it had faced in 1872, unable to offer a real Democrat to the nation. In 1900, the Democrats would not have to nominate another Republican.

**When 36-year-old William Jennings Bryan delivered his historic plea for the rights of labor and the coinage of silver currency at the Democratic Convention in Chicago in 1896, delegates were so moved that the ovation was said to have lasted for more than thirty minutes. This celebrated "Cross of Gold" speech won Bryan the nomination and catapulted him into the national arena, where he remained for many years.**

In his campaign for the presidency in 1900, William Jennings Bryan traveled relentlessly and delivered 546 speeches pleading in the name of the "great toiling masses" for an "awakened conscience against the tide of corruption." His oratorical flourishes, and his flair for dramatic metaphor, were the touchstones of his charismatic appeal and of his inspirational message.

# CHAPTER SIX

# *THE BEST...AND WORST OF TIMES*

## 1897–1920

### BY JOHN MILTON COOPER, JR.

For the Democratic Party, the years from 1897 to 1920 were, to borrow a phrase from a great writer of that time, Charles Dickens, "the best of times, the worst of times." They witnessed gratifying election victories, a spectacular record of domestic accomplishment, triumphant prosecution of a war and a formulation of a bold, far-sighted foreign policy. This period also saw the Party produce two of the greatest leaders in its history and two of the three most significant political figures of the first third of the twentieth century. But these years also witnessed defeats. Two of the presidential elections of this era ended in a pair of the worst beatings that Democratic candidates have ever suffered, before or since. And for most of this period, especially at the beginning and the end, the Party appeared to be mired in a hopeless minority status, excluded perhaps permanently from power. In short, the time from 1897 to 1920 compressed into a short space some of the most exhilarating and disheartening experiences in the history of the Democratic Party.

The first half of this era and a bit longer belonged unquestionably to William Jennings Bryan. By any measure, Bryan was one of the most remarkable figures to play a major role at any time in American poli-

tics. With his preferred nickname as "the Commoner," Bryan really believed he was just a common man gifted with oratorical powers and providentially raised to prominence. He was, arguably, the finest campaigner in the history of American politics. Sixteen or eighteen hour days on the hustings exhilarated him as he pressed the flesh, kissed babies and, above all, spoke over and over in his golden voice. The Democrats gave Bryan their presidential nomination twice more during this era, in 1900 and 1908, when he was still less than 50 years old. But only later, when the Democrats finally regained power and he was appointed secretary of state, did he hold public office. Nor did he play any formal role in the Party; he was mainly an orator and a champion of causes, or as one of his biographers has called him, a "political evangelist."

Bryan was responsible for two great accomplishments during his period of party dominance. His first and most important one was to keep the Democrats committed to the ideological position they had taken in 1896. Between then and 1912, when Bryan ceded leadership to Woodrow Wilson, he and his followers gave the Democrats their essential identity as a liberal party in the industrial era—that is, as a coalition of economically disadvantaged groups and regions that

Conservatives in both parties, including President Grover Cleveland, accused William Jennings Bryan in 1896 and 1900 of being a Populist, by which they meant that he was not a "real" Democrat but an ideological extremist. Although Bryan shared many of his egalitarian ideas with the Populists, he never belonged to or supported candidates of any party but the Democrats.

sought to use governmental power to redress inequities and enhance opportunities. No one in the twentieth century deserves greater credit than Bryan for making the Democratic Party what it has become in the domestic arena. To use a biblical analogy that he would have liked, Bryan was the Democrats' Moses. He was the prophet who led his followers through the wilderness and kept them faithful but was finally barred from entering the promised land.

Indeed, much of the story of the Party during the first decade of the twentieth century reads like the tribulations of Moses and his flock. The 1900 election largely amounted to a replay of 1896. The Republicans renominated President McKinley and hammered away again at their message of pro-business conservatism. The Democrats' domestic platform in 1900 virtually duplicated their 1896 document, and Bryan was renominated without contest. This suited the Republicans just fine. When Bryan tried to revive the currency issue, Mark Hanna gloated, "Now we've got him where we want him. Silver, silver, silver, that's our tar-

get." Domestically, the targets of both parties stayed the same as they had been four years before. Bryan again lambasted Republican "plutocracy," and now he charged that McKinley's protective tariff and gold standard policies had caused the explosive growth since 1897 of the big business combines known as "trusts." Thanks to their claim over the geese that laid the golden eggs of industrial prosperity, the Republicans once again carried the day with a majority of the voters. Bryan retained the Democrats' base in the South and border states, but he lost five western states that he had carried in 1896. In the popular vote, McKinley increased his majority by 100,000.

But 1900 was not a total repeat of 1896. A new issue and a new face introduced major changes. The new issue was foreign policy. Starting in the mid-1890s, thanks in part to the "yellow journalism" of Joseph Pulitzer and William Randolph Hearst, large numbers of people became stirred by the plight of the Cubans, who were revolting against Spain's colonial rule, so that by the time McKinley took office in 1897 the clamor for "free Cuba" posed a political and diplomatic problem for his administration. Eventually, McKinley gave in to pressures and led the country into the Spanish-American War in 1898. This "splendid little war" brought the United States not only sweeping victory in less than two months, with minuscule casualties, but also a new national hero in Theodore Roosevelt, who led his regiment of "Rough Riders" to a glorious charge up San Juan Hill and, unexpectedly, new colonial possessions in Puerto Rico and the Philippine Islands.

In 1897 and 1898, Bryan and the Democrats led the cry for "free Cuba," and the Commoner also raised a regiment to fight in the Spanish-American War. But he and his party adamantly opposed acquisition of the Philippines as a colony, and they attempted to make Republican "imperialism" a campaign issue in 1900. Their opponents met the challenge by sidestepping the issue and waving the flag. In fact, by the time of the election, foreign policy had already faded as a public concern. One farmer who listened to Bryan denouncing imperialism reportedly sniffed, "Price of hogs is 60 cents a pound. Guess we can stand it." After 1900, foreign policy sank still further from public and political consciousness, and it would remain submerged until World War One. But Bryan had attempted to define a Democratic Party position on foreign policy. This was his second great accomplishment as a party leader.

The other big change of 1900, the new face, belonged to Theodore Roosevelt. By any reckoning, this bespectacled, big-toothed New York aristocrat, who was only two years older than Bryan, was the second of the three most significant American political figures of the first third of the twentieth century. Although this refined, Harvard-educated urbanite seemed the antithesis of Bryan, he resembled his Democratic rival in important respects. No political organization man himself, Roosevelt owed his unorthodox political rise to an uncanny knack for attracting publicity. Even before the charge up San Juan Hill made him a war hero, Roosevelt had become a familiar personage through his western ranching and hunting exploits and his nighttime forays against the underworld as New York City police commissioner. His glasses, moustache, teeth and cowboy hat made him both a cartoonist's delight and the most readily recognizable man in politics. In all, Roosevelt showed how much impact a vivid appearance and personality could make on the

public consciousness even before the advent of the electronic media.

In 1900, the Republicans paid Bryan's new brand of personal campaigning the compliment of imitating it when they nominated Roosevelt for Vice President and sent him out on comparable barnstorming forays. Roosevelt was no trained orator, but his breathless speechmaking more than matched the Commoner's in attracting attention. He appealed for national greatness, preached "the strenuous life" for both individuals and the country and accused the Democrats of cowardice for wanting to get out of the Philippines. With Roosevelt's bursting onto the national scene in 1900, a new political star was born.

How large a leaf the Republicans had stolen from their opponents' book became apparent four years later. In September 1901, only six months into his second term, President McKinley was shot on a visit to Buffalo, New York, by an anarchist who fired a revolver concealed in his bandaged hand. After clinging to life for a week, McKinley died, making Roosevelt, at age 42, the youngest President in American history. His succession brought an enormous transformation in the visibility of the presidency. Roosevelt cultivated the press and allowed himself and his family to become household words.

Despite his showiness, Roosevelt's policies differed little during his first term from McKinley's pro-business conservatism, except in two notable areas. One was foreign affairs, where he wielded his "big stick," particularly in seizing the territory for the Panama Canal. The other was conservation of natural resources, in which his public preachments and preservation of public lands made him the first "ecology" President. By 1904, Roosevelt had made himself the main campaign issue.

That year, the Democrats could not have done worse in opposing Roosevelt in the election if they had tried. Bryan cheerfully stepped aside and let his conservative critics choose that year's nominee, while he and his followers concentrated on the platform. The nomination fell to one of the darkest horses ever to run for President. He was Alton B. Parker, a little known New York judge who faded into obscurity again after the election. Parker proceeded to repudiate the Bryanites' platform, especially on currency and anti-trust issues. He then conducted a lackluster campaign by attempting to attack Roosevelt's presidential

Alton Parker was a New York judge whose only run for major office was as the Democrats' presidential nominee in 1904. His running mate, Henry Davis, was a millionaire former Senator from West Virginia from whom the Party mistakenly expected a big campaign contribution. "Jeffersonian Principles" were code words attacking the alleged radicalism of Bryan and his Republican opponent, President Theodore Roosevelt.

"usurpations" in Panama and in conservation. Even fellow conservatives scoffed at these allegations. The only spark of life flared late in the campaign when Parker accused the President of "blackmailing Wall Street" for big campaign contributions. The charges were basically correct, but in presenting them Parker made factual errors that allowed an indignant Roosevelt to thunder back that they were "atrociously false." The flap made little impact on the results, as the Democrats suffered their worst defeat yet since the Civil War.

Events after 1904 seemed to offer some hope to Bryanite Democrats, at least at first. In his second term, Roosevelt had mounted his own "trustbusting" campaign and introduced legislation to regulate railroads and the quality of drugs and processed foods. "Progressive" Republican movements had sprung up in such states as Wisconsin and Iowa. Prices kept rising, and "muckraking" journalists, most notably Lincoln Steffens and Upton Sinclair, had exposed rampant political corruption, abuses by big business and oppression of workers and fraud in consumer products from patent medicines to life insurance. All these developments had lent far greater public acceptability to the views of Bryan and his Democratic followers. Moreover, Roosevelt was stepping down in 1908 and his

handpicked successor, William Howard Taft, had never run for office. This time, Bryan had no competition for his third presidential nomination.

The perennial Democratic candidate drew his usual large crowds and won applause as he lambasted probusiness Republican policies. The Commoner's performance alarmed Roosevelt so much that he ordered a reluctant Taft to hit the campaign trail and strike some reformist Republican chords. The results were predictable, as Bryan reduced his opponent's majority back to the 1900 level and recaptured three states lost in 1904. But shaving the Republicans' margin of victory seemed scant consolation in the face of a fourth straight defeat. The Democrats seemed destined to wander in the political wilderness forever.

American politics can change fast, however. By 1908, Democratic candidates were winning midwestern governorships, and their congressional strength was climbing back from the low point of 1904. This new strength sprang principally from two sources. First, despite continued Republican dominance at the presidential level, the Democrats' reformist message was making a dent in their opponents' majorities. Second, a new social issue, the recently revived question of Prohibition, was hurting the Republicans in certain states. The "drys"—who wanted to outlaw the manufacture and sale of alcoholic beverages—enjoyed large followings in both parties. Southern and Western Democrats counted probably a dry majority, including Bryan himself, but they soft-pedaled the issue at the national level, in deference to their mainly "wet" northern brethren. Prohibition hurt the Republicans at this time because they tried to straddle the issue in such states as Ohio, thus incurring the wrath of both wets and drys. Later, as a national issue in the 1920s, Prohibition would hurt the Democrats still more. The other great social issue of this period—votes for women, or "woman suffrage," as it was called then—divided both parties and suffered from a conspiracy of silence and avoidance by Republican and Democratic leaders alike, except for Bryan, who was the first major male politician to endorse suffrage.

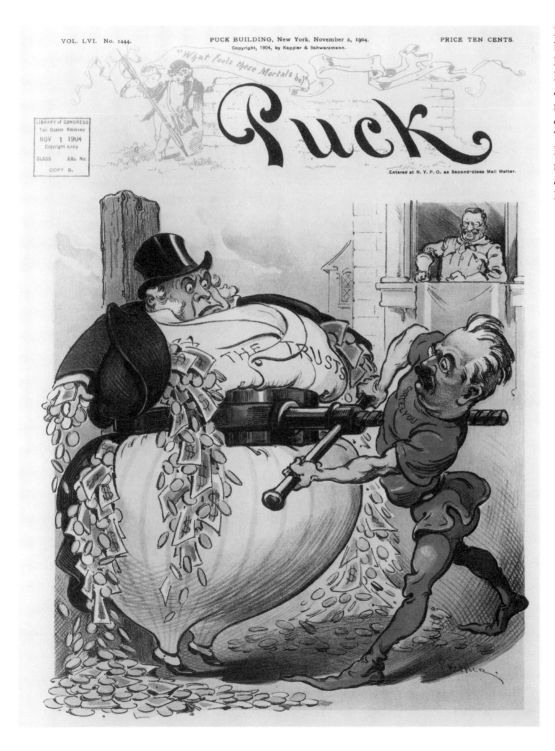

In the campaign of 1904, Democratic nominee Alton Parker accused President Roosevelt's campaign manager of coercing big business into shelling out huge campaign contributions. The charges were true, but Roosevelt indignantly denied them, denounced Parker and won in a landslide that November.

Although he was the most enthusiastic of campaigners and people came from miles around to witness his fabled forensic skills, William Jennings Bryan refused to speak on Sundays during the 1908 campaign. A deeply religious man, Bryan honored the Sabbath by not campaigning, and this taboo was widely observed by many other major politicians of the day.

By 1910, as often happens, the troubles and failings of the party in power helped the outs more than their own efforts did. Starting early in the Taft administration, the Republicans split into warring camps over tariff and business regulation issues. When insurgent progressive Republicans in the House and Senate tried to extend the reform program championed earlier by Roosevelt, they hit a stone wall of opposition from both their parties' conservative congressional leadership and from President Taft. Upon returning from his famous African safari in 1910, Roosevelt sided with the insurgents on the issues and called for even more sweeping reforms, including new graduated income

and inheritance taxes, abolition of child labor and congressional recall of judicial decisions. The ex-President did not openly criticize his successor, but their differences were plain to see, and the biggest question of the next year was whether Roosevelt would run against Taft for the Republican nomination in 1912.

These Republican troubles were grist for the Democrats' mill, and the state and congressional elections in 1910 witnessed a massive turnover, winning enough House seats for the Democrats to control a branch of Congress for the first time in sixteen years. Champ Clark of Missouri became Speaker of the House and, thereby, the Democrats' highest national

## "WET" OR "DRY"

"VOTE WET FOR MY SAKE!"

"VOTE DRY FOR MINE!"

BREWER

**Shall the Mothers and Children be Sacrificed to the Financial Greed of the Liquor Traffic?**

**IT IS UP TO YOU, VOTER, TO DECIDE**

# VOTE DRY

The "liquor question" agitated American politics through the early 1900s, as the foes of alcohol strove to prohibit its manufacture and sale. Southern and western Democrats counted a dry majority, but they soft-pedaled the issue out of deference to their mainly "wet" northern brethren.

Female activists for "woman suffrage" grew in numbers and determination throughout the beginning of the twentieth century. But it was an issue that divided both parties and suffered a conspiracy of silent avoidance by both Republican and Democratic leaders, except for Bryan.

office holder; Oscar W. Underwood of Alabama became majority leader and thus the Party's second-ranking national leader. In the Senate, Democrats fell short of a majority, but a coalition with insurgent Republicans gave them effective control. The most exciting changes came, however, in the governorships, where a crop of attractive new faces emerged from statehouse victories in the Northeast.

Curiously, the most politically attractive of these new faces belonged to a homely, long-jawed, bespectacled former professor of political science and president of Princeton University. He was the last of the three most significant figures of the first three decades of the twentieth century: Woodrow Wilson. Although he had won renown as a writer, lecturer and educational reformer, the 53-year-old Wilson made his first

run for office when he won the governorship of New Jersey in 1910. He proved to be both an exciting campaigner, with an informal manner and fluent speaking style, and a dynamic progressive governor, as he broke the influence of Democratic Party bosses and pushed through a spectacular program of political and economic reforms at the state level. Between his distinguished academic background and his flying start as a candidate and executive, Wilson quickly emerged as the early front-runner for the 1912 Democratic presidential nomination.

The nearer that election came, the worse the Republicans' troubles grew and, correspondingly, the brighter the Democrats' prospects looked. Republican insurgents declared open war against Taft, and at the beginning of 1912 Roosevelt threw his hat in the ring

When former President Theodore Roosevelt failed to win the Republican presidential nomination in 1912, he bolted the Party to form his own: the Progressive or "Bullmoose" Party, and ran as its candidate. Serious issues were involved, but Roosevelt never lived down charges that the new party only served his personal ambitions.

Because Woodrow Wilson struck most people as being cold and aloof at first, many were amazed by his effectiveness as a campaigner when he entered politics and won the governorship of New Jersey. The former president of Princeton pushed through a spectacular record of political and economic reform in the statehouse and went on to win the presidency in 1912.

for the nomination. When the ex-President failed to win at the tumultuous convention, he and his supporters bolted to form the new Progressive Party. For the Democrats, the lure of victory intensified the race for the nomination. As long as they faced an undivided Republican Party and probable defeat, established Party leaders were willing to let a newcomer like Wilson seek the nomination unopposed. But when the depth and bitterness of the Republicans' internecine strife began to bode a likely Democratic victory, both Speaker Clark and Majority Leader Underwood entered the race. Thanks to their much stronger ties to party organizations, they reaped a rich harvest of convention delegates, and Wilson's chances seemed to fade. The Democratic convention turned into a test of wills between the backers of Clark and Wilson as the convention consumed 46 ballots to choose the nomi-

nee. Clark reached a majority at one point, but the widely criticized two-thirds rule stopped him short of the nomination. Wilson's principal manager, William Gibbs McAdoo, held firm, won over nearly all of Underwood's delegates and induced enough Clark backers to switch so that the Wilsonians finally put their man over the top.

In choosing Woodrow Wilson, the Democrats put forward their strongest candidate. First, his stunning reputation as a progressive governor scotched any hopes of Roosevelt's Progressives that they might woo away reformist Democrats. During the Democratic convention, one of Roosevelt's sons confided, "Pop is praying for the nomination of Champ Clark." Meanwhile, Bryan was rumored to be discussing a bolt in the event of the nomination of Clark or Underwood, neither of whom enjoyed strong identification with

Wilson's Cabinet was led by Secretary of State William Jennings Bryan and Treasury Secretary William Gibbs McAdoo (at his right and left). With their assistance, Wilson compiled the most remarkable legislative record of any President up to that time, expanding the role of Federal Government with milestone laws which were to become the central pillars of American economic life.

progressive issues. Instead, Wilson's candidacy assured a united, enthusiastic Democratic party.

The other and perhaps even more impressive reason for Wilson's unmatched strength as the Democrats' candidate was his brilliant political mind. This enabled him to engage Roosevelt in the finest debate ever witnessed during a presidential campaign. In launching his new party, the ex-President advocated a stringent but essentially conservative reform program under the banner of his "New Nationalism." The Democratic standard-bearer responded by urging similar but essentially liberal reforms to foster greater economic competition and opportunity and, thereby, to promote social and economic mobility. Wilson dubbed

his program the "New Freedom," and he gave an intellectual elaboration and philosophical underpinning to the direction that Bryan had already given to the Democratic Party. Wilson made his main point best when he declared, "I am not afraid of the utmost exercise of government," so long as it was not "Big Brother government" but, rather, "a government that will make other men take their hands off me so I can take care of myself." Also, unusually for a Democrat less than 50 years after the Civil War, Wilson praised Lincoln as "the Great Emancipator" and vowed to emulate Lincoln by banishing economic "slavery just as emphatically as we have repudiated the other." In their debate, Roosevelt and Wilson made themselves twentieth century counterparts to Hamilton and Jefferson. It was a great moment in American politics.

Ironically, this debate seems to have had next to no effect on the outcome of the election. Wilson won in 1912, as almost everyone expected him to do, simply by holding the Democrats together. He swept the electoral college, carrying 40 states to Roosevelt's six and Taft's two. But Wilson won 100,000 fewer votes than Bryan had received in 1908. The only surprise in the returns came with the votes given to Socialist candidate Eugene V. Debs, who garnered over 900,000 votes—the biggest share ever won by a Socialist, before or since.

Despite their less than dramatic victory, President Wilson and the Democrats racked up a formidable record of achievement. In 1912, the Party also gained a huge majority in the House and a smaller one in the Senate. Wilson had long been a theorist of party government, and now he put his ideas into practice. Reviving the disused presidential practice of speaking to Congress in person, he appeared frequently to address joint sessions or special Senate sessions. Even before his inauguration, he drew up his legislative program, which consisted of tariff revision, banking reform and stronger anti-trust laws, and he pressed the Democratic leaders on Capitol Hill to enact measures that embodied this program. He relied upon Bryan, his secretary of state, to lobby for the administration's legisla-

In a historic ceremony, Wilson gathered with Bryan and a young assistant secretary of the Navy named Franklin Delano Roosevelt to commemorate Flag Day in Washington, June 4, 1914. These three men would run as the Democratic nominees for President in nine of the 13 elections held between 1896 and 1944, setting the course of the modern Democratic Party for half a century.

tion and to line up recalcitrant Democrats. As earlier during the campaign, he relied for expert advice about economic questions on the brilliant and controversial Boston attorney, Louis D. Brandeis. Finally, he kept Congress continuously in session from April 1913 to October 1914 until his initial program was completed.

This combination of approaches, together with good cooperation from the congressional leaders, wrought great achievements. During that session, Congress enacted milestone legislation in three areas. First, in the area of revenues, the Underwood-Simmons tariff lowered duties for the first time in 40 years and was paired with the first graduated income tax. Second, in the area of banking reform, the Federal Reserve Act established a new reserve system and central bank under government control. Third, in the area of anti-trust regulation, the Clayton Anti-Trust Act broadened and specified prohibited business practices, while a complementary act set up the Federal Trade Commission. Together, these acts and agencies altered and expanded the role of the Federal Government; most of them remain today as central pillars of American economic life. Then, in 1916, President Wilson pushed through a second legislative program that included Federal aid to agriculture, abolition of child labor, an eight-hour law for railroad workers and more sharply graduated taxes, together with the nomination of Brandeis to become the first Jewish justice of the Supreme Court. In his first term, Wilson had compiled the most remarkable legislative record of any President up to that time. If Bryan had been the Democrats' Moses, Wilson was their conquering Joshua.

The second segment of that legislative record required even more resourceful presidential leadership than the first. By 1916, two sets of difficulties were complicating Wilson's political life. The first set was domestic. In the 1914 elections, the progressives had virtually collapsed, while the Republican conservatives made a big comeback and shrank the Democratic majority in the House. The second set of difficulties was foreign. Revolutionary turmoil in Mexico had given President Wilson and Secretary of State Bryan headaches from their first days in office, and Roosevelt along with many other Republicans had excoriated their efforts to stay out of the factional violence south of the border. But the worst troubles came without warning when World War One broke out in Europe in August 1914. "This awful calamity came to us as lightning out of a clear sky," lamented one Democratic congressman. Horrendous as the war was, it seemed remote to most Americans until a German submarine sank the ocean liner *Lusitania* on May 7, 1915. That attack raised for the first time the danger of America being dragged into the war, and it resurrected foreign policy as a major political issue for the first time since 1900.

President Wilson tried to satisfy what he called the people's "double wish" for peace with honor. At first he urged Americans to be "too proud to fight," while he also warned the Germans that they would be held to "strict accountability" for their submarine attacks. Predictably, this policy drew fire from both sides. Roosevelt and hawkish Republicans attacked the President for failing to take a hard line that verged on war with Germany. Bryan resigned as secretary of state in protest against what he saw as the President's willingness to risk war. For nearly a year, until the spring of 1916, Wilson waged a two-front campaign on foreign policy and defense issues. At the same time as he stood up to hawkish Republican opposition, he battled Bryan and his congressional allies for control of the Democratic Party. In a deft series of compromises, appeals to public opinion and showdowns on Capitol Hill, Wilson prevailed over all his opponents, won enactment for his legislative program and secured his renomination. Diplomatic boldness and luck also allowed him to get the Germans to back down temporarily and dampen the danger of war. In all, by the middle of 1916, Wilson stood in a singularly fortunate position to run for a second term.

The 1916 election turned out to be one of the closest in American history. Wilson won slightly less than a majority of the popular vote, and he narrowly carried the electoral college by sweeping virtually the entire West and winning one big midwestern state, Ohio. Wilson's showing registered a remarkable improvement over 1912. He gained almost three million votes, bettering his Republican opponent, Charles Evans Hughes, by 600,000 votes. Foreign policy issues played an unclear role in the campaign. The Democrats rode the peace issue hard with their slogan, "He Kept Us Out of War," while Wilson asserted, "There is only one choice as against peace, and that is war." Yet they also condemned "disloyal" German-American groups, and Wilson called for "100% Americanism." The Republicans welcomed support both from such groups and from Roosevelt, who hewed to his increasingly shrill hawkish line, at one point taunting Wilson with "the shadows of men, women and children risen from the ooze of the ocean bottom." Voters in 1916 could be pardoned for finding foreign policy issues confusing.

By contrast, domestic issues cut clear and deep. Despite a few gestures toward their progressive insurgents, the Republicans reasserted their pro-business conservatism in 1916, and they spent much of the campaign attacking the Democrats' labor and tax records. Wilson and his party not only strengthened their established southern and western coalition, but they also won ardent labor union backing that boosted them in the Northeast and Midwest. Major elements were beginning to emerge for a future majority coalition.

It is fascinating but fruitless to speculate on what might have happened if the United States had remained at peace after 1916. Instead, in April 1917, Germany's renewal of submarine warfare plunged the nation into World War One. President Wilson had already tried to mediate the war and had presented his vision of a new world order through "peace without victory" and a "league of nations" to prevent war. Rather than abandon those objectives, he now pursued the complex and delicate course of seeking a liberal, non-punitive peace and reform of international affairs through war. Remarkably, Wilson succeeded up to a point at this daunting combination of diplomatic, military and political feats. Diplomatically, he stated his war aims in his Fourteen Points speech in January 1918 and used

**Wilson's second term, from 1917 to 1921, was overshadowed by World War One. Despite pressure from hawkish Republicans to respond to German provocations, Wilson won re-election with the slogan "He Kept Us Out Of War," but submarine attacks on the Allies finally forced him to declare war against Germany. "The world," he warned, "must be made safe for democracy."**

**Marshaling more than five million men and women in the armed forces within a year after entering the war, America manned the trenches alongside their European allies. Casualties were heavy—more than 120,000 allied troops in a single battle—but it was the last major offensive of the war. German resistance was crumbling, and by September of 1918, it would all be over.**

them as the basis for Germany's capitulation in the Armistice in November. Wilson spent the first half of 1919 in Paris negotiating a peace settlement that included establishment of a League of Nations. Both the apparent success of his liberal wartime diplomacy and his presence at Paris fed expectations around the world that this American President would build a new structure of peace, freedom and justice in the world. Wilson recognized that such hopes were excessive and unrealistic, but he became obsessed with the need to have the United States join and lead the League of Nations in order to prevent another world war.

Militarily, the Wilson administration ran a highly efficient war effort that raised armed forces of five mil-

lion men and women in a little over a year. But "Mr. Wilson's war" had a dark side as well. In order to bolster morale on the home front, a domestic propaganda agency, the Committee on Public Information, was created. Its director, George Creel, later called his work "how we advertised America," and critics charged that he and his agency not only sold the war to people like a commodity but also whipped up popular hysteria. Some cabinet officers resorted to censorship and repression of civil liberties. The most famous incident occurred in 1918, when Eugene Debs was convicted for violating the wartime laws that restricted free speech. Debs gladly went to jail declaring, "While there is a soul in prison, I am not free." The worst of-

*Address to Congress*
*8 January, 1918*

Once more, as repeatedly before, the spokesmen of the Central Empires have indicated their desire to discuss the objects of the war and the possible bases of a general peace. Parlies have been in progress at Brest-Litovsk between representatives of the Russian people and representatives of the Central Powers to which the attention of all the belligerents has been invited for the purpose of ascertaining whether it may be possible to extend *these parlies* into a general conference with regard to terms of peace and settlement. The Russian representatives presented at these parlies a perfectly definite statement *not only* of the principles upon which they would be willing to conclude peace but also an equally definite programme of the concrete application of those principles. The representatives of the Central Powers, on their part, presented an outline of settlement which, if much less definite, seemed susceptible of liberal interpretation until their specific programme of practical terms was added. That programme proposed no concessions at all either to the sovereignty of Russia or to the preferences of the populations with whose fortunes it dealt, but meant, in a word, that the Central Empires were to keep every foot of territory their armed forces had occupied, — every province, every city, every

fenses against domestic freedom occurred in the post-war Red Scare led by Attorney General A. Mitchell Palmer. Politically, Wilson did not use the war to promote his party's fortunes, but neither did he practice bipartisanship by including Republicans in major decisions. Partly as a result of their exclusion but more out of deep repugnance for Wilson's domestic and foreign policies, many Republicans were spoiling for a fight when the war ended and were determined to keep the United States out of the League of Nations.

The year 1919 still ranks as one of the worst in American history. Much of what went wrong was in some measure President Wilson's fault. Absent from the country for half the year and totally absorbed in foreign policy, he allowed the abrupt removal of wartime economic controls to spur inflation, and rapid demobilization to swell unemployment. Labor militancy collided with management intransigence to foment big strikes, and the administration did little to help the situation. Racial violence flared in a series of summer riots when whites in northern cities attacked newly arrived blacks from the South. The President and Senate Republicans, who had gained a one-vote majority in the 1918 elections, deadlocked over limits

In an attempt to define the Allied cause, President Wilson drafted his famous Fourteen Points calling for peace with honor. In an eloquent speech, delivered to Congress on January 8, 1918, he set forth his vision of a new world order based upon self-determination, disarmament and peaceful settlement of disputes by a League of Nations.

In a doomed effort to defuse Senate opposition to his peace plan, Wilson went directly to the people on a whirlwind cross-country speaking tour in September of 1919. But Wilson's health was failing, and he had to be rushed back to the White House, where he suffered the massive, crippling stroke that ended his career.

In 1920, the Democratic nominees, James M. Cox of Ohio and running mate Franklin D. Roosevelt of New York, waged a strenuous campaign against Republicans Warren Harding of Ohio and Calvin Coolidge of Massachusetts. But voters were in an isolationist mood after the hardships of a tragic war in Europe, and the Party was dealt one of its worst defeats in American history.

on American participation in the League.

In an attempt to break the deadlock with the senators, President Wilson took his case to the people on a whirlwind cross-country speaking tour in September 1919. It was a magnificent but doomed effort. The President gave 40 speeches in 21 days, traveling much farther and speaking more often than he had ever done before, even during his presidential campaigns. At first, the trip did not go well. Failing health diminished his previously superb oratorical abilities, but soon he hit his stride and delivered increasingly moving appeals to Americans to participate in maintaining the peace. "Ah, my fellow citizens," he urged, "do not forget the aching hearts that are behind discussions like this." Evoking memories of the fallen, he pleaded, "Do not forget the forlorn homes from which those boys went out." Warning against another, still more

terrible world war, he implored, "Ask any soldier if he wants to go through a hell like that again. The soldiers know what the next war would be." But Wilson's fragile health aborted the tour. He had to be rushed back to the White House, where he suffered a massive, crippling stroke on October 2, 1919. He never fully functioned as President again.

Nor did the United States ever join the League of Nations. The President had said that it would "break the heart of the world" if Americans failed to do their part in upholding the peace. But repeated efforts failed to forge a compromise between him and the Republican senators. Much of the fault again lay with Wilson. He could have won a limited form of League membership if he had been willing to accept senatorial reservations on ratification of the peace treaty. Instead, he refused to allow Democratic senators to accept those reservations, and the treaty failed to gain the Senate's consent. Wilson preferred to try to make the 1920 election "a great and solemn referendum" on membership in the League, and he even harbored delusions about running for a third term. Unfortunately, the President's stroke had affected his judgment and elevated his personal misfortune into a world tragedy. The political deadlock and the President's incapacity ended 1919 on the sourest of notes, especially when added to inflation, unemployment, strikes, race riots and the Red Scare. With all those troubles, one journalist could have won a prize for understatement when he wrote, "The country is in a mess."

In 1920, the Democrats were blamed for creating the mess. Party leaders wisely scotched President Wilson's notions about a referendum and a third term, but the 1920 convention witnessed a battle over Prohibition, and took 44 ballots to settle on a compromise candidate, Governor James M. Cox of Ohio. As a sop to Wilsonian loyalists, the vice presidential nomination went to Franklin Delano Roosevelt, a 38-year-old New Yorker who had served as assistant secretary of the Navy in the Wilson administration and was an ardent supporter of the League. He was related to his famous namesake, who had died early in 1919, distantly by blood and closely by marriage to Theodore's niece, Eleanor. A pleasant, well-liked man, Franklin Roosevelt was not a major political figure when he won the vice presidential nod.

The Democrats mounted an energetic campaign, but the Republicans vastly outspent and masterfully outadvertised them. Democratic appeals to liberal economic issues left the public cold, and Cox reluctantly switched to stress the League. The only surprise about the outcome was the massiveness of the

Democratic defeat. The Party suffered its worst popular loss ever, mustering only a third of the vote. In congressional races, no Democratic senatorial candidate won outside the South, while their House delegation fell to slightly over 100 seats. There could be no doubt that the result was an anti-Democratic protest. This was underscored by Eugene Debs' again receiving over 900,000 votes, even though he was in prison. "It wasn't a landslide," moaned one leading Democrat. "It was an earthquake."

Though this era ended on a gloomy note for Democrats, some could look beyond the despair of the moment. In the previous decade, they had broken the Republicans' seemingly endless lock on national power. Their President and congressional majorities had enacted monumental legislation that translated their party's domestic philosophy into action and set the agenda for succeeding generations. Their President, Woodrow Wilson, set forth an internationalist foreign policy program that the next generation would fulfill. Outside the main focus of domestic and foreign policy debate, the Party had also evolved in a more socially enlightened direction. Racism still haunted the Democrats in the South, but during the war, Wilson and others had swung a majority of the Party over to support suffrage, which finally gained congressional enactment in 1919 with the 19th Amendment. Also, a powerful new urban ethnic constituency had begun to emerge with the 1918 election of Alfred E. Smith as governor of New York. Although Smith lost his office in the rout of 1920, he and other Democrats quickly bounced back. So the end of this era may have been one of "the worst of times" for the Party, but "the best of times" would soon be here again.

Few would have predicted that Franklin Roosevelt—the pampered son of a wealthy landowner and a doting, aristocratic mother—would grow into the kind of inspirational leader who could lead America through the hardships of depression and world war. But he became the dominating figure of his time and one of the most important men in American history.

# CHAPTER SEVEN

# THE ROOSEVELT ERA

## 1921–1944

### BY ALAN BRINKLEY

Few would have predicted in 1921 that little more than a decade later, the Democratic Party would begin the most successful era in its modern history. Battered, divided and to some degree even discredited, the Democrats seemed destined for a long era of futility and discord.

One of the Party's problems was the legacy of World War One and the turbulent years that followed it. A Democratic President had taken the United States into the war: Even though the war was won, by the early 1920s, many Americans considered the country's intervention a colossal mistake. Democrats staked much of their claim to office in 1920 on a commitment to the new League of Nations: First the United States Senate, and then the entire electorate, repudiated that commitment. Woodrow Wilson's last years in office had coincided with a time of unprecedented social and economic turmoil: inflation, recession, racial conflicts, labor strife and a corrosive, hysterical Red Scare. In 1920, Democrats paid the price for what Warren G. Harding described as a popular yearning for a "return to normalcy."

But the problems of the Party in the 1920s went deeper than the controversies of the moment. For the Democrats were deeply, it often seemed irreconcilably, divided as seldom before in their history. Urban factions battled rural ones. "Wets" (opponents of Prohibition) battled "drys" (supporters of the "Noble Experiment"). Catholics battled Protestants. Recent immigrants battled native-stock Americans. Democrats made up a large proportion of the members of the Ku Klux Klan in the 1920s. Among the Klan's principal targets were Catholic immigrants, another important Democratic constituency.

For much of the 1920s, the bitter conflict at the heart of Democratic politics seemed to be personified by two men: William Gibbs McAdoo and Alfred E. Smith. McAdoo, Woodrow Wilson's son-in-law and secretary of the treasury, was the heir to William Jennings Bryan as the spokesman for the South and the West and for rural, traditionalist Americans. He supported Prohibition, tolerated the Ku Klux Klan and implied a sympathy with fundamentalists and anti-evolutionists. In reality, although born in Georgia and a resident of California, McAdoo was a quintessential member of the Eastern establishment: a wealthy, sophisticated lawyer closely connected with Wall Street. But he made skillful and effective use of populist rhetoric and

images nevertheless. He even attacked New York City, where he had himself lived for many years, as a "citadel of privilege . . . reactionary, sinister, unscrupulous, mercenary and sordid."

Al Smith, the governor of New York from 1919 to 1928 (with one two-year hiatus after the 1920 Republican landslide), came to personify another set of Democratic constituencies. Smith was born on the lower East Side of Manhattan and grew up in the shadow of the Brooklyn Bridge, among the burgeoning immigrant population that had begun transforming the New York Democratic Party in the 1870s and 1880s. A Catholic of Irish-Italian-German ancestry, he rose politically through New York City's Tammany Hall. By the

**A weathy, sophisticated lawyer with Wall Street connections and gilt-edged credentials as Wilson's son-in-law and secretary of the treasury, William Gibbs McAdoo was a quintessential member of the Eastern establishment. But in a failed bid for the Democratic nomination in 1924, he denounced his former home, New York City, as "a citadel of privilege" and tried to portray himself as an agent of change.**

**Enthusiastic supporters of New York's Governor Al Smith staged a floor demonstration during the tumultuous 1924 Democratic Convention, which was torn with controversy over race, religion and Prohibition. An engaging and dynamic leader with a progressive record, Smith won enough delegates to block McAdoo, but not enough to win the nomination for himself.**

Controversies over Prohibition, the Ku Klux Klan and the Catholic Church paralyzed the 1924 convention for 103 ballots. When Smith and McAdoo finally withdrew, the delegates turned in desperation to a colorless dark horse candidate, Wall Street lawyer John W. Davis. With Charles W. Bryan as his hapless running mate, Davis lost overwhelmingly to Republican President Calvin Coolidge.

early 1920s, he had become a leading champion of urban ethnic voters by virtue of his support for repeal of Prohibition, his hostility to the Ku Klux Klan and his work on behalf of progressive social-welfare initiatives that appealed to, among others, immigrant industrial workers. While McAdoo conveyed the stern, stiff rectitude of a Presbyterian moralist, Smith was a natty dresser known for his jaunty bow ties and an ebullient orator with a gravelly New York accent. To his admirers, he was the "Happy Warrior." To many Southern, Western and rural Democrats, however, he was more notable for being a representative of the "alien hordes" of what McAdoo once called the "imperial city."

The gulf between the two wings of the Party—and the rivalry between McAdoo and Smith—created a political disaster in 1924, when the Democrats gathered in New York's Madison Square Garden to nominate a candidate for President. McAdoo had the support of a majority of the delegates, but not the two-thirds necessary for nomination. Smith had enough support to block McAdoo, but not enough to win the prize himself. Controversies over the Klan, Prohibition and the Catholic Church paralyzed the convention for 103 ballots, until Smith and McAdoo both finally withdrew and the delegates turned instead to the colorless John W. Davis, a conservative Wall Street lawyer who lost overwhelmingly to Calvin Coolidge in November.

Four years later, with McAdoo out of the race,

Smith finally won the presidential nomination. But he remained crippled by the considerable anti-Catholic sentiment among the electorate and by his own, at times defiant, New York provincialism, which many voters resented. And like Davis in 1924, he faced the perhaps impossible task of defeating the candidate of a party that was presiding over booming prosperity. In November of 1928, Smith lost decisively to Herbert Hoover.

On the surface, therefore, what characterized the 1920s for the Democratic Party was a string of dismal political failures. But not far beneath the surface were signs of the greater success that was soon to come. Three developments, in particular, proved vital for the Party's future. First was the Democratic Party's growing identification with liberal and progressive ideas. By nominating John W. Davis in 1924, the Party had seemed to link itself to the conservative values of Wall Street. But Smith—an important reformer in New York—was in fact more nearly representative of the progressive sentiments of the Party as a whole. And while his 1928 campaign was a cautious one, Smith made it possible for voters to view the Democrats as the liberal alternative to the existing Republican order, as the party that promised change and progress. Four years later, when the need for change seemed much more compelling than it did in 1928, that would prove a decisive advantage.

Second was a significant realignment of voting pat-

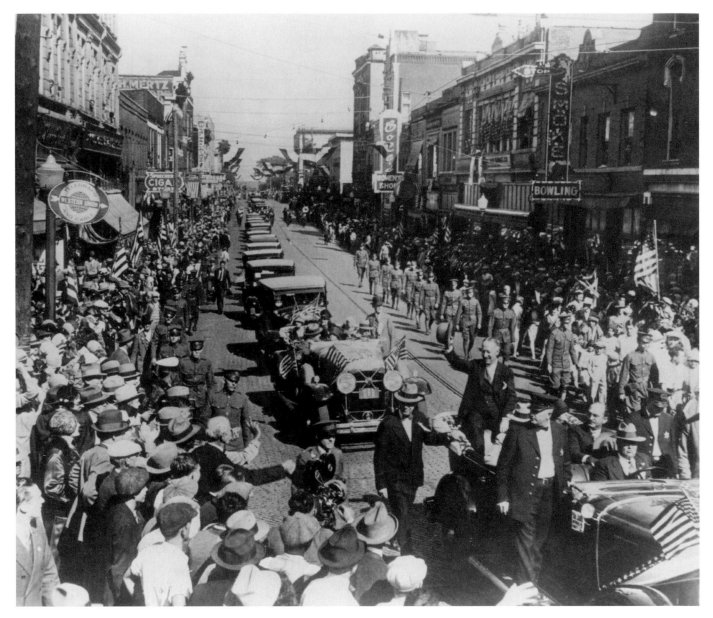

An ebullient orator, Al Smith attracted large crowds during his second campaign for the presidency in 1928, and effectively drew urban ethnic voters into the Democratic Party. In the end, however, his own Catholicism and his defiant New York provincialism cost him support almost everywhere outside the North, and Republican Herbert Hoover won in a landslide.

terns that began to become evident in the 1928 presidential election. Smith's Catholicism and provincialism were responsible for an important, but temporary, erosion of Democratic strength in the South. But his campaign also contributed to a substantial, and more durable, strengthening of the Party in other areas. American farmers, long an important part of the Republican coalition, were suffering the effects of more than five years of agricultural depression. Angry at the refusal of the Coolidge administration to support farm-relief legislation, they voted in large num-

bers for the Democrats in 1928. Voters in the West, where progressive and even radical sentiment remained high, also showed substantial movement toward the Democratic Party, which attracted many of those who had voted for Robert La Follette's third-party Progressive candidacy in 1924. Most of all, voters in urban, industrial areas flocked to the Democratic Party in substantial numbers in 1928—attracted by Smith himself (and by his urban, Catholic, ethnic background) and by the Party's emerging identification with immigrant, working-class concerns. Irish, Italian,

Jewish, German and Northern black voters showed a dramatically higher level of support for Democratic candidates in 1928 than they had in 1924 or 1920. The 1928 election, in short, began a redefinition of the Democratic Party's constituency that four years later would help it produce a solid majority.

Finally, the 1928 elections produced a new Party leader, destined to become one of the most important figures in its, and the nation's, history: Franklin Delano Roosevelt. An unlikely figure for the role he was to play, Roosevelt was the exquisitely pampered son of a wealthy railroad executive and a doting, aristocratic mother. After growing up on an estate in the Hudson Valley, which remained his principal home for the rest of his life, he went on to become an undistinguished student at Groton, Harvard and Columbia law

**John Nance Garner of Texas, often known by the nickname "Cactus Jack," was speaker of the House of Representatives when Roosevelt chose him as his vice presidential candidate in 1932. But after serving in the office for eight years, he grew increasingly unhappy with what he considered the excessive spending and the radicalism of the New Deal and ultimately became one of Roosevelt's most outspoken critics.**

schools; and, for a time, a lawyer in New York with a nondescript practice. In the beginning, at least, what political prominence he enjoyed was in large part a result of his family name. He was a distant cousin of Theodore Roosevelt, but he made up for the remoteness of the connection with a conspicuous and largely unreflective enthusiasm for TR (whose niece Eleanor he married in 1905). "My father and grandfather were Democrats," Franklin said years later, "but in 1904 when I cast my first vote for a President, I voted for the Republican candidate, Theodore Roosevelt, because I felt he was a better Democrat than the Democratic candidates."

But a more important influence, ultimately, was Woodrow Wilson, whom Roosevelt served as assistant secretary of the Navy during World War One. From his service in the Wilson administration, Roosevelt emerged finally as a figure of substance in his own right. He displayed considerable skill and substantial ambition in this important position; and he drew from Wilson a strengthened commitment to progressivism and internationalism. In 1920, Roosevelt was the Democratic nominee for Vice President on a ticket with James Cox; and while the Democrats suffered a crushing defeat, Roosevelt emerged from the campaign poised to play a major role in the Party's future.

Less than a year later, however, his career seemed to come to an end when he was stricken with poliomyelitis. He never walked again. But over the next seven years, encouraged by his wife and his most intimate advisor, Louis Howe, he gradually learned to compensate for and largely disguise his disability. He made a triumphant appearance before the 1924 Democratic Convention to nominate Al Smith; and in 1928, he ran successfully for governor of New York. His cautiously progressive record in Albany, and his landslide re-election victory in 1930, strengthened his claim to national leadership of the Party.

Roosevelt's great gift as a Democratic leader in the early 1930s was to turn the Party's gaze away from the divisive cultural issues that had so weakened it in the 1920s and toward the pressing economic concerns that the Great Depression had forced on most of its members. He took equivocal stands on Prohibition, religion, race and ethnicity. He built alliances with rural voters by citing his own experience as a "farmer" in the Hudson Valley. He solidified his standing among urban voters by emphasizing his experience in New York politics. Most of all, he called attention

after 1929 to the need for public action to fight the Great Depression, even if he remained vague and at times even contradictory about what that action would be.

He won the 1932 Democratic presidential nomination with relative ease and broke with tradition by flying to the Chicago convention and accepting the nomination in person—with a speech in which he promised "a new deal for the American people." He chose as his running mate the Speaker of the House of Representatives, John Nance Garner of Texas, a representative of the rural, Protestant wing of the Party that Bryan and McAdoo had once led. As head of the Democratic National Committee, he appointed James Farley, an Irish Catholic from New York. "He had become," the historian David Burner has written, "the representative of a party rather than a faction."

Any Democratic candidate in 1932 would likely have defeated Herbert Hoover, a man whom many voters had come to identify with the nation's failure to solve its economic problems. With unemployment approaching 25 percent, with industrial production dramatically reduced, with farm prices at historic lows and with the banking and financial system on the edge of collapse, Roosevelt needed only to avoid antagonizing the electorate to win. Critics accused him of being evasive and substanceless. Many considered him a political lightweight—or, in Walter Lippmann's famous description—"a pleasant man who, without any important qualifications for the office, would very much like to be President." But Roosevelt ignored them and ran a deliberately vague campaign. He won in November with over 57 percent of the popular vote and helped Democrats win substantial majorities in both houses of Congress.

Over the next twelve years, Roosevelt remade

**Left: With good reason, FDR and wife Eleanor exude confidence as they exit the polling booths after voting in the 1932 elections. Any Democrat would have been likely to defeat Herbert Hoover, whom many blamed for failing to avert or ameliorate the Depression that had brought America to the edge of ruin.**

**Surrounded by members of Congress and his administration in the Cabinet Room of the White House, President Roosevelt signed the historic Social Security Act of 1935, which established the basis for the American welfare state by creating Federal old-age pensions, unemployment insurance and aid to dependent children.**

New Yorkers gathered in Times Square on election night in November of 1936 to watch the news of Roosevelt's huge re-election victory. He won over 61 percent of the popular vote and carried all but two states, in one of the greatest landslides in the history of modern elections.

American government and remade the Democratic Party. His own ebullient public personality became one of the defining facts of American politics and encouraged millions of Americans to believe that the President shared their hopes and understood their frustrations. The achievements of the New Deal became the basis for the liberal orthodoxy that dominated the Party until at least the 1970s. And the constituencies that Roosevelt attracted to or solidified within the Party became the basis of Democratic victo-ries for the next four decades. The climactic election of 1896 had shattered the political order that dominated American politics in the late nineteenth century and replaced it with a new one, dominated by the Republican Party. The elections of 1928 and 1932 destroyed the Republican order of the early twentieth century and created what became known as the New Deal coalition, which left the Democrats the majority party for two generations to come.

The public image of Franklin Roosevelt—the dazzling smile, the upturned head, the jaunty cigarette holder, the strong, confident voice—began to reinvigorate the nation's politics beginning on his first day in office. The new President's inaugural address, with its assurance that "we have nothing to fear but fear itself," was the beginning of a crusade against panic and despair that continued for months. Roosevelt explained his programs to the public, and forged what many considered a personal bond with them, over the radio, through "fireside chats" in which he spoke simply and directly. He cultivated the press corps with frequent, informal press conferences and in effect recruited many reporters to his cause. It was an indication of Roosevelt's mutually supportive relationship with the press that never in the twelve years of his presidency did any newspaper publish a photograph of him in his wheelchair or being carried in and out of his car—even though reporters saw such scenes frequently. The President's energetic and compassionate wife, Eleanor, traveled the country and conveyed to millions of troubled Americans her own commitment to social justice. And the administration as a whole pioneered techniques of publicizing its own and the President's activities and achievements. For the next twelve years, Franklin Roosevelt himself was the Democratic Party's most important asset. Even when his policies grew unpopular or seemed not to be working, he himself continued to inspire confidence, loyalty and affection.

The concrete achievements of the New Deal—the laws it helped pass, the institutions it created, the policies it launched—are so diverse and even contradictory as to be almost bewildering. Many of the initiatives the New Deal launched proved unsuccessful or temporary. But out of what Richard Hofstadter once called this "chaos of experimentation" emerged sev-

Farmers wait to receive their government checks at an Agricultural Adjustment Administration office in 1939. The AAA, and several other agencies during Roosevelt's New Deal, were designed to create more purchasing power for farmers by establishing a system of Federal price supports and crop subsidies that permanently changed the face of American farming.

eral lasting changes in the nature of American government that helped shape the future of liberalism and of the Democratic Party. New Deal farm policies established a system by which the Government supported (and continues to support) agricultural prices through production limitations and subsidies. Banking reforms stabilized the nation's financial system, while Government insurance of bank deposits through the Federal Deposit Insurance Corporation helped stop the panic that had caused many banks to collapse in 1932. New regulatory agencies policed the stock market, broadcasting, air travel and other economic activities. The Wagner Act (or National Industrial Recovery Act) of 1935 guaranteed to American workers the right to form unions of their own choosing and, more important, required employers to recognize those unions and bargain with them in good faith. The Social Secu-

rity Act of 1935 created a system of social insurance—old-age pensions, unemployment insurance, aid to dependent children—that became the cornerstone of the new American welfare state and that continues today to define the nation's commitment to social assistance. The administration's use of public spending to stimulate economic growth—an idea the President seemed openly to embrace in 1938—helped establish the idea that the Federal Government has a responsibility for sustaining prosperity and high employment. The New Deal softened but did not end the Depression; not until the beginning of World War Two did full prosperity return. Nor did it do very much to help the most desperate members of society; its policies tended to protect and stabilize the middle class. But the Roosevelt administration took a government that in the past had lacked both the capacity and, usually, the will to ad-

Mexican-Americans and others line up outside a government relief office in San Antonio, Texas, in 1939. New Deal agencies made Federal assistance available for the first time to unemployed workers and farmers. In the past, such people had to rely on private charity to sustain them during hard times.

**Many could barely remember a time when FDR had not been President, and when he died of a cerebral hemorrhage in April 1945, millions reacted with shock and disbelief. The nation went into mourning, and thousands lined the streets of Washington to watch his funeral procession pass by, many weeping openly for the man who had guided them through tragedy and triumph.**

sevelt's illness were not exaggerated. On April 12, 1945, less than three months after the President's austere fourth inaugural (held not at the Capitol but on the south portico of the White House, with his new Vice President, Harry Truman, standing inconspicuously in the background), and a few weeks after his return from Yalta—where he had attempted to negotiate with Churchill and Stalin the framework for a new international order—Franklin Delano Roosevelt suffered a massive cerebral hemorrhage at his vacation home in Warm Springs, Georgia, and died. His passing brought to a close a remarkable era in the history of the nation, the Presidency and the Democratic Party.

# CHAPTER EIGHT

# NEW FRONTIERS

## 1945–1968

### BY ALONZO L. HAMBY

In the long cabinet room, he looked to me like a very little man as he sat waiting in a huge leather chair." Thus a White House aide recalled the stunned Vice President who, in the early evening of April 12, 1945, contemplated the office into which he was about to be sworn. Two days later, as the new President of the United States, he rode down Constitution Avenue in the funeral procession of Franklin D. Roosevelt.

Many of the spectators who lined the street wept openly. With the sound of muffled drums and slowly paced horses' hooves in the background, Arthur Godfrey described the event to a radio audience that stretched around the globe. In a broken voice, he recalled the way FDR had endured so much for all the ordinary people of the world, then solemnly declared: "God bless our new President, Harry Truman."

Truman was a man of average height and weight, but his modest demeanor and thick eyeglasses, his background in machine politics and, above all, his historical position in the shadow of Roosevelt made him appear considerably smaller in presidential stature than he actually was. By 1944, having established himself as perhaps the best-liked, hardest-working and

most influential Democrat in the Senate, he had been a consensus compromise choice to run as Roosevelt's vice presidential candidate. Many of his backers, cognizant of FDR's bad health, realized they probably were picking a President.

Not since Lincoln had anyone come to the presidency at so critical a moment in history, and never had any chief executive had so little preparation for the immediate tasks that lay before him. World War Two was nearing its end in Europe; Germany surrendered on May 8, Truman's 61st birthday. In the Pacific, the battle of Okinawa, the bloodiest of the Pacific war, went on until June 21; appalling casualties on both sides seemed to offer a foretaste of what an invasion of Japan would bring. That August, two atomic bombs brought the war to a sudden end, touching off mass jubilation across the country. Japan would sign the instrument of surrender on the great battleship named for the President's home state, the USS Missouri.

Truman had known virtually nothing of the atomic bomb project before becoming President, possessed only the most imperfect sense of just what he was authorizing and followed the advice of his top military aides. Still, he accepted full responsibility for the use

On April 12, 1945, 90 minutes after learning of the death of Roosevelt, a stunned Vice President, Harry Truman, took the oath of office as President of the United States. Never had anyone entered the Oval Office at so critical a moment in history with so little preparation for the monumental tasks that lay before him—but Truman proved himself more than equal to the job.

of the new weapon, believed that it had saved untold thousands of American lives and maintained until the end of his life that he felt no regrets. Perhaps not, but he clearly did not take the results lightly. He withheld permission for the use of the third bomb, scheduled for late August, because, as he told his Cabinet on August 10, the thought of wiping out another 100,000 people was too horrible to contemplate and he did not want to keep killing "all those kids." He seems never again to have seriously contemplated the use of nuclear weapons.

Six weeks before the end of the war, thanks largely to American leadership, the United Nations had been founded. The ideal of an international organization in which the United States would play a leading role had been intimately connected with the Democratic Party since Woodrow Wilson. Truman, an old Wilsonian, understood the role of military power in world affairs, but he also believed deeply in the UN and supported it strongly during his presidency.

The peace had hardly begun before the United States became enmeshed in a "Cold War" with its for-mer ally, the Soviet Union. With the United States pledged to individual freedom and national self-determination, it was impossible for Truman and his diplomats to watch without protest as the USSR imposed Communist dictatorships throughout Eastern Europe, kept troops in Northern Iran, pressured Turkey for control of the Dardanelles and lent at least moral support to a pro-Communist insurgency in Greece.

Little could be done about Eastern Europe, but strong diplomatic representations helped persuade the USSR to withdraw from Iran. In the spring of 1947, Truman prevailed on Congress to appropriate aid for Greece and Turkey, asserting what became known as the Truman Doctrine: "It must be the policy of the United States to support free peoples who are resisting attempted subjugation by armed minorities or by out-side pressures." Economic misery in Western Europe, accompanied by the rise of militant Communist parties in France and Italy, led quickly to the Marshall Plan, a massive aid program that helped the Conti-nent's democracies recover from the devastation of the

On August 6, 1945, Hiroshima was destroyed and 80,000 people were killed by the first atomic bomb ever dropped in warfare. Three days later, the United States dropped another bomb on Nagasaki, killing 60-70,000 more. A third bomb had been scheduled, but Truman withheld permission to use it because the thought of wiping out another 100,000 people was too horrible to contemplate.

A broken Japan accepted "the unendurable" and surrendered on August 14, 1945. A few days later, President Truman and the other architects of American victory—Secretary of the Navy James V. Forrestal, Secretary of War Henry L. Stimson and Army Chief of Staff General George C. Marshall (left to right)—inspected the articles of surrender signed by Japanese officials on the deck of the *USS Missouri*.

The United Nations General Assembly convened in a special session on April 28, 1947 to debate the Palestine question, a struggle between Arabs and Jews that confronted the Truman administration with perhaps its most intractable moral and political dilemma. Sixteen days later, against the advice of the State Department, Truman courageously recognized the new state of Israel.

On the campaign trail for re-election in 1948, Truman drew enthusiastic crowds everywhere he went, championing his "Fair Deal" domestic program of commitment to national medical insurance, aid to education, housing and civil rights. He hoped to rebuild the old FDR coalition, but political observers were convinced he would lose.

war and begin a process of economic integration. Truman named the plan for Secretary of State George C. Marshall, a retired World War Two general and a revered non-partisan figure. Refraining from taking credit for himself, he eased its path through a Republican Congress. It imposed a short-term sacrifice on Americans in return for the long-term benefits of freedom and prosperity in that part of Europe.

In June 1948, with the Western allies moving to establish an independent, democratic West German state, the Russians blockaded Allied ground routes to West Berlin. Truman authorized an airlift that supplied the city for a year. By the time the Russians abandoned the blockade in June 1949, the Western European nations and the United States had agreed on a mutual defense pact, the North Atlantic Treaty; the agreement established the North Atlantic Treaty Organization

(NATO) to provide a coordinated military capability.

NATO capped a series of epochal foreign policy departures that kept Western Europe free, democratic and, ultimately, prosperous. In the process, Truman had placed the United States at the head of a de facto empire that stretched across the Atlantic, but as the Norwegian historian Gier Lundestat has observed, the American empire, quite unlike the one the Soviets had established in Eastern Europe, was an "empire by invitation."

By then, Truman had become, as Robert Lovett put it, a midwife to the birth of Israel. On May 14, 1948, after protracted indecision on the Jewish-Arab conflict in Palestine, he announced that the United States would be the first nation to recognize the just-proclaimed Jewish state. Acting over the opposition of a State Department that did not want to antagonize the

**Truman was being dismissed as ordinary and uninspiring—"good field, no hit," wrote one commentator—but the feisty Missourian confounded critics by waging an aggressive whistle-stop campaign, lashing away at the "do-nothing, good-for-nothing Republican 80th Congress." In a major upset—and a coup for Democratic liberalism—he defeated the GOP's Thomas E. Dewey.**

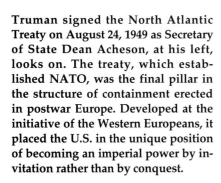

Truman signed the North Atlantic Treaty on August 24, 1949 as Secretary of State Dean Acheson, at his left, looks on. The treaty, which established NATO, was the final pillar in the structure of containment erected in postwar Europe. Developed at the initiative of the Western Europeans, it placed the U.S. in the unique position of becoming an imperial power by invitation rather than by conquest.

Arabs, he was motivated partly by strong concern for the displaced Jews of postwar Europe, partly by the importance of the Jewish constituency in the Democratic Party.

At home, Truman had initially fought a losing battle with the overwhelming difficulties of economic reconversion from the war. Tired of economic controls, shortages and strikes, the electorate gave the Republicans a strong victory in the 1946 congressional elections. For the next year and a half, the President worked hard to rebuild the New Deal Democratic coalition.

His domestic program, the Fair Deal, stressed continuance of Roosevelt's achievements and raised new issues: national medical insurance, Federal aid to education, housing and civil rights. Little would ever get through Congress, controlled by cautious moderates and conservatives throughout Truman's years in office. On civil rights, however, the President was able to take important action: desegregation of the armed forces and Justice Department arguments before the Supreme Court that laid the groundwork for the landmark Brown school desegregation decision of 1954. Thereby he cemented the loyalty of blacks to his party.

Truman's Fair Deal and his foreign policy established the content of a new style of "vital center" liberalism that stood for social reform at home and opposed all varieties of totalitarianism abroad. Espoused by a new organization of explicitly anti-

Communist liberals, Americans for Democratic Action (ADA), under the leadership of, among others, Eleanor Roosevelt and Hubert Humphrey, it would serve the Party well into the 1960s.

Nonetheless, most political observers thought Truman was sure to lose the 1948 election. He faced insurgent movements from both ends of the Party—on the left, Henry Wallace and the Progressives; on the right, Strom Thurmond and the southern States Righters. His Republican opponent, Governor Thomas E. Dewey of New York, had come close to beating Roosevelt in 1944. Truman himself, for all his accomplishments, seemed ordinary and uninspiring. Observing that "democracy is crying for daddy," journalist James Wechsler described Truman as a mediocre rookie: "good field, no hit." Many liberals tried to get General Dwight D. Eisenhower to run for the nomination.

Truman confounded his critics by waging an exhaustive whistle-stop campaign in which he traveled by train and made hundreds of hard-hitting speeches. "The Republican politicians . . . have never liked the New Deal," he declared in a representative address. "They are waiting eagerly for the time when they can go ahead with a Republican Congress and a Republican President and do a real hatchet job." On election day, he surprised a stunned nation, polling 49.6 percent of the vote to 45.1 percent for Dewey.

Truman's triumph has been viewed in two ways. It

was a win for the underdog, the "little guy," the ordinary person, over the slick organization man Dewey. But it was also a coup for the Democratic Party and the liberalism to which Truman had hitched it. After 1948, it was clear that the Democrats were the dominant party and that Roosevelt's New Deal was established beyond recall.

Truman would soon discover that the results were not a mandate for big new programs. In 1949 and 1950, he wrung important enlargements of several existing New Deal programs for Congress, but he had little luck with his own initiatives. Any hope that the mood might change was dashed by the Communist takeover of China, the Korean War and the rise of McCarthyism.

The Truman administration could do little to prevent the collapse of Chiang Kai-shek's Nationalist Chinese government and the establishment of a Communist regime that, in its early years, aligned itself with the USSR. There was much validity in Senator Tom Connally's purported remark that Generalissimo

Chiang needed to do more generaling and less "issimoing." Republicans, including many who had supported Truman's foreign policies to this point, saw it differently and asked, "Who lost China?"

In mid-1950, when Communist North Korea invaded pro-Western South Korea, Truman saw the action as naked aggression. Informed of the invasion by Secretary of State Dean Acheson, he said, as he later recalled it: "Dean, we've got to stop the sons of bitches right here and now." Fighting under the United Nations flag, South Korean and American troops, along with small detachments from many other nations, routed the North Koreans only to run into a massive Chinese intervention. After the battle lines stabilized near the prewar north-south boundary, the President opted for negotiations to end the war.

The move led to open criticism from his commander, General Douglas MacArthur. The great hero of the Pacific in World War Two, MacArthur was a living legend, frequently brilliant in his military decisions, blessed with formidable oratorical powers but also

When the American-sponsored government in South Korea was besieged by the invasion of an army of 90,000 troops from Communist North Korea in June of 1950—with backing from China and the Soviet Union—the U.S. responded with armed intervention to defend its containment policy in a land and air war that cost 100,000 American casualties and two million Korean lives.

vainglorious, incapable of admitting mistakes and unwilling to accept limitations from higher authority. He argued for total war against China, including the use of nuclear weapons.

On April 11, 1951, Truman fired MacArthur. Absolutely necessary to preserve the President's authority as civilian commander in chief, the decision was nonetheless highly unpopular. As truce negotiations with the Chinese bogged down, the war itself turned into a bloody stalemate that further eroded Truman's standing with the electorate.

At home, the President and his chief officials found themselves subjected to a constant pounding by Senator Joseph McCarthy and other Republicans, who made charges of Communist infiltration into the administration. More an opportunistic bully boy than a conservative ideologue, McCarthy nearly perfected what one observer called the technique of the "multiple untruth." Nonetheless, he probably would have faded quickly if Korea had not set off a mood of

intense public unease. Wartime economic controls, inflation and some instances of small-bore corruption all added to the political toll. On March 29, 1952, Truman announced that he would not seek re-election.

Perhaps, as the Republicans would claim in the fall, it was "time for a change" after 20 years of Democratic supremacy. Their candidate, Dwight D. Eisenhower, was surely unbeatable, but he took care in his own speeches to make it clear that he posed no threat to the fundamental legacy of the New Deal.

That promise was itself a measure of Truman's accomplishment. He left the presidency having made the New Deal part of the national consensus, and having entrenched the Democrats as the nation's majority party. He also had set the course of American foreign policy for a generation. In all, it was a remarkable record for a man whose detractors insisted was too little for the presidency.

Truman's successor as "titular" leader of the Democratic Party, Adlai Stevenson, shared his ideological

**Employing "the multiple untruth," Senator Joseph R. McCarthy launched scattershot charges of Communist influence in the Truman and Eisenhower administrations. At the notorious Army-McCarthy hearings in 1954, Army counsel Joseph Welch (seated) asked angrily: "Have you no sense of decency, Senator?" Outraged, the Senate censured McCarthy at the end of the year.**

**Adlai E. Stevenson, Truman's successor as titular leader of the Democratic Party, shared his political convictions but not his personal style. Witty and articulate, he inspired fervent allegiance from "liberal intellectuals" but lacked Harry's common touch—and he had the misfortune to run twice for President, in 1952 and 1956, against the unbeatable war hero Dwight Eisenhower.**

convictions but was vastly different in style. Articulate in his prose, eloquent in his speech, Stevenson lacked Truman's gut appeal to the "common person" but possessed the fervent allegiance of the "liberal intellectuals." Thinkers, public administrators, non-business-oriented professionals, this segment of the population became perhaps the fastest growing constituency of the party after World War Two, was usually at odds with old-style regulars and bosses and not altogether comfortable with the blue-collar classes and the unions. Still, pitted against anyone but Eisenhower, Stevenson might have been a winning candidate and a distinguished President. Instead, he became a transitional figure who paved the way for John F. Kennedy.

By virtue of family heritage, education and social status, Kennedy was more equipped than any Democratic leader of the twentieth century to bring together the liberal intellectuals with ordinary Northern Democrats who tended to be working class, non-Protestant and of immigrant background. A third-generation Irish-Catholic American, wealthy, Harvard-educated, articulate, polished, charismatic, Kennedy embodied the aspirations of the intellectuals. He was, as Massachusetts Governor Paul Dever observed, "the first Irish Brahmin." These qualities played poorly among traditional WASP southern Democrats, but no Democrat could win the enthusiasm of every constituency in so diverse a party; Kennedy achieved the adulation of its center of gravity.

Inevitably, his presidency is remembered for its

Campaigning for President in 1960, literally knee-deep in admirers, John F. Kennedy exuded the charismatic crowd appeal that enabled this junior senator from Massachusetts—a third generation Irish-Catholic "Boston Brahmin"—to win the nomination over a wide field of contenders at the Democratic Convention, then upstage Richard Nixon on television to take the election.

style and glamour. "The torch has been passed to a new generation of Americans," he declared in his inaugural address. Clearly, he considered himself the representative of that generation, tempered by depression, war and cold war; willing to "pay any price, bear any burden" in the defense of American ideals.

Remarkably suited for the new television media age that emerged about 1960, Kennedy probably could not have defeated Richard Nixon without the edge that TV gave him. As President, he employed television press conferences and other appearances to convey the image of a leader who was at once witty, self-possessed, an appropriate host for glittering White House social occasions and in command of his serious public duties. Yet there was much more to the Kennedy years. The President and his administration faced a wide range of issues at home and abroad, many of them inherited from Truman and Eisenhower,

some of them new challenges that seemed to demand, in Kennedy's memorable phrase, movement toward a "New Frontier."

No need was more fundamental, at least in a structural sense, than the imperative of stimulating economic growth, which had slowed perceptibly in the Eisenhower years. Kennedy responded pragmatically and flexibly, drawing in many respects on traditional Democratic doctrine. For the long term, he promoted freer international trade with the Trade Expansion Act of 1962. For the short term, he obtained an investment tax credit for business, then advocated a major tax cut to stimulate the economy. At Kennedy's death, the tax cut was moving through Congress; passed in 1964, it would contribute to the economic boom of the Sixties.

The other urgent issue was moral. By the time Kennedy became President, the black quest for full citizenship was approaching an activist peak. In the

**To stop the flow of refugees out of East Germany, Communist authorities built the Berlin Wall in 1961. Standing firm against Russian threats to eject the Western powers from the city, JFK delivered a ringing speech at the wall in 1964. Pledging support for the independence of West Berlin, JFK thrilled the Germans by declaring: "Ich bin ein Berliner!" ("I am a Berliner!")**

**Serving out his fallen predecessor's term, Lyndon Johnson signed the landmark Civil Rights Act of 1964, a broadly based attack against segregation and discrimination. His overwhelming election victory in 1964 mandated a flood of progressive legislation: Medicare, Medicaid, aid to education and urban America, and the historic Voting Rights Act of 1965.**

spring of 1963, responding to Birmingham police violence against civil rights demonstrators led by Dr. Martin Luther King, Jr., Kennedy proposed major civil rights legislation, thereby breaking decisively with the South. Northern Democrats in Congress predominantly supported the civil rights bill, and the administration worked hard to develop support among the Republicans. Kennedy nonetheless had taken a big political risk. Whether a civil rights law might pass and in what form remained uncertain when he left for Dallas just before Thanksgiving. If he hadn't died, it is impossible to know whether it could have passed through Congress in the form it finally took: the Civil Rights Act of 1964.

Kennedy had thought extensively about foreign policy issues during his years in the U.S. Senate and may have engaged in more working trips abroad than any other member of Congress. Wanting to take initiatives that expressed American idealism, he established

the Peace Corps and initiated the Alliance for Progress aid program for Latin America. Believing in the need for a strong defense, he ordered a buildup of the conventional armed forces. Nonetheless, faced with the first clear-cut Communist regime in the Western Hemisphere, Fidel Castro's Cuba, he slipped badly during the early months of his presidency. The poorly planned invasion by CIA-trained Cuban exiles at the Bay of Pigs became a major embarrassment.

On Berlin, the truly important focus of the U.S.-Soviet differences, Kennedy stood firm against Russian threats to eject the Western powers from the city. Unwilling to challenge the building of the Berlin Wall, he made it plain that the United States would fight any aggression against West Berlin, underscoring the pledge by visiting the city and declaring: "Ich bin ein Berliner!"

The Cuban Missile Crisis, in October 1962, established Kennedy's preeminence as a world leader. Firm but cautious, he displayed flexibility without ever backing away from his central objective, the withdrawal of Soviet missiles from Cuba. From a detached, analytical standpoint, the settlement was a compromise with benefits for Castro and the Russians. But to most of a world that had seemed poised on the brink of nuclear war, the outcome was clear. As Secretary of State Dean Rusk put it, "We were eyeball to eyeball, and the other side blinked."

Kennedy thereupon used his newfound prestige to push for a settlement of differences with the USSR. The first major breakthrough was an Atomic Test Ban treaty. "We all inhabit this small planet," he declared. "We all breathe the same air. We all cherish our children's future. And we all are mortal." Little more than a halting first step, it nonetheless gave rise to hopes that the end of the Cold War might be on the horizon.

Instead, a speck of a problem called South Vietnam became increasingly prominent. Kennedy had wisely disengaged American interests from Laos, but he remained committed to supporting South Vietnam's struggle against Communist rebels. He clearly wanted to avoid using American combat forces, but no one can declare with certainty how he might have reacted to the pressure of events that occurred after his death. By mid-November 1963, in the wake of a U.S.-sanctioned coup d'etat, the situation there was more precarious than ever.

Tragically cut down at the height of his achievements and power on November 22, 1963, Kennedy never had to face the issue. At the time of his assassination, President Kennedy was widely considered a great foreign policy leader and was vastly popular around the globe. The nation and the free world mourned him in a fashion that recalled the shock and grief that had accompanied the death of Roosevelt; it was perhaps even more intense in its realization that the young President's promise of greatness would forever remain unfulfilled.

Kennedy's successor, Lyndon Johnson, was to be sure a less attractive personality. According to legend, he once asked Dean Acheson why the American people didn't love him. The blunt-talking Acheson replied: "Mr. President, you are not a very lovable man." He was, however, a master of the legislative process who had excelled as Senate Democratic leader in the 1950s.

Above all, Johnson was a man of driving energy and ambition, who seemed in the words of one aide, to "have extra glands." Tough and domineering toward his subordinates, he liked to boast, "I don't get ulcers, I give 'em." He delighted in the trappings of power. Asked by a reporter to identify his helicopter from a group waiting on the White House lawn, he replied, "Son, they're all my helicopters!" His crude and profane style deeply offended many Kennedy loyalists.

Johnson nonetheless felt deep compassion for the poor and dispossessed. He came to the presidency determined not simply to realize the unfinished agenda of the Kennedy administration but to enact the most ambitious package of liberal reforms in American history and thereby make America into a "Great Society."

His first year was remarkable by old historical standards. At his urging, Congress passed the Kennedy tax cut and civil rights bills, then approved initial legislation for what became known as the War on Poverty. He was also lucky: In the election of 1964, his opponent was extremist Senator Barry Goldwater, the outspoken leader of a resurgent conservative movement that would lead eventually to the Reagan revolution. Unfortunately for Goldwater, however, was that as a candidate for the presidency, he lent himself to caricature as an angry right-wing zealot. Johnson's overwhelming victory, a personal and party triumph that rivaled Roosevelt's 1936 sweep, gave liberal Democrats a control of Congress beyond anything they had enjoyed in the postwar ear. The results, moreover, went beyond the Thirties in marginalizing the conservative South.

What followed was a flood of legislation that gave expression to all the blocked policy yearnings of Fair Dealers, liberal oppositionists in the Eisenhower era, and Kennedy New Frontier social activists. In a period of two years, Johnson and the Democratic Congress gave the nation Medicare, Medicaid, large-scale aid to education at all levels, vast additions to the War on Poverty, and assistance to urban America on a hitherto unimaginable scale. Perhaps most significant in the long run was the Voting Rights Act of 1965, a bill that would transform the Democratic Party in the South as blacks, finally able to participate in politics, flocked into it.

During this same period, the economy also boomed, creating employment levels that had not been known for a decade and setting new standards of the good life for most Americans. Yet by the midpoint

Sit-ins, marches and demonstrations, beginning with the Montgomery bus boycott of 1955 and culminating in the historic march for voting rights from Selma to Montgomery in March 1965 took the civil rights movement to the streets. The black struggle galvanized public opinion and the resulting legislation revolutionized American life and politics.

of Johnson's only full term, the country was in turmoil. Some of the reasons stemmed from the unexpected side effects of the Great Society and the social issues it addressed. Inflation put bigger paychecks into a race with higher prices. The civil rights bills emancipated Southern blacks, but seemed to do little for those who lived in Northern ghettos. The resulting anger and frustration erupted in inner-city riots across the country. Some critics charged Johnson with trying to do too many things too soon. Others asserted that he had produced only a small down payment on restitution for generations of oppression.

But the most palpable source of discontent was the war that had developed in Vietnam. Convinced that he was moving ahead with Kennedy's policies, Johnson engaged in a major escalation that, as David Halberstam put it, "led to the Americanization of Vietnam and the Vietnamization of America." By its very existence, the war imparted an atmosphere of conflict and violence to American politics.

Johnson hoped to persuade the North Vietnamese to agree to a compromise settlement at first through conciliation, then by escalating the war, but the Communist leaders in Hanoi were willing to pay any price for victory. In the end, South Vietnam was not impor-

tant enough to justify the great military and diplomatic risks vis-a-vis China and the Soviet Union that would come with an all-out offensive against the North. By 1968, the war had become a frustrating stalemate. That spring, after nearly losing the New Hampshire primary to peace candidate Eugene McCarthy, a chastened Johnson announced he would not run for re-election; shortly thereafter, the administration began negotiations with the North Vietnamese.

1968 was one of the most traumatic years in the history of American politics. Just days after Johnson announced his withdrawal, Martin Luther King, Jr. was assassinated in Memphis, prompting angry blacks to riot in dozens of cities across the country. A three-way race for the Democratic presidential nomination took shape between Senator Eugene McCarthy of Minnesota, the original leader of the war protesters; Senator Robert F. Kennedy of New York, JFK's younger brother and heir to his mantle; and Vice President Hubert Humphrey, long the happy warrior of American liberalism but now also saddled with all the discontents that clung to the Johnson administration.

On June 5, 1968, just minutes after he had proclaimed victory in the California primary, Bobby Kennedy was gunned down in Los Angeles. Heart-

Displaying the toll of nearly five years in the presidency, Lyndon Johnson confers on a halt to the bombing of North Vietnam, October 29, 1968. He had already decided not to run for re-election but hoped it might be possible to arrive at a peace settlement and in the process give a boost to Humphrey's presidential candidacy.

breaking as a personal tragedy, the second Kennedy assassination of the decade deprived the party of its most electable and charismatic candidate. He had been an exciting symbol of change and reconciliation, and his death created a void that plunged Democrats and their party into despair.

A bitter, riot-marred Democratic convention nominated Hubert Humphrey, who struggled valiantly to pull the Roosevelt coalition together and pledged himself to extrication from Vietnam. He came amazingly close to victory, in the end losing narrowly to Richard Nixon, who would inaugurate an era of Republican ascendancy in the presidency, but not on Capitol Hill. The Party, it seemed, had come full circle from the tragedy of Roosevelt's death to that of Bobby Kennedy. After 1968, it would face the difficult tasks of developing new leadership and remaking itself into a force that once again could inspire the allegiance of the majority of Americans.

The spiritual heir to JFK's mantle, Robert F. Kennedy was riding a wave of rising popularity in a string of primaries, tapping into the dreams of millions, in the spring of 1968. He seemed headed for the nomination and the White House. But in a nightmarish replay of his brother's death, Bobby was cut down, and the politics of hope died with him.

Jimmy Carter's declaration that it was time for the people to run the government, not the other way around, greatly appealed to a public who had grown distrustful of the system. Reminiscent of Jefferson's walk to his inauguration, he cast aside the trappings of the imperial presidency and strolled down Pennsylvania Avenue after taking the oath of office.

# CHAPTER NINE

# THE CHALLENGE OF DIVERSITY

## 1969–1992

### BY STEVEN M. GILLON

Th' demmycratic party ain't on speakin' terms with itself, "declared Finley Peter Dunne's fictitious character Dooley in his characteristic Irish dialect. Dooley's observation, made at the turn of the century, also described the state of the modern Democratic Party in the late Sixties. With the sudden loss of two of their most promising leaders by assassination, the Party's vying factions, which battled on the convention floor in 1968, continued their civil war into the 1970s and 1980s. The persistent conflict between a growing band of middle-class reformers, a diminished liberal group and an influential Southern wing prevented the Party from speaking with a single voice. As a result, the Democrats lost four of the next five presidential races after 1968, even though they retained a strong presence in Congress and in most states.

By any standard, the Sixties were an emotionally charged decade, and in 1969, no issue provoked more passion than the Vietnam War. Though a small number of hawks continued their calls for a military solution, most of the Democratic Party leadership rallied behind proposals to end the war. In 1970, Idaho Senator Frank Church proposed cutting off funding for American forces in Cambodia. The following year, one of the Senate's most vocal opponents of the war, George McGovern of South Dakota, sponsored an amendment which would have ended military operations in Cambodia and required the withdrawal of all U.S. forces from Vietnam by the end of the year. Opposition from Republicans and conservative Democrats defeated both amendments. Party liberals had more success in 1973 with passage of the War Powers Act, which required the President to notify Congress within 48 hours of American troop deployment to combat areas, and forced him to withdraw the soldiers after 60 days unless Congress specifically authorized them to stay.

In 1972, Democratic hopes of recapturing the presidency focused on Senator McGovern, a soft-spoken preacher's son whom Robert Kennedy once called "the most decent man in the Senate." Taking advantage of new party rules which expanded the number of primaries and increased the influence of minorities, women and the young, McGovern outmaneuvered Senator Edmund Muskie, his chief rival for the nomination.

In some ways, the convention that nominated

The 1968 Democratic National Convention opened in Chicago amidst the pandemonium of massive anti-war demonstrations that provoked what a presidential commission later branded as a police riot. The Vietnam War had polarized the nation and generated a wave of angry confrontations between protestors and the law that sometimes escalated into violence.

McGovern was the most representative of the country's populace in history. Women comprised nearly 40 percent of delegates; young people made up another quarter; and the number of black delegates doubled since 1968. But in its attempt to include marginalized groups, the party excluded prominent Democrats, powerful machine politicians and representatives of various ethnic groups that had long been the backbone of the Party. One labor leader grumbled, "There's too much hair and not enough cigars at this convention." Floor fights over controversial social issues—gay rights, legalization of marijuana, abortion and criminal rights—obscured the Party's commitment to end the Vietnam War, initiate tax reform and sustain social welfare programs. For the first time, the Party platform also included support for an equal rights amendment to the Constitution. Over the next decade, Democrats on the state and local levels embraced the cause of equal rights for women, but the amendment stalled in state legislatures, where Republicans

misrepresented the legislation as a challenge to family values.

The youthful supporters who waved placards reading "Saint George will slay the dragon" applauded McGovern's moral crusade against Nixon and the war. The recent passage of the 26th Amendment to the Constitution, which extended voting rights to 18-year-olds, buoyed McGovern's hopes of attracting an army of young antiwar activists to his peace candidacy. But his attempt to mobilize a coalition of minorities carried obvious political risks. It assumed that young people protesting on college campuses would translate their anger into votes. They did not. "Rarely in history has publicized activism been replaced so rapidly by apparent apathy, student dissent by silence," observed historian C. Vann Woodward. Also, many working-class Democrats felt betrayed by their party's enthusiasm for groups—college students, intellectuals and minorities—that were sometimes hostile to their interests. Nixon, nothing if not a shrewd politician, capitalized

Hubert H. Humphrey made his dramatic national debut at the 1948 Democratic Convention with a moving speech calling for civil rights. Elected senator from Minnesota that year, he went on to become Vice President under Lyndon Johnson. Though he ran unsuccessfully for President in 1968, the "Happy Warrior" remained a strong voice for liberalism until his death in 1978.

on this discontent by promising that "peace is at hand," and by pledging his fidelity to law and order and traditional values. Outpoliticked by the sitting President, McGovern suffered a decisive defeat in the general election. Nixon won over 60 percent of the popular vote, and his 521 electoral votes came within two votes of matching FDR's record. The electoral landslide precipitated another confrontation between rival factions vying to define the Democratic Party's mission in the 1970s.

While Party leaders debated the lessons of McGovern's defeat, congressional Democrats engaged in a historic confrontation with the President. In 1973, Senate Democrats established a committee to investigate charges that the executive branch had been involved

in a burglary of the Democratic headquarters in the Watergate building. North Carolina Democrat Sam

One of the Senate's most outspoken opponents of the Vietnam War, South Dakota's George McGovern—called "the most decent man in the Senate" by Robert Kennedy—embodied the ideals of his constituency at the 1972 Democratic Convention that chose him as its candidate for President. But his moral crusade against the Republicans and the war was buried in the landslide that re-elected Nixon.

It was soon after the election that the Nixon administration became embroiled in the firestorm of controversy that led from a burglary of Democratic Party headquarters in the Watergate building by members of the Committee to Re-elect the President. Sensational revelations of extralegal "dirty tricks" laid a trail of damning evidence that went straight into the White House.

Ervin, who endeared himself to the American people with his folksy manner and sharp wit, presided over the televised drama. Over the next few months, as the sordid details of White House "dirty tricks" emerged, the nation focused its attention on the question posed by Tennessee Republican Senator Howard Baker: "What did the President know and when did he know it?" The answer became clear in May when a reluctant Nixon released sanitized, "expletives deleted" transcripts of secret Oval Office conversations. The tapes contained talk of extortion, blackmail, cover-ups and hush money. Eminent journalist Eric Sevareid claimed that the tapes constituted "a moral indictment without known precedent in the history of American government."

As details of widespread violations emerged, and as an intransigent Nixon professed his innocence, the House Judiciary Committee considered impeachment. In July, following a Supreme Court order forcing the President to relinquish the remaining White House

tapes, committee Democrats voted unanimously for impeachment. No one was more eloquent than black Congresswoman Barbara Jordan, who forcefully defended a document that had once denied her ancestors' basic rights of citizenship. "My faith in the Constitution is whole," she told the hushed committee room in a voice filled with emotion. "It is total, and I am not going to sit here and be an idle spectator to the diminution, the subversion, the destruction of the Constitution." A few days later, Nixon became the first President in U.S. history to resign.

Though Nixon never admitted his guilt, and his hand-picked successor's presidential pardon prevented the public from knowing the full truth, the Watergate affair constituted the most serious political scandal in American history. The *New York Times* editorialized that the most important result of Watergate was that "the long and unmistakable drift toward concentration of power in the hands of one elected official, the President of the United States, has been stopped."

Congressional Democrats moved to prevent future abuses of executive power. These efforts were aided by the 75 freshmen Democrats elected to the House as part of the "class of '74." That year, Nixon's illegal impoundment of funds inspired passage of the Congressional Budget and Impoundment Act which, among other things, provided Congress with better economic management. In an effort to break its dependence on the executive branch for information, Democrats expanded the resources of the Congressional Research Service and the General Accounting Office, and created the Office of Technology Assessment. When Senators Frank Church and Walter Mondale uncovered a history of serious FBI and CIA abuses of individual rights, Democrats passed legislation that provided greater congressional oversight of the intelligence community.

The pervasive feeling of distrust aimed at the White House as a result of the Watergate affair, along with a stagnant economy, provided Democrats with the opportunity to put aside their differences and recapture the White House in 1976. Jimmy Carter, a former Georgia governor and a spokesman for the new South, emerged from a crowded pack of contenders. He fueled his campaign by tapping into the vast reservoir of public cynicism that followed in the wake of Vietnam and Watergate. "It is time for the people to run the government and not the other way around," he told audiences. Hoping to restore trust in government, the former peanut farmer shunned the accouterments of power and privilege and promised always to tell the truth. Running a grass-roots campaign that bypassed traditional power brokers, Carter touched a vital nerve with the American people. In his campaign against incumbent Gerald Ford, Carter emphasized general themes that were acceptable to all Democrats. While affirming the Party's historic commitment to help society's outcasts, Carter promised "a government as good as the American people" and offered a new vision of America's role in the world. In many states, including his native South, Carter pulled support from the remnants of the New

Veteran North Carolina Democrat Sam J. Ervin, Jr., a respected lawyer and chairman of the Watergate committee, challenged Nixon aide H. R. Haldeman on the stand at a dramatic moment in the televised 1973 Senate hearings, watched by millions, that led to indictments which engulfed the entire administration, precipitating threats of impeachment that forced Nixon to resign.

President Carter's tireless commitment to peace in the Middle East forged a historic treaty between Israel and Egypt. In a White House ceremony, Carter brought together the leaders of these two hostile nations to sign the Camp David Accords. Many of the President's most dramatic achievements were in the foreign policy arena, where he pursued an agenda of human rights for all.

Deal coalition and from independent voters who had defected to the Republicans in the two previous elections. More impressive, his message of racial healing appealed to blacks and whites eager to move beyond the social strife of the 1960s.

Once in office, Carter moved to institute his reform agenda. He named blacks and women to important positions in the administration, and he pushed through Congress legislation to stimulate the sluggish economy. Reflecting the discord that plagued the Party, a Democratic Congress refused to pass the President's proposals for welfare reform, national health care and energy conservation. Many of President Carter's most dramatic initiatives came in foreign policy. In a refreshing break with the realpolitik of the Nixon-Kissinger years, Carter announced that human

rights and not excessive fear of communism would guide American foreign policy. "Because we are free," Carter declared, "we can never be indifferent to the fate of freedom elsewhere." In Africa, Carter placed his administration firmly on the side of black nationalists struggling for political justice. As part of his effort to demonstrate support for rising nationalist sentiment in Latin America, the President successfully pushed the Panama Canal treaties through a reluctant Senate. In 1978, he engineered what one admiring observer called "the most remarkable and significant diplomatic achievement in the history of the Republic," when he brought together the leaders of Israel and Egypt for the signing of the Camp David Accords, the first formal non-aggression pact between these long-time and bitter enemies. Both Israeli Prime Minister

Menachem Begin and Egyptian President Anwar Sadat praised Carter for his deep commitment and tireless efforts. Begin told reporters that Carter worked "harder than our forefathers did in building the pyramids."

In the end, however, President Carter's administration fell victim to forces beyond its control. The 1970s witnessed the end of the sustained economic growth that had nourished social programs in the postwar period. The slowdown had many sources, but the main culprit was the dramatically rising price of oil. As Arab oil-producing nations decreased exports to the United States, the price of oil skyrocketed, sending inflationary shock waves through the U.S. economy. By May 1979, gasoline lines in California ran as long as 500 cars, and the price at the pumps climbed above a dollar a gallon for the first time ever.

There was no easy answer to be found to halt the deterioration of the economy, and Democrats were divided on how to respond. Carter, believing that inflation presented the greatest long-term risk to America's economic health, implored congressional Democrats to cut spending for social programs. But many liberals, convinced that the President had betrayed the Party's responsibility to protect the poor, argued for increased spending for jobs, health care and welfare. Underscoring the "crisis of confidence" within the Party, Senator Edward Kennedy challenged Carter, unsuccessfully, for the Democratic nomination.

Events abroad also conspired to undermine public confidence in the President's leadership. In November 1979, a crowd of 400 militants, whipped into a frenzy by the violently anti-American Ayatollah Khomeini, seized the American embassy in Iran and held 52 Americans hostage. Over the next few months, America watched horrifying scenes of delirious Islamic "students" burning American flags, chanting anti-American slogans and parading their prized hostages around the embassy compound in front of unblinking television cameras. Then, the following month, the Soviet Union sent troops into Afghanistan. These twin crises focused public attention on America's declining influence in the world, highlighted the confusion that sometimes characterized the administration's

On November 4, 1979, a mob of Iranian "students" seized the American embassy in Teheran, taking 52 Americans hostage. President Carter's diplomacy eventually secured their release, but only after humiliating scenes of blindfolded Americans paraded around the embassy overshadowed the President's foreign policy achievements and eroded support for his presidency.

approach to the world and obscured Carter's foreign policy triumphs. Gleeful Republicans, led by presidential nominee Ronald Reagan, translated the public's frustration and anger into a decisive victory at the polls in 1980.

President Reagan initiated a spirited assault on the Democratic Party's basic principles. In May 1981, the former California governor harnessed the emotional groundswell of sympathy generated by a failed assassination attempt into a significant legislative victory by forcing through Congress a budget resolution that called for deep cuts in social programs and increased spending for the military. In August, Congress passed Reagan's tax plan, which included a 25 percent reduction in tax rates over three years. Despite the opposition of the Democratic Party leadership, Reagan persuaded many Southern and conservative Democrats to support his radical program. "I expected him to cut me off at the knee," said a frustrated House Speaker Tip O'Neill, "but he cut me off at the hip."

Reagan's success confirmed the profound changes that had transformed American politics over the previous two decades. The buoyant optimism that characterized public attitudes in the early 1960s had given way to apathy and cynicism. Many Americans, doubtful that government offered solutions to vexing social problems, dropped out of the political process. The emergence of controversial social issues, such as school prayer, abortion, crime and homosexual rights, altered support from traditional Democratic appeals to economic self-interest and redrew the battle lines in American politics. Since 1968, Republicans convincingly represented the debate over these issues as a clash between the insurgent values of a liberal elite and the traditional values of middle-class Americans. This new conservative populism replaced contempt for greedy businessmen with a disdain for lenient judges, unresponsive bureaucrats and arrogant minorities. It would be almost ten more years before the realities of greed and deregulation, glorified as the cornerstones of the Reagan revolution, would lead the

After a start in the Massachusetts state legislature, Thomas P. "Tip" O'Neill won election to the House of Representatives in 1952, filling the seat vacated when John F. Kennedy ran for the Senate. Over 30 years, as Majority Leader and Speaker of the House, he effectively championed legislation designed to help minorities and the working class until his retirement in 1982.

Former Vice President Walter Mondale, a passionate advocate of the Party's mission to assist the needy, made history with his choice for running mate in 1984; Congresswoman Geraldine Ferraro, the first female vice presidential candidate ever nominated by a major party. But the Reagan tide was still running high, and the President was re-elected in a Republican sweep of 48 states.

nation into its longest recession since World War Two.

Race was the prism through which many of the new social issues were filtered. As the national Democratic Party became more identified with the civil rights struggles of the 1960s and 1970s, parts of the white South as well as many urban ethnics in the Northeast and Midwest moved comfortably into Republican hands. The Party's support for controversial policies such as affirmative action and busing, and fears about the emergence of a "black underclass," fed old racial stereotypes and further divided the voters.

During the 1980s, the Democrats continued their efforts to redefine the Party's mission. Neo-liberals, who sought an accommodation with Reaganism, appealed to independent, economically conservative voters. "The Democratic Party must govern well," declared Colorado Senator Gary Hart, "but it must not be the party of government." Many Southern Democrats, who created the Democratic Leadership Conference, continued to push the Party in a more conservative direction. Senator Edward Kennedy,

New York Governor Mario Cuomo and civil rights leader Jesse Jackson joined the chorus of eloquent defenders of the Party's commitment to protect society's less fortunate. "My constituency is the desperate, the damned, the disinherited, the disrespected and the despised," Jackson declared in a moving address at the Party's 1984 convention.

These philosophical differences produced two viable presidential candidates. In 1984, Gary Hart and former Vice President Walter Mondale engaged in a bitter primary fight. Hart, who challenged the Party's leadership with his campaign of "new ideas," appealed to younger, financially secure, politically independent voters. Mondale, a passionate advocate of the Party's mission to assist the needy, attracted support from many traditional Democrats. Mondale secured the nomination, and in a historic move he chose as his running mate Congresswoman Geraldine Ferraro, the first female vice presidential candidate of a major party. As she strode to the podium at the Democratic Convention in San Francisco, the crowd erupted in thunderous applause. Ferraro celebrated the Party's commitment to extend recognition to all groups by declaring that her selection proclaimed that "America is a land where dreams can come true for all of us." Unfortunately, her dream of becoming Vice President never materialized, as the Democrats won only in Minnesota and the District of Columbia.

In 1988, the Democrats nominated Michael Dukakis, the son of Greek immigrants who became a successful governor of Massachusetts, to lead the campaign against Vice President George Bush. Dukakis, who survived a prolonged and bruising primary battle against Jesse Jackson, hoped to make "competence, not ideology" the central message of his campaign. But Bush had a much different idea. While calling for a "kinder, gentler America," Bush launched one of the most vicious campaigns in history. Throughout the fall, Bush hammered away at Dukakis for opposing organized school prayer and compulsory recitation of the Pledge of Allegiance in public schools. "The Pledge and the flag are little hammer taps directed just below the knee of the electorate," wrote Richard Cohen. "They are designed to elicit a reflexive reaction, to obscure rather than explain, to camouflage a lust for office with the drop cloth made of red, white and blue." On election day, Bush won 426 electoral

Long a champion of the Party's commitment to society's less fortunate, civil rights leader Jesse Jackson electrified delegates with his message of revival to the 1984 Democratic Convention. His "Rainbow Coalition" carried him into the campaign four years later as a serious candidate for President with the broad-based support of Americans who shared his commitment to social and economic justice for all.

votes and continued the Republican dominance of presidential elections begun in 1968.

Though Democrats failed to win the White House, they maintained their dominance in congressional and state races. "If someone were to write a musical about the Democratic Party of the last generation," quipped Massachusetts Congressman Barney Frank, "it could be called How to Win Everything in Politics Except the Presidency." Democrats retained control of key state houses in every region of the country. In 1989, Democrat Douglas Wilder became Virginia's first black governor. In 1990, Ann Richards became only the second female governor in Texas history. In Congress, Democrats have also controlled the House since 1954, and the Senate for all but four years since 1931.

Democratic success on the state and congressional levels pushed a new generation of leaders into public view. In the Senate, Sam Nunn earned bipartisan respect for his mastery of the intricacies of military and defense issues. Bill Bradley of New Jersey, a former Rhodes scholar and professional basketball player, emerged as a leading expert on tax policy. Edward Kennedy, an outspoken advocate of health care reform for more than two decades, was joined by Jay Rockefeller of West Virginia and Robert Kerrey of Nebraska. Oklahoma's David Boren, also a Rhodes scholar, distinguished himself as a thoughtful proponent of campaign finance reform. A number of successful governors, including Bill Clinton of Arkansas and Raymond Mabus of Mississippi, gained national praise for their reform initiatives.

By 1990, the Democrats showed signs of overcoming past differences and forging a new consensus. The end of the Cold War allowed them to refocus public attention on unmet social needs at home. Seizing the initiative, Party leaders proposed a number of new programs—Federal health insurance, family leave policy and aid for education—designed to help the middle class that had abandoned the Party in the 1970s and 1980s. Capitalizing on evidence that the rich gained unfair advantage from Republican economic policies over the past twelve years, Democrats revived their populist heritage by proposing tax cuts geared to average workers. At the same time, the Party refused to compromise on its support of abortion rights and civil rights. In 1987, a number of key southern Democrats helped block the Supreme Court nomination of Robert Bork because of his controversial stand on civil rights. As Senator Richard Shelby of Alabama declared: "In the South, we've made a lot of progress. We do not want to go back and revisit old issues." In 1990, Democrats passed a civil rights bill that overturned recent Supreme Court decisions limiting the scope of affirmative action.

Thomas Jefferson, the father of the Democratic Party, once said that the purpose of government was "to secure the greatest degree of happiness possible to the general mass of those associated under it." For most of this century, the Democratic Party has struggled to extend to all of its citizens the rights and privileges enjoyed by the few. Woodrow Wilson's New Freedom employed the power of the state to tame the excesses of corporate greed and to lead the nation to victory in the Great War "to make the world safe for democracy." Franklin Roosevelt rescued millions from the ravages of a debilitating Depression and successfully battled the forces of Nazi tyranny. Harry Truman, John F. Kennedy and Lyndon Johnson secured the New Deal agenda and extended its benefits to other disadvantaged groups. In recent years the Democratic Party has paid a heavy political price for its efforts. But at the dawn of their third century, Democrats are bristling with fresh faces and new ideas. They stand ready to lead this great nation once again.

"The test of our progress is not whether we add more to the abundance of those who have much; it is whether we provide enough for those who have too little."

—Franklin Delano Roosevelt

# CHAPTER TEN

# DOMESTIC POLICY: A CALL FOR COMPASSION

## BY WILLIAM E. LEUCHTENBURG

For most of the past two centuries, the Democrats have been the party of the common people. In their early years, they were the party of "country folk, fishermen and the poorer classes generally," as one historian has said. And for more than half a century after the Civil War, another writer has observed, the Democrats "would gather together the discontented on the farms, in the factories, in the mines and among the recently arrived to these shores."

That tradition has been carried on into the twentieth century. In the 1932 campaign, Franklin Roosevelt asserted that "these unhappy times call for . . . plans . . . that build from the bottom up and not from the top down, that put their faith once more in the forgotten man at the bottom of the economic pyramid." In the 1952 campaign, Adlai Stevenson reminded a Minnesota audience, "A hungry man is not a free man." In his inaugural address, John F. Kennedy declared, "If a free society cannot help the many who are poor, it cannot save the few who are rich." And in his very first State of the Union message, Lyndon Johnson said, "Unfortunately, many Americans live on the outskirts of hope—some because of their poverty, some because of their color, and all too many because of both. Our task is to help replace their despair with opportunity."

The patron saint of the Party, Thomas Jefferson, drew the lines sharply at the very outset when he opposed the schemes of Alexander Hamilton, who was to become a leader of the Federalists. In the Federal Convention debates, Hamilton advocated giving to "the rich and wellborn . . . a distinct, permanent share in the government" so that they might check "the mass of the people . . . [who] . . . seldom judge or determine right." Jefferson, in contrast, had a fundamental faith in the capacity of the people to rule. "Sometimes it is said that man can not be trusted with the government of himself," he observed. "Can he, then, be trusted with the government of others? Or have we found angels in the forms of kings to govern him? Let history answer that question." A historian has said of Jefferson: "His sympathies were never with the great planters who aped the English squires, but with the farmers, trappers and hunters of the western counties, whose cause he championed so effectively as never to be forgiven by the salt-water aristocracy."

In 1932, an army of World War One veterans marched on Washington to demand immediate payment of the postwar bonuses Congress had promised to them fourteen years before. In an order issued by Republican Herbert Hoover, they were routed from their makeshift camps by U.S. forces under Douglas MacArthur—an episode that helped oust Hoover and elect Franklin Roosevelt.

Anointed by the Party's liberal establishment as their candidate for the presidency in 1952 and 1956, former Illinois Governor Adlai E. Stevenson eloquently articulated his vision of government's role as the champion of the oppressed. He lost twice, but even in defeat he endeared himself with the bittersweet admission, "It hurts too much to laugh, and I'm too proud to cry."

As a consequence of this attitude, the Democrats have been opposed throughout most of their history to concentrated financial power, typified in Andrew Jackson's day by "the Monster"—the Second Bank of the United States—and in later years by, in an all-embracing phrase, "Wall Street." Jackson, who aligned himself with "honest laborers," not with the "monied aristocracy of the few," had a frontier suspicion of financiers, and he especially distrusted the Second Bank of the United States, a gigantic private monopoly. When in 1832 he boldly vetoed a bill to recharter the bank, he did so, he explained, on behalf of "the humble members of society—the farmers, mechanics and laborers."

In the Jacksonian era, Democrats raised the banner, "Equal rights for all, special privileges for none." They pushed for free public schools, abolition of imprisonment for debt and an end to property requirements for voting. They eased naturalization requirements for recently arrived immigrants, and espoused rotation in office as a way to dislodge a cadre of officials who regarded their fiefdoms as lifetime grants of power. In 1834 a Democratic campaign song implored:

> "Mechanics, Carters, Laborers
> > Must form a close connection
> And show the rich Aristocrats
> > Their powers at this election.
> Yankee Doodle, smoke 'em out
> > The proud, the banking faction.
> None but such as Hartford Feds
> > Oppose the poor and Jackson."

Democrats kept these Jacksonian distinctions alive for generations afterward. In the 1890s, William Jennings Bryan warned against "the enslavement of the farmers, merchants, manufacturers and laboring classes to the most merciless and unscrupulous gang of speculators on earth—the money power." And at the 1912 convention, Democratic delegates adopted a resolution introduced by Bryan declaring themselves "opposed to the nomination of a candidate for President who is the representative of or under obligation to J. Pierpont Morgan . . . or any other member of the privilege-hunting and favor-seeking class." In his inaugural address in 1913, Woodrow Wilson stated, "The great Government we loved has too often been made use of for private and selfish purposes, and

those who used it had forgotten the people." Two decades later, Franklin Delano Roosevelt, in his 1933 inaugural address, scourged "the moneychangers," and in 1936 he lashed out at "economic royalists" and "entrenched greed." Similarly, Harry S. Truman told the 1948 Democratic Convention that the Republican Party "helps the rich and sticks a knife in the back of the poor," and in his "Give-'em-Hell-Harry" campaign that year, he excoriated "gluttons of privilege."

To the generalization that Democrats have been the party of the people against the interests, there is, though, one unhappy exception. Much of the Democratic leadership in the mid-nineteenth century ardently defended slavery, and for generations after the Civil War, Democrats in the South were the party of white supremacy. In the 1840s and 1850s, Democratic presidential nominees were "Northerners with Southern principles," men who sought to conciliate the slavocracy. Not even these concessions, or the compromises advanced by Stephen Douglas, were enough for Deep South Democrats such as Jefferson Davis, who demanded enactment of a congressional slave code. When they did not get their way, they led their states out of the Union. During the Civil War, some Democrats, who earned the epithet "Copperheads," sought to undermine Lincoln and sue for peace on Confederate terms. Nor was the record of Party leaders toward Native Americans one in which Democrats today take pride. Andrew Jackson, in particular, sanctioned the removal of Indians from their ancient homelands in Georgia and Alabama.

Yet even in the nineteenth century, numbers of Democrats opposed slavery, and in the twentieth century the Democratic Party became committed first to fair treatment for blacks and then to legislation to wipe out racial discrimination. In the 1930s Franklin D. Roosevelt's New Deal dispensed relief funds to millions of blacks who were down-and-out, and Eleanor Roosevelt became an outspoken champion of racial equality. When the gifted black contralto, Marian Anderson, was denied a concert hall in Washington, D.C., solely because of the color of her skin, the Democratic administration arranged for her to sing at the steps of the Lincoln Memorial in the nation's capital. Blacks, in response to such deeds, began to move massively out of the Party of the Great Emancipator and into the party of FDR. "Go turn Lincoln's picture to the wall," a black editor advised black voters. "That debt has been paid in full." "Under the charismatic Franklin Delano Roosevelt and the New Deal," Alex Haley has written, "for . . . the first time ever, really, the black masses were being dealt with . . . as Americans with the same needs and rights as white people."

Roosevelt's successors markedly improved upon his record. Harry Truman broke new ground by appointing a President's Committee on Civil Rights in 1946, and at the 1948 Democratic Convention, the young mayor of Minneapolis, Hubert Humphrey, led a movement that resulted in the strongest civil rights plank in the Party's history. John F. Kennedy called upon Congress to enact far-reaching legislation to curb racial discrimination and segregation, and when that effort was tragically cut short, Lyndon B. Johnson asked Congress to approve a civil rights bill as a memorial to the slain President. As a result of Johnson's determination and the efforts of the Reverend Martin Luther King, Jr., Congress enacted landmark civil rights laws in 1964, 1965 and 1968. The 1964 act also included an important section to assure equality for women. When former Georgia Governor Jimmy Carter entered the White House, he made a point of naming blacks, as well as women, to high office.

The Democratic Party has also undergone a sea change with respect to what role it deemed appropriate for the national government. Jefferson inaugurated a tradition of limited national power and respect for the rights of the states. Circumscribing the scope of the Federal Government, he and his followers believed, would deny grasping speculators an opportunity to enrich themselves at public expense by obtaining special favors. Jefferson favored a "wise and frugal government, which shall restrain men from injuring one another," but "which shall leave them otherwise free to regulate their own pursuits." With military expenditures rising and the national debt mounting, Jefferson cut spending and taxes, reduced the size of the diplomatic corps, and sold off much of the navy.

Alarmed that the Federalists had been aping the monarchical style of Europe, Jefferson set an example of republican simplicity by walking to his inauguration from his boardinghouse through the muddy streets of the new capital of Washington, still a raw village, to the drumbeat of a flag-bearing militia. Having "sworn upon the altar of God eternal hostility against every form of tyranny over the mind of man," Jefferson went on to pardon political prisoners who had been jailed under the Federalists' Alien and Sedition Acts, and stoutly defended the Bill of Rights. "If there be any among us who would wish to dissolve this Union or change its republican form," he declared, "let them stand undisturbed as monuments of the safety with which error of opinion may be tolerated where reason is left free to combat it."

Jefferson's nineteenth century successors—from James Madison through Grover Cleveland—adhered to these Jeffersonian precepts: states' rights, free trade, hard money and, at least in theory, strict construction of the Constitution. Both Andrew Jackson and Grover Cleveland vetoed internal improvements bills as "pork barrel" legislation that would benefit avaricious

A black farmer in Arkansas receives a government check from the Farm Security Administration. One of the most inventive of the programs engineered under FDR's New Deal, the FSA was scrupulously fair to blacks.

The Democratic Party's most eloquent orator and one of its most passionate idealists, William Jennings Bryan championed the old Jacksonian theme of "Equal Rights to All, Special Privileges to None." In his high-minded but ill-fated campaign for the presidency in 1900, he inveighed against "imperialism," America's empire building expansion in the wake of the Spanish-American War.

Suffragists marched down Pennsylvania Avenue in 1913, the year Wilson restored the Democrats to power. In 1916, Democrats endorsed suffrage, and in 1919 Congress approved the 19th Amendment, finally granting women the right to vote.

special interests. In his second inaugural address in 1893, Cleveland insisted, "The lessons of paternalism ought to be unlearned and the better lesson taught that while the people should patriotically and cheerfully support their government, its functions do not include the support of the people."

But in the very next national campaign, under the leadership of "the Boy Orator of the Platte," the young Nebraska congressman, William Jennings Bryan, the Democrats began to turn in a different direction. They continued to embrace the Jeffersonian ideals of liberty, equality and justice, but experience had taught that in an age of industrialization and mass communication, of crowded cities and mighty trusts, these ideals were best fulfilled not by decentralized government but by strengthened authority in Washington. At the 1896 Democratic Convention, Bryan asked, "Upon which side will the Democratic Party stand: upon the side of 'idle holders of idle capital' or upon the side of the struggling masses?" The delegates responded by choosing Bryan as their standard-bearer, and adopting a platform that came out for prosecution of the trusts, tariff reform and a graduated income tax. Bryan's quest for the presidency fell short, but for years to come, in the pages of his weekly, *The Commoner*, he railed against the trusts and advocated such innovations as women's suffrage, direct election of senators

and a Cabinet-level department of labor.

Bryan's efforts, together with those of courageous women in the settlement houses, helped pave the way for the big transition in Democratic policy that took place in Woodrow Wilson's administrations. Wilson took office as the advocate of a "New Freedom" which envisioned, in the tradition of Jefferson and Jackson, a role for government restricted to opening up opportunities for entrepreneurs in a competitive economy. So in his first two years, he put through measures lowering the tariff, curbing the trusts and setting up a Federal Reserve banking system that would make it easier for new investors, especially in the South and West, to enter the marketplace. By the time his first term had ended, however, he had embraced measures such as the Child Labor Act of 1916 that looked toward the welfare state, and during World War One he set up a number of emergency agencies that were forerunners of Franklin D. Roosevelt's New Deal. The War Industries Board later served as a model for the National Industrial Recovery Act (NRA); the War Finance Corporation led to the Reconstruction Finance Corporation (RFC), a 1932 creation that took on new functions when the Democrats came to power; and some of the features of the War Labor Board were revived in the National Labor Relations Board (NLRB) established under the 1935 Wagner Act.

When Franklin Roosevelt came to power on March 4, 1933, in the depths of the Great Depression, he employed the national government in the interests of the American people in a myriad of ways beyond anything Wilson had ever imagined. He entered the White House at a desperate time—industries paralyzed, the countryside devastated, the banks shut down, upwards of 15 million jobless. In rapid fashion during the electrifying First Hundred Days of 1933, with the aid of his advisors, whom the press dubbed the "Brain Trust," he sent fifteen recommendations up to the Hill, and Congress enacted all fifteen. Swiftly he resolved the bank crisis, gave succor to the thirsty with a beer bill while a constitutional amendment repealing Prohibition was making its way through the states, launched an ambitious experiment for industry under the frenetic former cavalry officer Hugh Johnson and

another for agriculture, took the country off the gold standard, created the Tennessee Valley Authority, and brought relief to the unemployed, in part by an imaginative program, the Civilian Conservation Corps, to put jobless youth to work in the forests.

In commenting on the First Hundred Days, the French writer, Andre Maurols, remarked: "One cannot help calling to mind, as one writes the history of these three crowded months, the biblical account of the Creation. The first day, the Brain Trust put an embargo on gold; the second day, it peopled the forests; the third day, it created three point two beer; the fourth day, it broke the bonds that tied the dollar to gold; the fifth day, it set the farmers free; the sixth day, it created General Johnson, and then looking upon what it had made of America, it saw it was good."

In ensuing years, Roosevelt expanded on this pro-

In 1932, future First Lady Eleanor Roosevelt dispensed help in a soup kitchen, an institution that gave way to Federal Depression relief programs when her husband was elected President that fall. She was to become not only a champion of the oppressed, but a lifelong spokesperson for minority rights.

gram by putting the Stock Exchange under Federal regulation for the first time; breaking up utility holding companies; building huge power projects at Grand Coulee and Bonneville; electrifying the countryside; finding Federal jobs for artists and writers (among them Saul Bellow, Ralph Ellison, Jackson Pollock and Katherine Dunham); persuading the Supreme Court to approve a vast expanse of Federal power; creating an "Indian New Deal"; setting up a National Youth Administration that helped destitute young people work their way through college (one was the budding playwright, Arthur Miller, another a Duke Law School student named Richard Nixon); serving hot lunches to school kids; and, above all, enacting the Social Security law that gave the country its first statute authorizing old-age pensions, unemployment compensation and aid to dependent children. In his annual message to Congress in 1938, Roosevelt declared: "Government has a final responsibility for the well-being of its citizenship. If private co-operative endeavor fails to provide work for willing hands and relief for the unfortunate, those suffering hardship from no fault of their own have a right to call upon the Government for aid; and a government worthy of its name must make fitting response."

Each of the Democratic Presidents who succeeded

FDR has augmented his legacy. Harry Truman not only took a strong stand on civil rights, especially by desegregating the armed forces, but also advocated a "Fair Deal," including medical care for the aged, a proposal that would be enacted into law some years later. John F. Kennedy, in the final days granted him, sketched out what would be Lyndon Johnson's War on Poverty. And Jimmy Carter called our attention to the need to husband our resources in an age of limits, especially when, in one notable address on the energy crisis, he borrowed a phrase from Chicken Little to warn, "The sky is falling."

Lyndon Johnson made an especially large contribution by espousing a "Great Society." He defined it, in Tom Wicker's words, as "a promised land in which there will be no poverty, no illiteracy, no unemployment, no prejudice, no slums, no polluted streams, no delinquency, and few Republicans." In 1964, Johnson's first full year in office, he put through a huge tax cut that gave a great lift to the economy; initiated a war on poverty; and, most important, succeeded in persuading Congress to pass the historic Civil Rights Act of 1964. In 1965, after having been returned to office in a landslide, he persuaded "the fabulous 89th Congress" to pass an extraordinary array of legislation: the Voting Rights Act, Medicare, Medicaid,

**The dedication of Chicago's Outer Drive Bridge in 1937 marked one of the many moments when the public works projects of Roosevelt's New Deal brought to completion a series of mammoth projects ranging from the Grand Coulee Dam and Fort Knox to New York's East River Drive and the Lincoln Tunnel connecting Manhattan and New Jersey under the Hudson River.**

President John F. Kennedy and his Vice President, Lyndon B. Johnson, could hardly have been less alike in style and temperament, but the two former rivals shared common ideals that moved Johnson to pick up the fallen torch when JFK was killed and fulfill his ambitious social agenda with sweeping civil rights legislation, health-care reform and anti-poverty programs.

an Elementary and Secondary Education Act, a Higher Education Act, legislation for clean air and clean rivers, a Highway Beautification Act (a favorite project of Lady Bird Johnson's), creation of two new Cabinet-level agencies (HUD and the Department of Transportation), a more generous immigration law, and Federal aid to the arts. Johnson signed the Federal aid to elementary education bill in the one-room Texas schoolhouse he had attended as a boy, and put his name to the new immigration bill in the shadow of the Statue of Liberty.

For 200 years, then, the Democratic Party has been committed to the cause of the people. In the course of those two centuries, it has built a constructive record of achievement, especially in the past two generations as it extended to disadvantaged groups the maxims Thomas Jefferson wrote into the Declaration of Independence. Sometimes it has faltered. Sometimes it has strayed from its finest principles. But more often, it has been true to its fundamental ideals. And it will continue to be in the future, so long as it holds fast to the conviction that Franklin D. Roosevelt set forth in his second inaugural: "The test of our progress is not whether we add more to the abundance of those who have much; it is whether we provide enough for those who have too little."

On April 4, 1949, President Harry S. Truman addressed the delegates gathered in Washington for the signing of the North Atlantic Treaty. A bulwark against Cold War expansionism by the Soviet Union, NATO was the first formal alliance in which the U.S. had participated since 1800, and has proven to be one of history's most enduring military defense pacts.

# CHAPTER ELEVEN

# FOREIGN POLICY: A BEACON OF FREEDOM

## BY GEORGE C. HERRING

From the beginning of the Republic, the Democratic Party has set the tone for and charted the course of the nation's foreign policy, guiding it along the path to world leadership and leaving a record of major achievement.

America's first secretary of state and third President, Thomas Jefferson, best exemplifies the national spirit in foreign policy. The "Sage of Monticello" drew a sharp distinction between the high moral purpose he thought animated the United States and the less exalted motives he felt drove other nations. A confirmed idealist, he was certain that his country's destiny was to set an example for other nations through the principles on which it operated at home and the policies it pursued abroad. America, in his view, was the "sole depository of the sacred fire of freedom and self-government."

In terms of tangible accomplishments as well as the ideals he stood for, Jefferson left a rich legacy. He refused to pay tribute to the so-called Barbary "pirates," as his predecessors had done, because their behavior violated his commitment to free trade and his notions of proper behavior. Despite his abhorrence of war, he sent military forces to "chastise their insolence," and his eventual success enhanced the reputation of the United States abroad and confirmed Americans' view of themselves as agents of a new order of justice and fair play.

Through shrewd diplomacy, well-timed threats and extreme good fortune, with the assistance of James Monroe, his minister to France, Jefferson also pulled off in the Louisiana Purchase one of history's great real estate steals, nearly doubling the nation's territory at a cost of roughly 13.5 cents per acre. His Northwest Ordinance of 1787 had already provided a mechanism for incorporating this territory into the Union on an equal basis, an "empire of liberty," he called it, and a radical departure from the exploitative empires of European tradition.

The refusal of Jefferson and his successor James Madison to submit to French and British harassment of American shipping eventually forced the United States to abandon its firmly held precept of neutrality in Europe's wars. Again, however, through a combination of good fortune, timely military victories and skillful diplomacy, the United States under Madison survived the War of 1812 with its pride and territory intact and emerged from this "Second War of Independence" much stronger than before.

The nation's first secretary of state and third President, Thomas Jefferson blended high-minded idealism and hard-headed pragmatism in a way that has typified the American approach to foreign policy. In both an ideological and a practical sense, he established the foundation for an "empire of liberty."

French Finance Minister Francois Barbe-Marbois, special U.S. Minister James Monroe, and U.S. Minister to France Robert Livingston contemplate a map of the Louisiana Territory in 1803. Monroe was authorized to purchase only New Orleans and west Florida, but jumped at the chance when Napoleon impulsively offered to sell the entire territory for the bargain price of $15,000,000.

The Franco-American Convention of 1800, signed in Paris, released the United States from obligations under the French alliance of 1778 and provided new commercial arrangements for the two nations, ending two years of undeclared war.

Monroe, the third President from the so-called Virginia Dynasty, elevated his mentor's principles into doctrine. Faced with the threat of Russian intrusion in the Pacific Northwest and European intervention to restore Spanish authority in Latin America, Monroe in 1823 proclaimed that the New World was no longer subject to European colonization and that the United States would look with disfavor upon European intervention in the Western Hemisphere. Although the United States lacked the power to enforce it, this so-called Monroe Doctrine constituted a second declaration of independence, and affirmed for the New World a destiny separate from that of the Old.

The nineteenth century was the great age of continental expansion for the United States, and the Democrats were in the vanguard. The phrase Manifest Destiny was indeed coined by Democratic publicist John L. O'Sullivan to justify annexation of Oregon, Texas and California. The United States, he proclaimed, had the "manifest destiny to overspread the continent allotted by Providence to the free development of our yearly multiplying millions."

Manifest Destiny expressed the exuberant optimism and brash self-confidence of the age. In the eyes of Americans, at least, it gave them a superior claim to contested lands and lent an air of inevitability to their expansion. It served as a rationalization for a variety of motives from simple greed for land to the extension of slavery, and it was heavily tinged with racism, especially as it applied to Indians and Mexicans.

The nineteenth century was the great age of continental expansion for the United States, and Democrats were in the vanguard. Their rallying cry was "Manifest Destiny," a phrase that expressed the exuberant optimism and brash self-confidence of the age. Though it was used to rationalize the greed for land, it also marked the beginning of America's emergence as a modern empire.

At the same time, Manifest Destiny was a product of genuine idealism. To some American expansionists, the acquisition of new lands and the admission of new peoples to the Union were seen as God-given obligations. To others, additional territory was needed so that the United States could continue to serve as a haven for the oppressed from other continents. Whatever its precise meaning, Manifest Destiny reflected a growing appreciation on the part of Americans of their nation's impending grandeur. In O'Sullivan's words, "The far-reaching, the boundless future will be the era of American greatness."

Democratic President James K. Polk was the instrument of Manifest Destiny. Taciturn and enigmatic, ambitious and doggedly persistent, Polk ran for the presidency in 1844 on the dubious platform of the

On September 13, 1847, U.S. troops stormed Mexican fortifications on Chapultepec, a hill guarding Mexico City. The summit was taken in hours, opening the way for conquest of the capital and the end of the Mexican-American War. Mexican President Santa Anna lamented that if "we were to plant our batteries in hell, the damned Yankees would take them from us."

"re-annexation of Texas" and the "re-occupation of Oregon." His aggressive diplomacy took the United States to the brink of war with Britain over the Oregon country and with Mexico over the Texas boundary and California.

Polk wisely retreated from the weak claim to 54° 40', compromising with Britain at the 49th parallel. In the South and West, however, he pushed Mexico into a war that would secure California and Texas to the Rio Grande for the United States but would also have fateful internal consequences, helping to set off the irreconcilable conflict over slavery that led directly to the Civil War.

Ardent continentalists in the antebellum period, the Democrats generally opposed overseas expansion after the Civil War. Sometimes they were motivated by partisanship, sometimes by race, sometimes principle. Accurately perceiving that an 1893 treaty providing for the annexation of Hawaii had been extracted from the Hawaiians after a "revolution" instigated by Americans, incoming Democratic President Grover Cleveland, a man of principle and courage, took the unusual step of withdrawing the treaty from consideration.

Democrats like Cleveland and 1896 presidential candidate William Jennings Bryan were among the leading "anti-imperialists" who opposed annexation of the Philippines after the Spanish-American War. And senatorial Democrats attempted unsuccessfully to block Theodore Roosevelt's imposition of a protectorate on Santo Domingo in 1904.

In the twentieth century, adapting to their nation's emerging status as a major world power, the Democrats formulated, articulated and put into practice a new internationalism that called upon the United States to play a leading role in shaping a world order based on its own principles. No individual was more important in this regard than Woodrow Wilson. Taking office in 1913 on a platform of domestic reform, Wilson initially adhered to tradition, declaring the United States neutral and appealing to Americans to remain "impartial in thought as well as in action." But this proclamation proved impossible for Wilson and the nation to uphold. While remaining technically neutral between 1914 and 1917, the United States moved closer to the Allies.

Persuaded by April 1917 that further efforts to re-

**During Republican President William McKinley's bid for re-election in 1900, the Democrats accused him of a new imperialism: The U.S. had won the Spanish-American War only two years before, and now he had sent American troops to quell an uprising in the Philippines. This Democratic cartoon shows McKinley fitting a puffed-up Uncle Sam with a new set of expansionist clothes.**

main neutral would endanger America's interests and undermine its ideals, a reluctant Wilson led the United States into the war on the side of the Allies, elevating American participation into a great crusade "to make the world safe for democracy." Once at war, he broke even more sharply with the past. Wilson insisted that his nation must take a leading role in the peace settlement and that a lasting peace must be built upon American principles. The Great War had demonstrated to him the bankruptcy of European power politics and imperialism. He found equally abhorrent the radical notions of Vladimir Ilyich Lenin, who took power in Russia in 1917, that the international system could be freed of conflict and war only through revolutions that eliminated capitalism.

In Wilson's view, only a world purged of imperialism and ultra-nationalism, and reformed along liberal-capitalist lines, would serve the needs of humanity. Economic nationalism must give way to commercial

**When Democratic President Woodrow Wilson journeyed to Europe in 1918 to begin negotiations for a treaty ending World War One, he received triumphal welcomes in every city he visited. The warm reception misled Wilson into believing that the peoples and governments of that war-torn continent shared his dreams of a new world order.**

internationalism, in which all nations would have equal access to markets and raw materials, tariff barriers would be removed and freedom of the seas guaranteed by law. Colonial empires must be eliminated and all peoples given the right to self-determination. Balance-of-power politics must give way to a new world order maintained by an organization of like-minded nations joined together to resolve disputes and prevent aggression. "These are American principles . . . ," Wilson affirmed, "and they are also the principles of forward-looking men and women everywhere, of every modern nation, of every enlightened community. They are the principles of all mankind and must prevail."

Between 1917 and 1920, Wilson fought determinedly to implement his ideas. In a series of public statements, most notably his Fourteen Points address of January 1918, he shaped his broad principles into a concrete peace program. At the peace conference, which opened in Paris in January 1919, he fought for a just peace and new world order against unrepentant enemies and vengeful allies. He made crucial concessions on such issues as German reparations and the disposition of colonial empires while redrawing the map of Eastern and Central Europe and eventually securing Allied acceptance of his plans for a League of Nations.

Aware of the limitations of his handiwork, Wilson still felt, perhaps correctly, that it was the best that could be attained. His hand trembled on June 28, 1919, as he signed the document in the elegant Hall of Mirrors at Versailles. Speaking before the Congress on July 10, he defended the Treaty of Versailles as "the last best hope of mankind" and issued a ringing challenge: "Dare we reject it and break the heart of the world?" The answer was not long in coming. Ironically, although he had won at least qualified acceptance of his hard work abroad, Wilson met crushing defeat at home. Isolationist and internationalist Republicans opposed Wilson on the grounds of partisanship and principle, and the President's own partisanship, his high-handedness and his reluctance to accommodate his critics, intensified the opposition.

Convinced that only a massive show of popular support could move the Senate, Wilson in September 1919 began an 8,000-mile speaking tour. Illness and exhaustion forced him to stop in Colorado, and after returning to Washington he suffered a stroke that left him partially paralyzed. An ill and embittered President rejected last-minute efforts to compromise and in-

MAYBE IT'S A CASE OF TOO MANY COOKS.

This 1939 cartoon by Clifford Berryman suggests the confusion that prevailed in U.S. foreign policy in the days before the outbreak of World War Two. The chef, Democratic President Roosevelt, is beset with many other cooks pushing their own foreign policy "recipes."

sisted that his Democratic followers do the same. In three separate votes, the Senate narrowly rejected the Treaty of Versailles.

Franklin Delano Roosevelt had served in Wilson's administration and inherited his mantle of internationalist leadership. Taking office in the depths of the Great Depression, Roosevelt initially acquiesced in the isolationist mood that swept the nation in the 1930s. Gradually perceiving the threat from Nazi Germany and Japan, Roosevelt from 1937 to 1941 skillfully led a deeply divided nation from neutrality to intervention, modifying the Neutrality Acts to permit limited aid to the Allies and then, in a daring and ingenious stroke called Lend-Lease, making the United States the great "arsenal of democracy." The Japanese attack on Pearl Harbor and Germany's subsequent declaration of war on the United States resolved the issue of war and peace, and united America as perhaps nothing else could have done.

Like Wilson before him, Roosevelt used the exigencies of war to convert his nation to internationalism and promote a new order of peace and harmony based on American principles. "I dream dreams," he once said, "but I am an immensely practical man." Less ideological than Wilson and more disposed to compromise, he nevertheless sought, like Wilson, to extend

German torpedo attacks on U.S. ships in the Atlantic, beginning with the *USS Greer* on September 4, 1941, eventually led to a repeal of the Neutrality Acts. According to this cartoon, such attacks also exploded the myth that the United States could remain safely neutral in a time of global war.

EXPLODING A MYTH!

On Flag Day, June 1942, Franklin Delano Roosevelt gathered in a historic meeting with representatives from the international coalition that was waging war against the Axis. These same allies formed the nucleus of a global organization designed to "out-law" aggression anywhere in the world that might unleash another world war: the United Nations.

The end of World War Two was months away when FDR, Churchill and Stalin met at Yalta to pave the way for a meaningful UN, to persuade Stalin to declare war on Japan, and to resolve the fate of Eastern Europe. In the wake of the conference, the Soviets occupied Manchuria, Mongolia and Korea—and solidified their hold on Eastern Europe.

Three months after Roosevelt's death, Churchill and Stalin met in Potsdam with his successor, Harry Truman, to discuss the impending Allied campaign against Japan. The resulting declaration warned Japan to surrender or risk "prompt and utter destruction." It failed to reveal the nature of a secret weapon that had just been developed for that purpose: the atomic bomb.

the American concepts of free trade and self-determination as the guiding principles of the new order and to establish a United Nations organization to oversee it. He was prepared to use American influence and leverage to reform Germany and to persuade his allies, Great Britain and the Soviet Union, to accept his principles.

Roosevelt's dreams, like Wilson's, went unrealized. Learning from the mistakes of his illustrious predecessor, capitalizing on what seemed the obvious lessons of America's rejection of the League, and employing his own considerable political skills, he secured overwhelming American acceptance of the United Nations. But his vision of a new world order and indeed of the United Nations itself broke down amidst the Soviet-American conflict that, by his death in April 1945, had assumed overriding importance in the politics of the Grand Alliance and by the end of the war had become

the dominant feature of the new postwar international system.

Under the pressure of what came to be called the Cold War, Roosevelt's Democratic successor Harry Truman established the foundation for a generation of global involvement quite without precedent in United States history. Persuaded that the Soviet Union was committed to a policy of world domination, the Truman administration in the aftermath of World War Two adopted a policy of "containment" that called for the United States to thwart Soviet expansionism through economic assistance, political influence and, if necessary, military intervention.

Between 1947 and 1949, the administration applied containment in Europe. The Truman Doctrine provided economic and military aid to Greece and Turkey; the Marshall Plan rebuilt Western Europe and integrated it into the American economic system; and the North Atlantic Treaty Organization (NATO), the first formal alliance to which the United States had been a party in a century and a half, committed the nation to the defense of Western Europe.

Subsequently extending the policy of East Asia, Truman sent military forces to repel North Korea's invasion of South Korea in June of 1950. As a result of the policy of containment, the United States was committed to defend 42 nations across the globe by 1953 and had a military budget of more than $60 billion.

John F. Kennedy guided the United States through the most perilous days of the Cold War, and before his untimely death pointed the nation and the world in a new direction. Kennedy struggled through a crisis-strewn first year, suffering embarrassment in the ill-conceived and abortive Bay of Pigs operation against Cuba and from Soviet erection of the Berlin Wall. In 1962, in the Cuban missile crisis, he averted—perhaps narrowly—the most menacing of Cold War confrontations. Perceiving more clearly than ever the dangers of the Cold War and nuclear weaponry, Kennedy negotiated with the Soviets a nuclear test-ban treaty in his

last year, and in a major speech at American University called for a rethinking of the conventional wisdom of the Cold War.

In the late 1960s, the Democrats split among themselves over the direction the nation's foreign policy should take. Following the broad outlines set by Truman and Kennedy, Lyndon Johnson extended the containment policy to Vietnam in Southeast Asia, sending economic and military assistance and then thousands of troops to assist the beleaguered government of South Vietnam to hold off an indigenous Communist-led insurgency supported by North Vietnam. By 1967, the cost of the commitment in terms of blood and treasure had become high, and the nation was torn apart by a bloody and brutal conflict that appeared to have no end.

Some Democrats insisted that the United States must stay the course in Vietnam to maintain its credibility and uphold the world order it had created in the face of a persisting Communist challenge. Other Democratic internationalists who had supported World War Two, Korea and the Cold War argued that

**When the Berlin Wall was erected in August 1961, sealing off the West from East Berlin, the resulting crisis escalated into a war scare that was defused only after meetings between President Kennedy and Soviet Foreign Minister Andrei Gromyko. Said Kennedy later: "The Wall is the most obvious and vivid demonstration of the failure of the Communist system."**

Emerging from 13 days of intensive private negotiations with President Carter at the presidential retreat in Camp David, Maryland, Egypt's President Anwar Sadat and Israel's Prime Minister Menachem Begin issued the historic Camp David Accords, which ended the state of war between their countries and laid the foundation for an uneasy peace in the Middle East.

by backing a corrupt, authoritarian regime in South Vietnam, the United States was betraying its own principles. They also questioned the war on practical grounds, contending that it was essentially an internal struggle in an area of marginal significance whose connection with the Cold War was peripheral at best. Democratic critics increasingly insisted that the huge investment in Vietnam was diverting attention from more urgent problems at home, damaging America's relations with its allies, and inhibiting the development of a more constructive relationship with the Soviet Union.

The Democratic critique of Vietnam quickly broadened into an indictment of American "globalism." The nation had fallen victim to the "arrogance of power," Senator J. William Fulbright of Arkansas maintained, and was showing "signs of that fatal presumption, that over extension of power and mission which brought ruin to ancient Athens, to Napoleonic France and to Nazi Germany."

Jimmy Carter, the first Democratic President after Vietnam, attempted to repair the damage inflicted by that conflict and to chart a new course for the nation's foreign policy. Eventually, he was consumed by the Iranian hostage crisis and by the Cold War fires he had tried to extinguish, but he left a legacy that is only now fully appreciated. His Panama Canal Treaty set an important precedent for the liquidation of outdated, colonialist institutions. The Camp David agreement he helped to negotiate between Egypt and Israel in 1979 marked a major step toward peace in the strife-torn Middle East. His stress on human rights reclaimed the moral high ground taken by Jefferson two centuries earlier and put the United States on the side of the democratic revolutions that would erupt in the 1980s and 1990s.

Throughout U.S. history, the Democrats have assumed leadership in framing the nation's approach toward a rapidly changing world. With the end of the Cold War, the principles that Jefferson, Wilson and Roosevelt proclaimed with such eloquence are now being realized on a global scale. The challenge for the Democratic Party today is to draw upon its rich heritage of internationalist leadership and support for human rights, freedom and democracy, to shape new policies for the uncertain world of the twenty-first century.

# CHAPTER TWELVE

# *PORTRAITS OF TEN GREAT DEMOCRATS*

BY LARRY DUBOIS

THOMAS JEFFERSON

JAMES MADISON

JAMES MONROE

ANDREW JACKSON

WILLIAM JENNINGS BRYAN

WOODROW WILSON

FRANKLIN DELANO ROOSEVELT

HARRY S. TRUMAN

JOHN FITZGERALD KENNEDY

LYNDON BAINES JOHNSON

# THOMAS JEFFERSON 1743–1826

During his presidency, Thomas Jefferson once performed emergency surgery on a man who'd gashed his leg with an axe. Afterward, he wondered aloud how the human body might be better designed to protect against such injuries. Hearing that, one of his political enemies complained: "What is this world coming to? Here this fellow, Jefferson, after turning upside down everything on Earth, is now quarreling with God Almighty himself!" Jefferson was accustomed to the scorn of those who didn't share his extraordinary range of talents. One of the most gifted men of his era—or any era—he was an accomplished philosopher, inventor, architect, farmer, lawyer, musician and writer.

Raised on a 2500-acre family estate in Virginia, Jefferson was the son of a planter who was married to one of the state's most distinguished families. The third of ten children, he showed his abilities at a young age. By the time he was 14, he spoke Latin and Greek and when he entered William and Mary College at 16, he was befriended by the governor of Virginia and two distinguished professors—of mathematics and law—who soon came to treat him as an equal.

Studying law after graduation, the redheaded bachelor found plenty of time for livelier pursuits, including fox hunting and romance, and he admitted to friends that he enjoyed the "comforts of a single state." Then he fell in love with a beautiful young widow named Martha Skelton. One day when two of her many suitors arrived to pay their respects, they heard from her drawing room the sounds of a violin and a man and woman singing. "We're wasting our time," one of them wisely said. "We may as well go home." They knew that Jefferson was the only accomplished male violinist around.

But the talent for which he will be best remembered was writing. Prevailed upon by his elders at the age of 33 to draft the Declaration of Independence, Jefferson at first demurred, asking John Adams why he didn't assign himself the honor. Because, Adams replied, "You can write ten times better than I can." Working at a portable writing table he had invented, Jefferson "turned to neither book nor pamphlet" in drawing from within himself what he regarded as his crowning achievement—an eloquent proclamation declaring man's right to "Life, Liberty and the Pursuit of Happiness."

But even then he couldn't resist sharing the credit for the Declaration's success. He gleefully told a friend that he owed its acceptance to the swarms of flies buzzing around the humid congressional meeting hall. In their jackets, breeches and silk stockings, the delegates were so uncomfortable and hot that they couldn't wait to sign the document on July 4, 1776.

On March 4, 1801, Jefferson went to his inauguration as President on foot—and then returned the same way to his boarding house when the ceremony was over. This informal style scandalized a British minister when he arrived at the White House for a diplomatic meeting only to be greeted by the President wearing a dressing gown and "down at the heel" slippers. When the minister spoke out about this "utter slovenliness," Jefferson straight-facedly professed that he was attempting to strip his office of its royalist trappings and endow it with some good "republican simplicity."

Jefferson didn't rank his two terms as President among his greatest accomplishments. He called the office "a splendid misery" and couldn't wait to slip from "the shackles of power." Not a moment too soon for his own tastes, he returned to his beloved Monticello and his great loves of farming and philosophy. For the last 17 years of his life, he carried on a prolific correspondence with statesmen and scientists and friends, while he designed, down to the smallest detail of academics and architecture, his last great legacy: the University of Virginia.

For his epitaph, he forbade any mention of his presidency. He instructed that there be "not one word more" than:

*Here was buried Thomas Jefferson*
*Author of the Declaration of American Independence*
*Of the Statute of Virginia for Religious Freedom*
*And Father of the University of Virginia.*

# JAMES MADISON
## 1751–1836

When admirers called him "the Father of the Constitution," James Madison, in his modest way, declined the compliment. "This was not," he wrote, "like the fabled Goddess of Wisdom, the offspring of a single brain. It ought to be regarded as the work of many heads and many hands." But Madison's mind was perhaps foremost. The 36-year-old Virginian spoke on 71 of 86 days at the Constitutional Convention of 1787, and his "Virginia Plan," as it was called—based on his voluminous study of historical confederations—became the foundation for the Constitution. Madison would get so enthralled in his speeches that he asked a friend to give him a tug on the coattails when it was time to sit down. Once, when he asked his friend why he hadn't stopped Madison from talking, the man replied: "I would have rather laid finger on the lightning."

The son of a planter, Madison was born and raised on the family plantation, Montpelier. As a young state legislator, he met fellow Virginian Thomas Jefferson and discovered that they shared much in common, including their political philosophy. They remained friends for the rest of their lives. Jefferson praised Madison as "the greatest farmer in the world," and John Quincy Adams, who opposed them both politically, called him "in truth a greater man" than Jefferson.

From all accounts, Madison was a consummate gentleman who relied on intellect rather than presence to command a following. Though he could be relaxed and brimming with warm conversation among friends, he was a bit stiff and uncomfortable in public. As one historian noted, he always wore black "and was considered old-fashioned in his garb, reminding an English visitor of a schoolmaster dressed up for a funeral."

But what he lacked in charisma, Madison made up for in his choice of a wife, an attractive widow, Dolley Payne Todd, who was 17 years younger. Held in high esteem for her character and high-spirited charm, she aided her husband's career when he was secretary of state by serving as hostess for the widowed President Jefferson, and was a powerful sustaining force for Madison as President during the War of 1812.

Dolley Madison was also the heroine who saved Clifford Stuart's treasured painting of George Washington from the British in 1814. With her husband away in Virginia, when she learned the troops were nearing the White House, she delayed her escape until the portrait was removed from its frame and ready for her to deliver into safe-keeping. It was a close call. The British soldiers ate the hot meal she'd been preparing for herself.

The national trauma of the war was a shattering experience for Madison, but John Quincy Adams spoke of his "imperturbable patience," and when he returned to Washington after the British departure in 1814, he still managed to appear, in the words of one contemporary, "tranquil as usual, and 'tho much distressed by the dreadful event, which had taken place, not dispirited." One historian wrote: "Madison was one of the most conscientious, fair-minded and even-tempered of all our Presidents."

Madison and Dolley had a long and happy retirement at Montpelier, entertaining a wide circle of friends, one of whom wrote that to listen to Madison was to hear "a stream of history," so rich in anecdote as to make him one of the most compelling conversationalists alive. Remaining active in his intellectual pursuits, when his old friend Jefferson died, Madison stepped in to become Rector of the University of Virginia.

Madison was the last of the Founding Fathers to serve as President and the last survivor among them. When he died at 85 in 1836, Dolley sold to the government his priceless secret notes from the 1787 Constitutional Convention. They represented one last national treasure created by "the Father of the Constitution." In his notes, Madison had written his own tribute to the founding fathers: "There never was an assembly of men, charged with a great and arduous trust, who were more pure in their motives. . .of devising and proposing a constitutional system which should. . .best secure the permanent liberty and happiness of their country."

# JAMES MONROE
# 1758–1831

Thomas Jefferson said that James Monroe was "a man whose soul might be turned wrongside outward, without discovering a blemish to the world." Jefferson undoubtedly overstated the case for his protégé, but Monroe was indeed a hero of the Revolutionary War who was held in high esteem by his peers over a long and illustrious career.

The son of a Virginia planter—as were Washington, Jefferson and Madison—Monroe was born in 1758 in Westmoreland County, the first of five children, and entered the College of William and Mary when he was sixteen. But when the Revolution began, he received a lieutenant's commission in a Virginia regiment and fought alongside Washington's troops in New York and New Jersey, winning the general's promotion to captain after being wounded in the shoulder at the Battle of Trenton.

After the war, Monroe studied law under Jefferson's tutelage and was elected to Congress in 1782, the same year he married Elizabeth Kottright, a businessman's daughter. He left politics after one term to practice law in Fredericksburg and raise their two daughters. Knowing that Monroe was sympathetic to the French Revolution, Washington soon named him ambassador to France, but Monroe's enthusiasm swept him far beyond the more neutral stance Washington wanted in European affairs, and when Monroe was abruptly summoned home, he was so outraged he wrote a 500-page book blaming his former commander-in-chief for the decline in French-American relations.

After a term as governor of Virginia, Monroe was dispatched as President Jefferson's envoy to England, where he was snubbed at a state dinner. When a toast was made to the King, Monroe proceeded to drop his wine glass into his finger bowl, splashing water everywhere and creating a great commotion. "James Monroe doesn't care where he eats dinner," he said later, "but to find the American minister put at the bottom of the table between two little principalities no bigger than my farm in Albemarle made me mad." In Paris, he received a warmer reception, dining with Napoleon and pulling off one of his great coups. Authorized to negotiate the purchase of New Orleans, Monroe vastly exceeded his authority and snapped up the entire Louisiana Territory for a cool $15 million.

At 58, he was elected President in 1816, precisely as America was entering a period so tranquil that it came to be known as "the Era of Good Feelings." Seizing the moment, Monroe set off on a three-and-a-half month nineteenth century version of a barnstorming tour through New England, and all the way West to Detroit, which was so well received that a critic sneeringly labeled it "a political jubilee." "Even Harvard was friendly, " one historian noted wyrly. Later that year, when the damage inflicted by the British back in the War of 1812 was repaired, the Monroes moved into the White House, including among its furnishings some of Marie Antoinette's furniture and silverware purchased at auction after her execution.

Like Jefferson, Monroe favored "republican simplicity" in his presidential manners and appearance, surprising one European diplomat whose first impression was that the man he saw wearing an ink-spotted waistcoat and worn slippers must be a slovenly clerk worthy of reprimand. The last President to wear a cocked hat, one historian wrote, "with his ancient knee breeches, silk stockings, cockade and sword, he was a hangover from the age of Revolution." But Monroe's style suited Americans fine. He was one of only two Presidents ever to win a second term unopposed, receiving all but one of the electoral college's 232 votes. The lone dissenter, it was said, merely wanted George Washington to retain the honor as the only unanimously elected President.

Retiring to Oak Hill, his mansion near Leesburg, Monroe remained close with Jefferson and Madison. But he was not spared misery in his later years. Severe financial setbacks plagued him as he fought to collect money that he claimed was owed him by the government for his expenses during his years in public life. After the death of his wife in 1830, Monroe could no longer maintain Oak Hill and was forced to move in with a married daughter in New York City. After his death in 1831, at age 78, his former secretary of state, John Quincy Adams, lamented that his public's veneration of America's last great Revolutionary had not followed him into retirement. "His life for the last six years," Adams wrote, "has been one of abject penury and distress, and they have brought him to a premature grave."

# ANDREW JACKSON
# 1767–1845

When Andrew Jackson was running for President in 1828, the Whigs circulated a pamphlet enumerating "General Jackson's Youthful Indiscretions, between the Ages of Twenty-Three and Sixty." It included a number of brawls, duels and knife-fights in which Jackson was said to have "killed, slashed and clawed various citizens." And there was more than a little bit of truth in the accusations, for Jackson seems to have taken his mother's advice: "Never sue for assault or slander; settle them cases yourself."

As far as is known, Jackson never backed down from a fight — or a party. Born to poverty on the Carolina frontier and orphaned as a boy, Jackson was soon enrolled at a dancing school to learn social graces, but as a prank invited two prostitutes just "to see what would come of it." What came of it was a severe reprimand and the beginnings of his local legend. "Andrew Jackson," said one local years later, "was the most roaring, rollicking, game-cocking, horse-racing, card-playing, mischievous fellow that ever lived in Salisbury."

As a teenager, the money he inherited from a grandfather in Ireland was quickly squandered on whiskey, women, song and gambling. Then he settled into the study of law—whenever he could spare time from his self-acclaimed position as "head of the rowdies." Clients beat a path to his door, for he was a lawyer as skilled at collecting debts outside the courtroom as in. As a judge, he once attacked the governor of Tennessee and had to be talked out of killing him on the spot. Once, a wild man, standing in front of the courthouse waving a pistol, intimidated onlookers until Jackson faced him down at gunpoint. Asked why he surrendered, the man said: "I looked him in the eye and I saw shoot."

So did a lot of others. He fought more than one duel over a perceived slight to his beloved wife Rachel. "For the man who dared breathe her name except in honor," one contemporary remarked, "he kept pistols in perfect condition for 37 years." His victory over the British in the Battle of New Orleans lifted the spirits of the entire nation. And he was a ruthless Indian fighter. But his skill and ferocity as a military commander was matched by his ability to win the loyalty of his troops, who nicknamed their general "Old Hickory" for his insistence on enduring the same deprivations they did. But Jackson wasn't above making sure he won affluence in his private affairs. He was a canny land speculator and slave owner.

His presidency started with an appropriate bang, when thousands of his devoted admirers stormed the executive mansion for what surely was the wildest shindig ever held in Washington, D.C. "It was like the inundation of the northern barbarians into Rome," wrote one eyewitness. But Jackson was still grieving for Rachel, who had died just as they were scheduled to head north to the nation's capital. Jackson talked of having nothing left to live for, and his friends feared that he might die in office. At 61, he suffered from tuberculosis, and his condition wasn't helped by the bullets he carried inside him from old gunfights. But he worked to improve his regimen, telling his doctor that he'd give up everything except coffee and tobacco.

Despite his weakened condition, "Old Hickory" still intimidated his enemies for the next eight years. Although he was capable of aristocratic manners when he wished, as one historian wrote, upper-class Americans saw him as a roughneck who "would probably shoot down White House visitors in cold blood if they said something he didn't like." It was an image that Jackson used to full political advantage. When John Calhoun spoke of secession by South Carolina, Jackson mobilized his troops and threatened to hang his former Vice President from the first tree he could find. South Carolina backed off. And when he threw a temper tantrum in front of a group of businessmen complaining of his anti-bank policies, they scurried away in a hurry. "They thought I was mad," said Jackson with a laugh. A friend of 40 years summed him up: "No man knew better than Andrew Jackson when to get into a passion and when not."

The grizzled old frontier hero who had survived bullets and arrows outlived even many of those who thought he'd never make it through his first term. At age 78, after eight years of retirement at the Hermitage, his plantation near Nashville, he died peacefully in bed, surrounded by his household staff. His last words were: "I hope to see you all in heaven, white and black."

# WILLIAM JENNINGS BRYAN 1860–1925

William Jennings Bryan arrived at the Democratic Convention in 1896 with $100 in his pocket. But the "Silver-Tongued Orator" was also armed with his most powerful weapon—the famous "Cross of Gold" speech. The packed crowd of 20,000 in the Chicago Coliseum didn't need their ear trumpets to hear him thunder his denunciation of "the money kings" on Wall Street, whose greed was strangling American workers and farmers. Thrusting his arms out and leaning his head back in a Christ-like pose, Bryan captured the moment in one of the most powerful lines ever spoken in American political history: "You shall not press down upon the brow of labor this crown of thorns. You shall not crucify mankind upon a Cross of Gold."

Bryan won the nomination and went forth, stumping the country by train and delivering hundreds of his famous stem-winders in support of "the common man." In an era of Populist revolt, his was a potent message. With 80 percent of those eligible voting, Bryan received more votes than any presidential candidate before him. It wasn't enough to defeat William McKinley, but some historians believe that Bryan's wide appeal may have saved the Democratic Party from the same fate that met the Whigs before the Civil War: extinction.

Nominated twice more, he never won the presidency but, as journalist William Allen White wrote, Bryan "influenced the thinking of the American people more profoundly than any other man of his generation." In his 1900 campaign, he delivered 546 speeches pleading in the name of the "great toiling masses" for "an awakened conscience against the tide of corruption." In 1908 his progressivist attack on "the trusts" was eloquently framed: "Shall The People Rule?"

One of two surviving children of a respected Baptist farmer, politician and judge who prayed and read Scripture at least three times a day, Bryan was born on a 500-acre farm in southcentral Illinois. Accepting unquestioningly the verities of religious faith, hard work and stern morality, he grew up secure in his belief that he lived "in the greatest of ages" and "the greatest of all lands." At a local college, Bryan became so smitten with Mary Baird, a student at a nearby female academy, that he violated the rule against unchaperoned dating, causing her suspension. But they soon married and she was forever after the center of his life. They had three children.

After law school in Chicago, he quickly made his name as an orator. Tall and handsome with a mane of black hair and a rich, deep voice, he had perfected his skills with private instruction and long hours of practice, even learning to speak with pebbles in his mouth and walking alone deep into the woods where he could boom his voice without being overheard—except for the time he alarmed a group of picnickers who feared he was an escapee from an asylum. "His ringing eloquence, his uncanny ability to paint understandable and strikingly vivid word pictures, and his superbly resonant voice invariably brought listeners to their feet," one historian wrote.

In 1890, Bryan became known as the boy wonder of Nebraska politics, becoming, at 30, only the second Democrat from the state to win a seat in Congress. During two terms, he was labeled "a promising newcomer" in national politics—a promise that seemed fulfilled when even after losses in three Presidential campaigns he was regarded by friends and foes alike as one of the most charismatic grass-roots leaders of his generation.

As the Roaring Twenties began, Bryan trumpeted old-time religion as the savior in an era of declining morals. Bryan's motives were complex—and well-meaning. He feared that the rich had seized upon "survival of the fittest" as their justification for preying upon the poor in the economic jungle. But his last moral crusade led Bryan to his famous debacle fighting the case against teaching evolution in schools at the Scopes "monkey trial." On the stand testifying about Scriptural truths, he was devastated on cross-examination by his former admirer, Clarence Darrow. A few days later, Bryan died in his sleep.

As his funeral train moved from Tennessee toward Arlington National Cemetery, thousands lined up along the tracks to pay their respects and mourn for the man whose life had been devoted to "the commoner." "They had lost a friend," one historian wrote. "And they were mourning the end of an era as well."

# WOODROW WILSON 1856–1924

Woodrow Wilson's earliest childhood memory was a warning of war. As a four-year-old boy in Augusta, Georgia, he heard a man outside his home shouting that Lincoln had been elected; they'd have to fight now. He would recall watching Confederate soldiers brought to the make-shift hospital in the Presbyterian church where his father was a minister. And with Southern schools in disarray, Wilson couldn't begin his education until he was nine.

His childhood experience left him with a deep hatred of war. As a student at Presbyterian College in New Jersey, he decided to become a statesman, devoting his life to the cause of peace. After briefly practicing law, he found it "as monotonous as . . . hash," and gave way to his scholarly bent, becoming a professor at a new woman's college, Bryn Mawr. He married Ellen Louise Axson, whose father was also a Presbyterian minister, and they soon had three daughters. Appointed professor of jurisprudence and history at Princeton, he was popular with students, rode his bike to class every day.

Named president of Princeton at 45, he immediately precipitated a decline in enrollment by demanding higher standards of scholarship. The conservative alumni got their revenge by defeating his attempt to abolish private eating clubs—but the incident brought Wilson to prominence when newspapers portrayed him as a fighter for democratic values. In 1910, the alumni were ready to rise in rebellion when Wilson again made national headlines with a speech criticizing private universities for not providing "opportunities to serve the people" and Protestant churches for "serving the classes and not the masses." The New Jersey Democratic machine greased Wilson's path to a graceful exit: the governorship. But they, too, soon discovered that he wasn't for sale. He took on the machine boss in public and won, while newspapers reported that "the long-haired bookworm of a professor" had "licked the gang to a frazzle." With the public behind him, he pushed through reform legislation for matters as basic as labor regulations for women and children.

Wilson was successful despite his austere personality. "Calvinists may bear tidings of great joy," one historian wrote of him, "but they are not usually very cheerful about it. Wilson struck most people as being cold, reserved, distant and aloof, not to say vain and self-righteous." Wilson protested that he actually had a happy Irish temperament—and he did get off a witty line now and then—but he knew that the most he could hope for from Americans was respect, not love.

His eloquence, however, provided inspiration to millions. His inaugural address as President in 1913 ranks as one of the greatest ever. With a use of language not heard since Lincoln, it strikes resonant chords even today: "With riches has come inexcusable waste," Wilson said. "We have squandered a great part of what we might have used, and not stopped to conserve the exceeding bounty of nature, without which our genius for enterprise would have been worthless and impotent." He went on to state: "The great Government we loved has too often been made use of for private and selfish purposes, and those who used it had forgotten the people."

In his first term, Wilson passed through Congress a greater number of laws designed to promote social justice than any President before him. But after the death of his wife in 1914, he was despondent until he met Edith Bolling Galt, a 43-year-old widow, in 1915. He fell deeply in love and even admitted that he broke into song for her during their courtship: "Oh, You Beautiful Doll." Nine months later they were married in her Washington home.

But dark days were on the horizon. The tragedy of Wilson's life was that events in Europe overwhelmed his love of peace and his desire to provide a better life for Americans. Against every fiber of his being—crying out as if in pain about the "brutality" it would inflict at home as well as abroad—Wilson sent American troops into the slaughter of World War One. His lifelong dream of world peace crushed, Wilson crusaded futilely at war's end for a League of Nations that would spare the world from future horrors. But after a speech in Pueblo, Colorado in September 1919, he collapsed and two weeks later was felled by a stroke that left him an invalid. At the end of his term, Wilson retired with his wife to a small house in Washington, and in 1924, four years after receiving a Nobel Prize, he died at the age of 67.

# FRANKLIN DELANO ROOSEVELT 1882–1945

Franklin Delano Roosevelt loved to tell the story about the Republican commuter from Westchester County who paid his quarter for the *New York Herald-Tribune* every morning, glanced at the front page and handed the paper back. Finally the newspaper boy asked what he was doing. "Looking for an obituary." "But they're on page 24." "Boy," said the Republican, "the son of a bitch I'm looking for will be on page one."

That was FDR's kind of story. His eyes twinkling with mischief, he'd wave his cigarette around in its long-stemmed holder and beam with delight while he exuberantly shared the fun to be poked—at himself and the Republican—in that soothing "Fireside Chat" voice of his. "The voice," as he was fond of saying, "that Wall Street uses to inculcate fear in the breasts of their little grandchildren."

There was truth in Roosevelt's jest. As a leader he was more concerned with ending suffering than protecting the privileges of the rich. In the first 100 days after becoming President during the darkest moment of the Depression in 1933, his "New Deal for the American people" showed his true and lasting colors, forcing the country through its greatest peacetime upheaval in history. When he was gearing up his massive programs to provide relief to the needy and put the unemployed to work, an aide asked him if they could include artists. "Why not?" FDR responded. "They are human beings. They have to live. I guess the only thing they can do is paint, but surely there must be some public places where paintings are wanted."

The only son of a railroad executive, Roosevelt was himself born to a life of privilege on his family's estate in Hyde Park, New York. As a boy, he was educated by governesses and tutors and taken on European travels. Like cousin Teddy, he attended Harvard, where he spent as much time on social life as studies and regarded his highest accomplishment as becoming editor of the *Harvard Crimson*. While at college, he was engaged to his distant cousin, Eleanor Roosevelt, and they were married in 1905. They had six children, one of whom died as an infant. A brilliant and energetic woman known for her many causes, Eleanor became a major figure in her own right. But Roosevelt enjoyed teasing his wife almost as much as the Republicans. When he became the first President to appoint a woman to the Cabinet, Eleanor mentioned the terrible time that labor leaders must have given him. "Oh, that's all right," FDR replied. "I'd rather have trouble with them for an hour than trouble with you for the rest of my life."

The only man ever elected to four terms as President didn't even enter politics until he was 28. Though the Roosevelts were known as Republicans, his own branch of the family was Democratic. In 1910, after he made a sizable contribution, the Party surprised him with a nomination for the state senate in Dutchess County. There was speculation that they meant it as a joke; no Democrat had won in Dutchess for about fifty years. But Roosevelt had the last laugh, traveling the rural backroads by car and charming the farmers enough to win by more than a thousand votes. Two years later, President Woodrow Wilson named Roosevelt an assistant secretary of the Navy.

Stricken with polio in 1921 when he was 39, Roosevelt never regained the use of his legs, but three years later he showed his unconquerable spirit when he struggled from his wheelchair at the Democratic Convention in Madison Square Garden and walked to the rostrum with crutches to deliver a nominating speech for Al Smith, calling him "the Happy Warrior of the political battlefield." In later years Roosevelt talked of his battle with polio as a source of his indomitability. Asked if the weight of the world's problems ever got too heavy, he said: "If you had spent two years in bed trying to wiggle your big toe, after that anything would seem easy."

In more than a decade of fighting the Depression and World War Two, Roosevelt's supremely confident optimism never wavered. But by early 1945, when he returned from his Yalta Conference with Churchill and Stalin, his exhaustion showed, and in March, he traveled to Warm Springs, Georgia, for a rest. On April 12, writing at his desk while his portrait was painted, he complained of "a terrific headache" and at 4:45 p.m., he died. The nation went into mourning. After services in Washington, he was buried at Hyde Park, leaving behind the last words he wrote: "The only limit to our realization of tomorrow will be our doubts of today. Let us move forward with strong and active faith."

# HARRY S. TRUMAN
# 1884–1972

Just before leaving the White House, Harry Truman told his daughter Margaret that he'd never be recorded among the great Presidents, but that his feelings were captured by a Boot Hill epitaph in Tombstone, Arizona: "Here lies Jack Williams; he done his damndest."

Harry Truman did just that—and two generations later, he looks better than ever. As one historian wrote: "Once called a liar, cheat, fool, coddler of subversive and the worst President in history, he began to appear in retrospect refreshingly independent, straightforward, decisive and courageous."

Certainly no President ever took office under worse circumstances with less cause for high expectations. Not even Truman had wanted himself to be in destiny's way. In 1944, when he heard that FDR wanted him as his running mate, Truman's answer was typically direct: "Tell him to go to hell." Truman had been Vice President for only 82 days—and had barely spoken with the President—when Eleanor Roosevelt gave him the news that her husband had died. "Is there anything I can do for you?" Truman asked. "You're the one in trouble now," she replied. After taking the oath, he told reporters: "I don't know whether you fellows ever had a load of hay fall on you, but when they told me yesterday what had happened, I felt like the moon, the stars and all the planets had fallen on me."

Much of the nation felt the same way. Even without the whole world in crisis, Truman just didn't seem presidential. The son of a mule trader, he hadn't started school until he was eight — and never made it to college. He swore, even in public, like the World War One artillery man and Missouri dirt farmer he'd been. He had also been a small-town suit salesman— and looked the part—with more than one failed business behind him. And his rise in politics from county judge to U.S. Senate was helped by the notoriously corrupt Pendergast machine in Kansas City.

No wonder the skeptics feared the country was in trouble. But what the skeptics didn't know was that Truman's cranky honesty had driven even Boss Pendergast to distraction. "He's the contrariest cuss in Missouri," Pendergast complained. And this owly-looking, straight-talking little man was a regular dynamo. He kept a dirt farmer's hours, rising at 5:30 a.m. and leaving the White House grounds to walk a mile or two—often with reporters who trotted to keep up with him—before his morning swim and breakfast.

As President, Truman quickly rose to the occasion. "If you can't stand the heat, stay out of the kitchen," he was fond of saying. And the plaque on his desk became a part of the language: "The buck stops here." Truman's salty talk, free of any media niceties, became a hallmark of his presidency. His "hells" and "damns" and "s.o.b.'s" were always getting him into hot water, even with his wife, Bess. His greatest ire was reserved for the *Washington Post* columnist who dared to ridicule his daughter Margaret's singing. "Westbrook Pegler, a guttersnipe, is a gentleman compared to you," Truman wrote in a letter. "I never met you, but if I do, you'll need a new nose and a supporter below."

And he was just as feisty with his political foes. Truman loved nothing better than denouncing Republicans. Counted out in the 1948 campaign, he went on a whistle-stop train campaign across the country from Labor Day until Election Day, telling ordinary Americans in the most sincere way he knew how: "If the Republicans win, they'll tear you to pieces." Ordinary Americans responded with the now-famous phrase: "Give 'em Hell, Harry." He did—and he won.

When Truman and Bess left the White House, they rode the train home to Independence, Missouri, where he proceeded to take over his fair share of the housework. But he hated mowing the lawn, so he started doing it on Sunday mornings, when the neighbors were passing by on their way to church, until Bess was embarrassed enough to find someone else to do it. He wrote two volumes of memoirs and made speeches for the Democrats—with the same old fire in his belly— even stirring up one last hornet's nest when he observed while campaigning for JFK in 1960 that any Texan who voted for Nixon should "go to hell."

He was an American original, the likes of which won't pass our way again any time soon. But it was left to Winston Churchill to pay the ultimate compliment to the former haberdasher who had successfully faced the monumental task of stepping into FDR's shoes and leading the Allies to victory in World War Two. "You, more than any other man," said Churchill, "have saved Western civilization."

# JOHN FITZGERALD KENNEDY 1917–1963

As a sickly boy recovering from scarlet fever, John Fitzgerald Kennedy read books—a habit that stayed with him the rest of his life. He fell in love with history. And heroes. But his most cherished mythology was provided by the Knights of the Round Table. Sometimes at night years later, when his back was hurting, his wife Jackie would climb out of bed and turn on their old Victrola and play his favorite show tune: "Don't let it be forgot, that once there was a spot, for one brief shining moment that was Camelot."

A few days after his death, she told that story to author Theodore White, who immortalized it in *Life* magazine. But as White sadly conceded, there were no Merlins or Galahads in Kennedy's court. There was no Camelot. But there was certainly a national tragedy that causes pain even today for those who lived through the loss of America's youngest, handsomest, most dashing—and perhaps wittiest—Chief Executive. The first President born in the twentieth century, Kennedy was only 43 when he took office and challenged the country to chart a "New Frontier."

The second of nine children of Rose and Joseph P. Kennedy, one of America's wealthiest—and most controversial—men, young John Kennedy seemed charmed: winters in Palm Beach, summers in Hyannisport, surrounded by a close-knit clan. In his first three years at Harvard, his grades were gentlemanly Cs. With his looks and charm, the fun-loving Kennedy could have enjoyed a successful career as a dilettante. But war threatened and he was accepted as a Navy seaman three months before Pearl Harbor.

Eventually winning a lieutenant's commission, Kennedy was commanding a torpedo boat in the South Pacific in 1943 when a Japanese destroyer slashed through it, killing two of his crew and leaving Kennedy to swim for his life to the nearest island. Asked about his heroics, he said: "It was absolutely involuntary. They sank my boat." The beginnings of the Jack Kennedy legend emerged in John Hersey's memorialization of the PT-109 saga in *The New Yorker*.

When Kennedy was 28, "the poor little rich kid," as one opponent called him, won a seat in Congress. In 1952, with his brother Bobby as campaign manager, he won a seat in the Senate. A year later he married Jacqueline Lee Bouvier, a 24-year-old George Washington University coed when they met, and they had three children, one of whom died shortly after birth.

By 1958, Senator Jack Kennedy was hot in pursuit of the presidency, and the Gridiron Club in Washington showed him what they thought with a skit called: "Just send the bill to Daddy." Kennedy responded in his usual disarming way, reading a telegram he said he'd just received from his father: "Dear Jack: Don't buy a single vote more than necessary. I'll be damned if I'm going to pay for a landslide."

Kennedy paid his dues, slogging across the country through backwoods and back rooms for more than a year, fighting an uphill battle in a country that had never before elected a Catholic as President. He surrounded himself with a world-class brain trust, and was "a realistic leader of men, a master of games who understood the importance of ideas."

On of the day of his inaugural, Kennedy stood before the nation in the brisk cold and uttered his ringing words about passing the torch to a new generation. It was an inspiring moment. But he quickly discovered the enormity of the dangers America faced. "The only thing that really surprised us when we got into office," he said, "was that things were just as bad as we had been saying they were."

In two years and ten months as President, even Kennedy's critics enjoyed the sparkling wit of his press conferences. In what now seems a more innocent time, not even the threat of the Cold War turning hot could dampen the nation's optimism that anything was possible—even Kennedy's promise that we would put a man on the Moon before the end of the decade.

The entire world mourned his death. In words that ring as true now as they did then, President Lyndon Johnson captured the feelings of a grieving nation in his address to a joint session of Congress a few days after the assassination: "The greatest leader of our time has been struck down by the foulest deed of our time. Today John Fitzgerald Kennedy lives on in the immortal words and works that he left behind. He lives on in the minds and memories of mankind. He lives on in the hearts of his countrymen."

# LYNDON BAINES JOHNSON 1908–1973

Averill Harriman said that if it hadn't been for Vietnam, Lyndon Johnson would "have been the greatest President ever." Even Johnson later admitted: "I knew from the start that if I left the woman I really loved—the Great Society—in order to fight that bitch of a war, then I would lose everything at home. All my hopes . . . my dreams."

And Lyndon Johnson's dreams were larger than life. He saw the country soaring to new heights as he led the civil rights revolution and fought his War on Poverty. A man governed by his passions, the outsized Texan—a strapping 6'3"—had a personality as extravagant as his vision for America. "LBJ seemed like the quintessential Texan to many Americans: big, loud, brash, friendly, informal, folksy, pushy, vulgar and combative," wrote one historian. "He was all these things, and more. He had a remarkable memory, a razor-sharp mind, great comic gifts and a populist bent that made him eager as President to make life better for the masses of people."

Politics was in his blood. The first of five children, he was born on a ranch outside Stonewall, Texas, the son and grandson of men who had served in the Texas legislature. As a teenager, he earned movie money shining shoes and picking cotton, and after finishing high school at fifteen, he lived a hobo's life in California for a year, picking oranges and washing dishes, before returning to Johnson City. With $75 borrowed from the local bank, he entered Southwest State Teachers College in San Marcos, Texas.

He was teaching high school debate and public speaking in Houston when opportunity knocked: A Congressman offered him a job as a $3000-a-year secretary in Washington. Caught up in the whirlwind just as FDR was unleashing the New Deal, he mastered the intricacies—and personalities—of how the Capitol worked.

Back home in Texas in 1934, Johnson married a 20-year-old named Claudia Alta Taylor, known as Lady Bird. They had two daughters, Luci and Lynda.

After Johnson's enthusiastic support of the New Deal won him a seat in Congress in 1937, Roosevelt helped him find his way to the right committees—joining House Majority Leader Sam Rayburn, who became one of his mentors. Johnson won his next three terms unopposed. In 1948 he was elected to the Senate by 87 votes out of nearly a million cast.

But to this day his performance as a senator is legendary. His famous motto, "Let Us Reason Together," was a tribute for his admirers, black humor to his enemies. In polite company, they told stories of his genius at persuading legislators of divergent views to reach consensus. But when the boys were alone in the back room with their feet on the desk drinking bourbon and branch water, they regaled one another with earthier accounts of this arm-twisting, profane, manipulative and ingratiating horse-trader who played politics as a physical contact sport, like football. Barry Goldwater said affectionately that Johnson had two methods of persuasion: the Half-Johnson and the Full-Johnson, which were variations of a bear hug.

By 1955, Johnson was the youngest Majority Leader in the history of the Senate. But he was also a chain smoker and workaholic and on July 4, when he was only 46 he suffered a massive heart attack. He quit smoking, but soon returned to his compulsive work habits. His ambition was to be the presidential nominee in 1960, but after Jack Kennedy outspent, outflanked and outfoxed him, he surprised everyone by accepting the number two spot on the ticket. On the night of November 22, 1963, Johnson was humble in his first public words as President to the American people: "I will do my best. That is all I can do. I ask your help, and God's."

His landslide victory over Barry Goldwater in 1964 made it appear that Johnson's dreams of a Great Society would come true. But "that bitch of a war" stole him—and America—away from those dreams. Three years and two months after his inauguration, Johnson stunned the nation by announcing—in a paragraph that he tacked on to a televised address at the last minute—that he would not seek another term. It was a saddened and subdued Johnson who departed the White House in January 1969 for a quiet retirement. He started smoking again. And in January 1973, when he was only 64, he died of a heart attack. After services in the Capitol, he was buried in the family graveyard a few hundred feet from his birthplace in his beloved hill country of Stonewall, Texas.

# CHAPTER THIRTEEN

# *WHY I'M A DEMOCRAT...*

### INTERVIEWED BY DANICA KIRKA

SENATOR BILL BRADLEY

PRESIDENT JIMMY CARTER

GOVERNOR BILL CLINTON

CONGRESSWOMAN GERALDINE FERRARO

SENATOR ALBERT GORE

REVEREND JESSE L. JACKSON

CONGRESSWOMAN BARBARA JORDAN

SENATOR EDWARD M. KENNEDY

SENATOR GEORGE MCGOVERN

SENATE MAJORITY LEADER GEORGE J. MITCHELL

SPEAKER THOMAS P. "TIP" O'NEILL

GOVERNOR ANN RICHARDS

# SENATOR
# BILL BRADLEY

I remember the hot summer night in 1964 when the Civil Rights Act passed. I was a student intern, between my junior and senior years in college, and I was in the Senate Chamber as the roll call was read. I remember thinking that America is a better place because of this bill, that all Americans, white or black, are better off. I remember the presidential elections that year, too, when Senator Goldwater made the Civil Rights Act an issue in his campaign. I recall the separate restrooms and drinking fountains for black and white. And some believed blacks should eat on the kitchen steps of restaurants rather than in the dining rooms. I had come to Washington that summer as a Republican. I left as a Democrat.

Looking through the prism of history at our contemporary circumstances, I'd have to say that the Democratic Party should take heart from the progress and determination to fight the obstacles that remain in the path before us. Achieving the ideals of the Declaration of Independence means assuming that everyone has a right to influence outcomes in our society, and to shape our common future through the vote.

The whole history of American democracy, I believe, has been the history of broadening the franchise—the fulcrum of democracy—by enabling people to take control of their destinies at the voting booth. That's what the Democratic Party is all about. It's about playing to the best in all of us, about supporting tolerance toward others, about making a commitment to civic virtue. It's about believing that pluralism has a chance to be realized.

In my home state of New Jersey, there are students in the public school system who come from homes representing 120 different languages and almost every cultural background in the world. But it's the same all over this country. In San Jose, there are more families with the Vietnamese surname Nguyen than there are Joneses. In Houston, there is a Korean-owned restaurant that employs Latino immigrants to prepare Chinese food for a predominantly black clientele.

In all of our history, we are at our finest when we live what we believe—that race and color are irrelevant to our nationality. As the Democratic Party leads the nation into the twenty-first century, it must recognize—and champion—the interdependence that binds us all together, for the best of what we are as Democrats, and as Americans, embraces first and foremost our common heritage as human beings.

# PRESIDENT
# JIMMY CARTER

There were 50 some officers in submarine training in New London, Connecticut, when I was a young naval officer in 1948. I was the only one who was openly for Harry Truman. I thought he was honest and told the truth, even when it was politically damaging to him. He was a man of the people in that he had faith in the ability of people to improve themselves. He made it possible to go into an era of peace and understanding with former adversaries. When he defeated Dewey, it was a wonderful time in my life. Later, when I got out of the Navy, I didn't have any need to change my opinion.

With my own personal private, religious and social commitments, I've never felt uncomfortable as a Democrat. I still feel that way. But I've never been a Party man. I have always felt more constrained than liberated by the trappings of the Democratic Party leadership. But the principles of the party made me feel compatible. The Democratic Party is one of such wide diversity that there's room for multiple beliefs and multiple emphases. The Republican Party is much more narrow and restricted and self-contained, much more controlled from the top with much less breathing room for the accommodation of diversity.

One Democratic principle that stands alone is the faith that, if given a chance, people can utilize their lives in overcoming the handicaps of poverty and race deprivation and prejudice. Working through Habitat for Humanity—building homes side-by-side with people who in the past have been scorned or com-

pletely homeless or living in pasteboard boxes or under plastic sheets on the sidewalk—I've seen their lives transformed.

It's always seemed to me that the Democratic Party was more attuned to alleviating the suffering of people who are in need, giving people a chance to capitalize on their own native ability, improving public education, providing job opportunities for people who wanted to work, giving a better chance for those who are trying to move up in life and being more dedicated to environmental quality. My own feelings of a more integrated society were confirmed by the principles of the Democratic Party—to bind together rather than separate them.

# GOVERNOR BILL CLINTON

I was born into a Democratic family in a small town in the South. I was told by my grandfather when I was a very young boy that he was a Democrat because Franklin Roosevelt, in the Great Depression, cared enough to try to save the average working people of America—the small business people, the farmers and the factory workers—and give them a chance to be rewarded for their work.

I decided to be a Democrat starting in the Presidential elections of 1960 when John Kennedy excited me with a promise to get the country moving again. I think he gave people the sense that they could make a difference and that the President could make a difference. And he did it without ever promising that all the problems could be solved—just that tomorrow would be better than today. He convinced me that he and Lyndon Johnson wanted to do something about civil rights problems, particularly in the South, my own region. As a young man, the two great issues of my times were race and the war in Vietnam. I agreed that we should be pro–civil rights and that we should withdraw from the war. So I stayed in the Party. In the aftermath, I think the Democrats came to be viewed as kind of an elitist party of people who were not interested in the day-to-day concerns of most Americans. That made me very sad. But I'm a Democrat because I never believed there was an alternative in the Republican Party. I thought it was better to keep trying to change the Democratic Party and make it a pro-growth, pro-middle class party that was still committed to equal opportunity for all Americans and doing something for the poor and disadvantaged.

I'm proud I stayed, because now I think we've got a chance to rebuild the elements of the Democratic coalition and add to it. Thoughtful Independents and Republicans, who want to have a genuine strategy of economic growth and opportunity for America, desperately want to end the long, dark night of racial division which has paralyzed our country and our politics, and which has enabled us to go on denying our real problems. We've got to do something about children who are shooting each other in schools and the kids we're losing to drugs and to violence. We've got to do something about the hard-working people who are playing by the rules and still getting the shaft. Only a party that believes government can be a full partner with the private sector in promoting growth and equality of opportunity can do that. That's the Democrats.

The Democratic Party believes that every man and woman should be able to live to the fullest of their God-given capacities. To do that in the world in which we live requires making America competitive in the global economy. We have to make a real commitment to economic growth, to affordable health care, to education for all, to preserving our environment and to uniting across racial, gender, age and income lines. We have to make a commitment to be one nation again.

# CONGRESSWOMAN GERALDINE FERRARO

I look back with a tremendous amount of pride in the fact that my mother was strong enough to make the decision to be a Democrat, and that I was smart enough to continue in her tradition. She was my first role model in the Democratic Party. My second was Eleanor Roosevelt. I remember being so impressed by this woman. I was newly married. I was rather a new lawyer. I met her at a neighborhood church in Manhattan where she had come to speak. She was brilliant. I remember going up to her afterward and telling her what an inspiration she was to me. I look at the young women who come up to me and say things like, "Thank you for running. The campaign of '84 was very important to me." And when I see people doing that, I see myself going up to Eleanor Roosevelt. I know how much it took to come up and tell me that. I know how uncomfortable they must be and how shy they must feel about doing that. So I'm very, very grateful to them because I remember how difficult it was for me to go up to this woman whom I respected so deeply.

Mrs. Roosevelt was a woman who could easily have stayed home and lived a life of luxury, but she felt a tremendous obligation toward humanity. She left her mark and made a difference. This was a woman who was well ahead of her time and certainly one of the foremost women leaders of the Democratic Party.

This is a party that has recognized equality and has always pushed for legislation and principles that address the equal rights of women, whether it's the Equal Rights Amendment or the rights of women to equal pay or equal credit. They've also recognized women who have the ability to move forward in the political system. We have had women chairing the important committees of the Democratic National Committee for years. And, obviously, we had the first woman on a national ticket. You could not expect Republicans to do that. That is what Democrats do. Democrats open doors of opportunity, whether it's civil rights or women's rights or workers' rights. It is the party that has reached out to women and the party to which women have responded.

It's a party that looks to national security as not only the strength of our weapons but also the strength of its people. And it spends time and energy paying attention to the strength of its people. I truly believe that the Democratic Party stands not only for working people, but for bringing people who are poor and disenfranchised into the system to make us all a part of a better society. We've never been a party that has said to anyone, "You're excluded." And we've been criticized for that. Our detractors say, "You're trying to be all things to all people." No, we're not. We're trying to be open. And we're trying to say that in this world, we're entitled to reach as far as our dreams will take us.

# SENATOR
# ALBERT GORE

Coming from Tennessee, I guess I have a particular appreciation for the Jackson legacy and for trusting in the people. Jefferson and Jackson were the founders of the Party. Jefferson was responsible for the principles and values that are still at the heart of the Party and Jackson was responsible for giving people control of their government.

I learned at a very early age that being a Democrat means caring about people, caring about the future of our country. It is the Democratic Party which always has and always will fight for American families, for their jobs and for their futures. The Democratic Party has always been about facing the future with courage and with vision, and a commitment to leadership, in contrast to the other party's reluctance to ever challenge the status quo, especially when it affects the wealthy or the comfortable. Our party has consistently searched for creative and effective solutions to the nation's problems and has never been reluctant to fight for change.

Both of my parents and my older sister were steeped in Democratic politics and theory, and I remember sitting around the dinner table listening to conversations about the hopes and dreams of a better life. About those who were struggling to make ends meet and get health care for their children and good jobs. The conviction and the sincerity with which their battles were fought made a deep impression on me.

Take the environment. I believe there is a deep connection between individual freedom and the protection of the environment. All over the world, the democracy and environmental movements have become intertwined. Here at home, the most effective way to protect the environment is to fight alongside the Democratic Party for political and economic empowerment so that people can aquire the ability to protect the environment in which they live, and secure a better future for themselves and their children.

For many of us, the initial choice of political affiliation flows out of one's family experiences, and I won't pretend that this wasn't a factor for me, at least in the beginning. But I have quite deliberately chosen to remain a Democrat. I have deepened my conviction that the Democratic Party is where I want to spend my energies and talents. Why? For one principal reason: It is the party which identifies with the concerns of the average person and especially the concerns of those whose interests will never be attended to by the powerful and the self-interested in our society. I believe deeply that our country prospers when all Americans are doing well and withers when the interest of the many are subordinated to the interests of the wealthy and powerful few.

# REVEREND JESSE L. JACKSON

I went to jail on July 17, 1960, for trying to use a library in Greenville, South Carolina. But 24 years afterward to the day, I spoke to the Democratic National Convention in San Francisco as a presidential candidate. It was an historic breakthrough for African-American participation, for those who had been locked out at the level of political participation. There were people who feared that if ever an African-American had that platform, what would happen to the Party—to the country? What would the reaction be? And yet we made the case for the coal miner in West Virginia, and the rural farmer in Iowa, and for the working mother who could not afford health insurance. We made the case for those who had been last and least and left out. We made the case for the damned and the disinherited. It touched something deep in the conscience of the people of our country. They responded with a great sense of unity and hope.

The Democratic Party, at its best, is the party of inclusion and expansion. In the last 60 years, it is the party that led the drive after the Great Depression for Social Security for seniors, for jobs for the common people, for mass-based education. It is the party that led the drive for civil rights in planks of its platform in 1948; the party that led the drive for civil rights bills of the Sixties.

The Party is at its best when it unifies red, yellow, brown, black and white. That's why I often say the Democratic Party must lead the people and allow them to move from racial battleground to economic common ground and then on to moral higher ground. The Democratic Party's credo is that people should go forward, not backward, that they should vote their hopes, not their fears. If the Democratic Party fulfills this vision, it will win and deserve to win. The Republicans feed fears. They have been the party that has used those fears to divide the nation and to conquer it.

The Democratic Party accepts the challenge of building a culturally diverse party. It is the place where African-Americans, Jewish-Americans, Hispanic-Americans, Asian-Americans, Arab-Americans, Irish-Americans, Italian-Americans, women, gays, lesbians, working people and youth—the new majority—can find common ground.

The Republican Party is like a sheet. It's all one piece of white cloth. The Democratic Party is like a quilt—many patches, many colors, many textures, many different sizes, but bound together by a commitment to racial and social justice and gender equality. You compare the quilt with the sheet, and it speaks volumes. While the Republican Party will appoint some African-Americans, some Hispanics and some women, from the top down—on the condition they pass the ideological litmus test—the Democratic Party represents the potential for growth from the bottom up. It is a party of hope.

# CONGRESSWOMAN BARBARA JORDAN

For as long as I can remember, I was always a Democrat. I never had to make a choice, because the alternative was totally unacceptable. I lived in Houston, Texas, and the Republican Party was just a very, very minor player in any politics, so it was a given that I was a Democrat. Then, as I began to discern the legitimate differences between the two parties, I knew my comfort zone would remain in the Democratic Party.

I remember my father in 1948 talking about the attachment he felt for the civil rights program of Harry Truman. I recall him saying that supporting civil rights was such a unique and new and different thing for a national politician to talk about. After I graduated from law school and returned to Houston, I searched to find people who were trying to help John Kennedy and Lyndon Johnson. It was necessary for us to call out the black area of Houston and develop a black worker program. We went almost door to door and to neighborhood churches, talking to people about the importance of the contest. It was this experience that made me think I might one day want to run for office myself.

I knew very early that I wanted to be able to do things that would have an impact on large numbers of people, and the best way to do that was to become active in politics. It became clear immediately that most of the people who were doing things that were helpful and beneficial to people were Democrats. This solidified my commitment.

I believe the fact of race has been, for me, all of the stimulation I needed to work hard and push myself as far as I desire to go. I deliberately did not consider race as an impediment. I have always thought of race as a challenge and an opportunity rather than as a barrier to achievement, and I think this attitude has served me well throughout my life.

The Democratic Party, I feel, cares about me. That is the driving focus. I believe this is a party which is not so weighted with highly touted and high-flung people and ideas that they have become disconnected from what I care about. And it's not just for me as an individual, but also for the average person who gets up in the morning and goes to work and does the best job he or she can do.

I believe the Democratic Party can still be the Big Tent and that there is still room for everybody under the tent. We need to know that there is a party that hasn't forgotten about us. We cannot forsake our roots.

# SENATOR EDWARD M. KENNEDY

Allegiance to the Democratic Party is second nature for my family. For Irish immigrants in Boston, politics was one of the few avenues to a better life. It was the Democratic Party—the party of the common citizen, the party of the American dream—that gave them the voice and the opportunity they sought. My grandfathers, P. J. Kennedy and John Fitzgerald, "Honey Fitz," served together in the Massachusetts Senate in the 1890s, and "Honey Fitz" went on to serve for many years in Congress and as mayor of Boston.

My father joined Franklin D. Roosevelt's administration in the 1930s as the first chairman of the newly created Securities and Exchange Commission, and later served as ambassador to Great Britain on the eve of World War Two. I grew up in a home where discussions of politics and current events were nightly topics at the dinner table, and I learned the value of party principle and party organization by working in President Kennedy's campaigns for Congress, the Senate and the White House.

Circumstances change, but enduring values remain the same. In the two centuries of its history, the fundamental appeal of the Democratic Party has always been grounded in the principles of fairness, opportunity, equal justice for all and a firm belief that the mission of Government is not to stand on the sidelines, but to be active in pursuing these goals for the people.

From Jefferson to Jackson, from Wilson to FDR, from Truman to John Kennedy to Lyndon Johnson and Jimmy Carter, Democratic Presidents have led our country toward the fulfillment of these ideals at home and around the world.

Our heritage and history as Democrats are among our greatest assets in meeting and mastering the challenges ahead. People are not asking much from government—a job where they can work, not a place in the unemployment line; decent health care and education for their families; safe streets where they can walk at night; a fair opportunity to share in the blessings of this land.

The issues today are no more difficult than those which America faced in the past. What the country needs most is presidential leadership that brings us together and moves us forward, not drives us apart and holds us back. Like the New Deal in the 1930s and the New Frontier in the 1960s, the 1990s can be a new era of progress for our Party, our ideals and our country.

# SENATOR GEORGE McGOVERN

My mother and father lived and died as South Dakota Republicans. But I saw with my own eyes in the 1930s, as I was growing up, that the Democratic leadership was responding to the needs of the people I knew in my everyday life, dealing with the Depression and putting people to work on government projects. They were confronting a disastrous farm crisis. They brought rural electricity to the farm, to our state. It was a responsive party that was oriented to meet the needs of ordinary people—and the Republican Party was not. They were ignoring all those things, and that's when I first began to think my parents were in the wrong party.

I think the Rural Electrification Program was the one I found the most dramatically impressive. There's just no question that the conservative interest in the country opposed that program, and so did the big, private power companies. I just literally saw the lights come on in the barns and the farms and the little towns of South Dakota. Instead of people straining over kerosene lanterns and doing all the labor around the farmhouse by hand, all of a sudden, the lights began to come on across the prairies and the Great Plains. To me, that was one of the most dramatic reasons why I wanted to become a Democrat.

I thought Franklin Roosevelt provided equally brilliant leadership in World War Two. He was the only President I ever knew as a child growing up. I thought the leadership of Roosevelt was an inspiration to the American people, and that's what really reaffirmed my decision to go after the Democratic Party rather than the Republican Party. In later years, during the Kennedy-Johnson era, in particular, the Democratic Party was outstanding on the civil rights issue. So that was a big factor in my decision to stay with the Democrats.

Still today, by and large, the Democratic Party comes down on the side of the ordinary American more than the Republican Party does. The Republicans tend to resolve questions in favor of the rich and the powerful and the established. The Democrats have more of a sense of compassion and concern for ordinary citizens: the working people, the small business people, the farmers, those who are poor or handicapped in some way. Unless you're in the top 10 percent economically, the Democrats will better serve your interest than the Republicans.

Let me put it this way. When I think about the public programs that are now generally endorsed by both Republicans and Democrats, whether it's Social Security or student loans or civil rights or Medicare or collective bargaining—all of those things that are now accepted by just about everybody—began as Democratic initiatives over Republican opposition. I mean, eventually, the Republicans come around, but not until after years of foot dragging in opposition. So, I see the Democrats on the cutting edge of progress and the Republicans ordinarily delaying it.

# SENATE MAJORITY LEADER GEORGE J. MITCHELL

Mine was a working-class family. My father worked as a janitor and Mom worked nights in a textile mill through the dark days of the Depression. So it's not surprising that our family hero was Franklin Roosevelt and that my earliest political awareness was of FDR's vision for the Democratic Party—a party committed to social justice, to the economic well-being of the common man, to an agenda that gave all of us the same opportunity to share in the American dream.

That's what one of my heroes as a young man, John Kennedy, stood for and fought for during his years in office. So did another mentor and role model for whom I had the honor to work during my early years in politics: Senator Edmund Muskie. From both of these men, I learned that the government could help to promote the kind of society I thought America should become, the kind of community in which I wanted to live. It's in this belief, toward this end, that I've devoted my life as a Democrat.

The Democratic Party, I've come to understand, is an inclusive and diverse party whose principles are drawn from the same roots that guided the men who wrote our Constitution, from the enduring strengths and traditions of the American nation itself—the principle of an equal voice for everyone, of respect for the liberty of individual conscience and of tolerance for the liberties of others.

Throughout its history—and the nation's—the Democratic Party has been the party of expanded opportunity. It is Democrats who have worked to vindicate the civil rights of all Americans. Democrats have fought to empower the workers of this country, to ensure them of a share in the material prosperity of America, to give the children of plumbers and bricklayers—and janitors like my father—the chance to go to college with the sons and daughters of industrialists and governors.

In my lifetime, nine-year-old boys worked in coal mines and ten-year-old girls worked in textile mills. Democrats changed all that. We passed child-labor laws and fair-labor laws so that American boys and girls can spend their early years in school where they belong. It used to be that most Americans who reached the age of 65 could look forward only to a few years of poverty and misery. Democrats passed Social Security and Medicare to help elderly Americans keep their dignity and self-respect. We passed environmental laws that cleaned up our polluted rivers and began the clean-up of our polluted air.

The Democratic Party has made mistakes. It has sometimes strayed from its own beliefs. Its diversity had been known to tear it with dissension from within and without. But in the two-century span of American history, no institution, no organization has done as much to preserve the principles of democratic representative government on which our nation is founded. I'm proud to be a part of that tradition, and proud to share in that same commitment for the future.

# SPEAKER THOMAS P. "TIP" O'NEILL

I was born into the Party. What kept me there was the fact that I came from the other side of the tracks. It was the Depression of the Thirties, and unless you lived in it, you can't believe how miserable it was. You know, they talk about the "good old times," but the fact is that during the Depression, only three percent of America had health insurance and eight percent had pensions, and if you were fortunate enough to graduate from high school, only three percent went on to college. And 50 percent of America was impoverished, 25 percent were unemployed. It was Franklin Roosevelt who showed the way to the underclass and the needy of America. I was born in that neighborhood, and so I grew up in the Democratic Party and their beliefs and their feelings and concerns—that you never pull the ladder out from the guy behind you, that you try to help him.

When I was fourteen, I was getting seventeen cents an hour, mowing lawns, cutting bushes and spraying the flowers at Harvard. I remember graduation there one year, I was out working on the lawn while the graduates stood around in their Palm Beach suits drinking champagne. Champagne was then against the law, but the police blinked at them, and so did the officers at Harvard. I just thought it was the wrong thing to do. It was something I resented very, very much. I said to myself, some day I hope I can be a part of changing America.

It's something you feel deeply when you're from the other side of the yard, particularly in a city like Cambridge which is one-third industrial, one-third university and one-third working people in an area of six-and-a-half square miles. My people were the firemen and the policemen and the people who did the menial work. Our avenue to success was the Democratic Party. That's what it was all about.

When I was a youngster, there was always some needy family in the neighborhood. At Easter and at Christmas and at Thanksgiving, your political organization delivered baskets to those who needed them, and either your political party or your church ran the social activities of the area. So when I say I was born into it, there's no question about it. I loved it, and I loved what it stood for.

I saw America pull itself out of poverty and become the most powerful nation in the world. I remember in 1941 when we got into the war. We were unprepared, yet we became the arsenal of the world. I remember in 1951 when Harry Truman said we're not going to allow the expansion of communism, and so we went into Korea. I remember when Sputnik went up and Jack Kennedy became President and said we'd put a man on the moon and we did within ten years. So I've been a witness to many great events and great achievements in the course of my lifetime as a Democrat. And I've even lived to see that boyhood dream of mine come true—the dream that I would live to play a small part in changing America, in moving toward a more just society, a society that offers the same opportunities for everyone.

# GOVERNOR
# ANN RICHARDS

I grew up in a Texas where people might vote for a Republican presidential candidate once in a while, but card-carrying Republicans were so scarce that they were an endangered species. John Henry Faulk used to say that they were in such short supply, we should put them on a reservation where they could be protected from the real world. Winning the Democratic nomination was tantamount to winning the office. The serious fights were within the Party—where I was often on the losing but righteous side. I was in my thirties before a Republican won a statewide race—and that was because the Democrats were divided.

From our courting days, my husband and I attended political meetings like other couples go bowling or join dance clubs. We loved politics. We were active in the Young Democrats during graduate school at the University of Texas and, once our four kids arrived, we took the whole family to marches and rallies.

It was civil rights that drew us to politics, and the feeling that we could change people's lives for the better kept us involved. This country is still midway in a journey toward equality for minorities and women, but we have made progress. I am living proof. There was a time in her life when my grandmother did not have the right to vote. Less than one lifetime later, I am Governor of Texas. As the modern champion of the rights of minorities, women and working families, the Democratic Party opened the door for me. And in my public service, I am holding that door open wide for others who have been excluded in the past.

Like Adlai Stevenson, I make no pretense about the "wisdom, virtue or infallibility of Democrats." But Democrats have a right to be proud of their party and its leaders. The name Franklin Roosevelt still evokes a sense of common purpose and a government that can act to help when people are in need. Harry Truman gave the presidency back to the people and reminded us that common sense can make government work. John Kennedy's Peace Corps created a whole new way of looking at foreign relations—a personal, one-on-one approach that showed us we could move beyond the

diplomatic straightjacket and toward a new frontier of international cooperation. Lyndon Johnson demanded that, as a nation, we give more than lip-service to equality. He applied his immense legislative skills to the fulfillment of the American dream of liberty and justice for all. Jimmy Carter reminded us of the value of direct service to those who need help. Watching him build houses for the homeless instead of jetting here and there for one celebrity event after another makes us all proud.

One of my favorite Democrats is Eleanor Roosevelt. There's a wonderful story about Mrs. Roosevelt traveling by train across the country years ago. She looked out the window and saw clothes on a line drooping against the horizon. She made a note in her journal: two children's play suits, a denim workshirt, a pair of faded dungarees and a plain cotton dress. "Not much left to waste here." Others might have seen only clothes hanging on a line, but Eleanor saw the family.

That kind of insight is what this party is all about. Our party and our nation will always be strong when we have leaders who look beyond the statistics, whose commitment is to more than rhetoric, who actually see the families affected by their government. I believe that every bit as much as I did the day I cast my first vote.

# A F T E R W O R D

# *FACING THE CHALLENGES AHEAD*

## BY ROBERT B. REICH

Throughout its history, the Democratic Party has resisted escapism. Its mission has been to focus the public's attention on what must be done, and to mobilize the public to act. That mission is perhaps more vital today than ever before, for the tendency toward escapism in American society has grown. The great challenge ahead is to refocus America's energies on our life together.

America's two most recent Republican Presidents have assured the public that there is no cause for alarm: America has no major problems, faces no large challenges here or abroad, need not change in any fundamental way. Its remaining blemishes will disappear if we only allow them to be entrusted to the "magic of the marketplace" in which the lure of private profits automatically improves everyone's lives. To the extent that imperfections remain, we can count on individual acts of generosity to rectify them. There is simply no reason to join together as a nation, to mobilize our collective will and resources. We could not afford to do so in any event, it is said; we have more will than wallet.

Democrats do not agree with this cheerful diagnosis. They see growing poverty at home: Between 1973 and 1990, the median income of young families with children plunged by nearly one-third. By 1992, almost 30 percent of American children were living in poverty, more than a third of Americans were without health insurance and the level of infant mortality in the United States was higher than in 17 other nations. Democrats also are aware of the growing impoverishment of the Third World: Throughout the 1980s, family incomes in Latin America and sub-Sahara Africa have dropped. At this writing, the survival of many of the citizens of the former Soviet Union is precarious as well. Democrats see worsening environmental devastation; they witness the spreading scourge of AIDS; they acknowledge the problem of drugs and crime; they feel the intransigence of racism and sexism in society; they comprehend the danger of continued proliferation of nuclear weapons, the growing trade in armaments and the fragmentation of nations into warring tribes.

But Democrats are equally aware of this nation's capacities to address such problems—perhaps not to solve them immediately, or ever, but at least to ameliorate them. No civilization in history has possessed the resources available to the United States at the close of the twentieth century: the material resources of an economy generating six trillion dollars of wealth each year, with an average family income of $71,000 and the highest level of productivity among all nations; the intellectual resources of the world's largest network of colleges, universities, and public and private research laboratories, within which are found the largest concentration of scientific and technical knowledge in the history of mankind; the resilience of a system of democratic governance that has withstood two centuries of political conflict, founded on a set of constitutional principles still commanding widespread allegiance. And all of these resources are available at a time when the United State faces no foreign threat, when the Soviet Union has vanished from the earth.

Before it is possible to mobilize these capacities to address these problems, the American public as a whole must acknowledge both the problems and the capacities. The true test of Democratic leadership in the years to come—the essential challenge facing the Democratic Party and the vision it offers to America—will thus be to reengage the American people in its common task. The difficulty of doing so should not be underestimated, however. Escapism is now rampant. The mechanisms of avoidance and denial have taken firm hold in American society. They come in three forms, each of which threatens our survival as much if not more than any of the substantive problems now facing American society.

The first form of escapism—the trivialization of public discourse—is the diversion of the public's attention from serious discussion of public matters to personal details of public figures. The first challenge of Democratic leadership, accordingly, is to refocus public attention on the large questions of American life, and away from lesser important, yet more widely reported, "scandalous" revelations and titillations. "News" like this, which has dominated headlines, must be understood for what it is: a means of avoiding the real news. It not only replaces serious discourse, but it exists precisely in order to take the mind off more weighty matters. It thus fulfills the same diversionary function in society as does a music video.

Elections in recent years have displayed a similar diversionary quality. Surely a candidate's "character" is relevant to making an informed judgment about the candidate's capacity to function once in office. The potential mischief comes in determining what aspects of the candidate's personal history are relevant to the issue of "character." Here is where titillating "news" has become a means of diverting attention from real news—where gossip and innuendo have provided subtle means of avoiding the more difficult tasks of acknowledging the nation's problems and examining whether a candidate's ideas and temperament appear to be up the challenge.

The trivialization of public discourse is not entirely the fault of broadcast and print journalists—although, admittedly, the frantic media acquisitions of the 1980s transformed much of the American press corps from professionals into entertainers. The American public has been conditioned to want entertainment—to regard the news of the day as a form of escape from real life.

The conditioning has come gradually. The public's interest in the private peccadillos of a 1984 presidential candidate was, at most, ambivalent—inspired partly by the candidate's brashness about such matters. By 1992, not even the most intimate detail of personal history dredged up from decades before was out of bounds. How to explain the public's growing desire for personal revelation in place of substance? This aspect of escapism is a legacy of the Reagan presidency, during which time the public came to confuse leadership with celebrity.

Although the U.S. Presidents have always had certain ceremonial functions—much like the roles played by kings and queens in constitutional monarchies—Ronald Reagan, the experienced entertainer, played this ceremonial role so masterfully that the American public began to equate ceremony with political authority and to confuse personality with serious discourse about the nation's problems. Under Reagan, the President became the nation's toastmaster, the host and narrator of America's unfolding TV docudrama. As redefined by Reagan, the President's role was to welcome home brave soldiers, comfort the families of fallen heroes, celebrate the birthdays of national monuments, exult the nation's friends and condemn its enemies. He was the reflection of the nation's preferred self-image—bountiful, buoyant, effervescent. His was a presidency of carefully staged visuals, photo opportunities and pageantry.

Thus, when it came time to replace Ronald Reagan, or even to fill other elected offices, the public instinctively was more interested in personality—"character" in the sense of *People* magazine-type revelations about tastes, hobbies, pets, habits and friends—than in a candidate's record or positions on issues. And it became likewise legitimate for political opponents, and for the media, to dredge up whatever detail of a candidate's life that some members of the public might find distasteful—regardless of its relevance to the candidate's capacity to handle the nation's real problems once in office. By the early 1990s, serious political discourse in America had been supplanted by gossip.

A public accustomed to pageantry and gossip does not want to hear about America's larger problems. It does not want to be told that it must sacrifice today's pleasures for the sake of the future. The first task of Democratic leadership, therefore, is to tell Americans the truth.

The second form of escapism—the externalization of public responsibility—is the attribution of America's problems to malevolent forces beyond the nation's borders. Thus the second challenge to Democrats and the nation: to bring responsibility back home.

This tendency to blame others has a long history in America, of course, but it has grown in recent years as the United States has joined an increasingly interdependent world. It has led the nation to concentrate its efforts on warding off outside perils, often at the expense of tending to perils within. Too often in recent years, America has found it easier to feel righteous than responsible. That the nation could plan to spend upwards of $280 billion on weapons and troops in 1993 in order to defend itself against foreign dangers—more than the nation spent on defense in 1980 (adjusted for inflation) when the Soviet threat still existed, and far more than it planned to spend on the health and nutrition of its children—is the clearest evidence.

The same inclination can be found in other domains. In the 1980s, for example, the United States launched a major offensive against international drug trafficking. Enforcers resorted to all the techniques of modern warfare—spies, informants, fancy electronics, armored vehicles, helicopters. The effort cost the lives of several Andean peasants, drug runners and narcotics agents in the field; jeopardized American relations with several Latin American nations which we periodically accused of harboring drug traffickers; and culminated in an invasion of Panama.

There is no question about the dangerousness of drugs such as cocaine. But by defining the problem primarily as one of intercepting cocaine before it arrives in the United States, the evil has been declared external. Less emphasis has been placed on curbing the drug appetite of American citizens, who by 1992 were spending an estimated $110 billion a year on illegal drugs. With Americans willing and able to pay such sums to muddle their minds, no strategy to wreck the trade could be expected to succeed. Capitalism is a sturdy institution; enterprising drug traffickers are only slightly deterred by border patrols and helicopter gunships when so lucrative a market beckons. Drugs are at least half our problem. A fixation on the evil threatening our shores has diverted attention from this unsettling fact.

Americans employed in making textiles, steel, automobiles and other items, meanwhile, have become increasingly concerned about foreign goods arriving on American shores, and the consequential loss of jobs to Americans. This problem is understood, once again, as of foreign origin. Japanese and Third World producers are said to be "stealing our jobs" and "flooding our market" with their wares. We are being had, somehow. The apparent solution: Coerce them into holding back their wares to us and buying more of ours, and threaten them that, if they won't, we will put up higher barriers and close our borders more tightly.

There remains, though, the disconcerting fact that Americans want to buy these goods, and often do not make them as cheaply or as well as foreigners. If we did not have such an overwhelming desire for Japanese cars or South Korean steel or Taiwanese shirts, much of the "problem" would cease. Nor is it particularly useful to rail at "them" for not buying more of our products when American manufacturers fail to tailor their products to foreign markets. That American automakers have been unsuccessful in selling their products in Japan may have something to do with the fact that Japanese consumers prefer their steering wheels on the right, while the Big Three steadfastly prefer them on the left.

If foreign governments keep out American goods, it is perfectly reasonable for America to threaten retaliation. But if foreigners can do something better and more cheaply than Americans, the solution lies at home: We had best learn to do it as well, or learn to do something else that foreigners cannot so easily rival. To blame "them" for our competitive difficulties diverts attention from the real challenge. It is difficult to be competitive internationally when one out of every five American eighteen-year-olds is functionally illiterate and one out of four fails to graduate from high school, when Americans do not train their non-college employees or otherwise invest for the long term and when Wall Street withdraws money from any enterprise unable to demonstrate split-second profitability.

The nation's dependency on oil imports is another aspect of this externalization of responsibility. America has demonstrated steely resolve in defending the sovereignty of desert sheikdoms willing to supply us with oil—even to the extent of assembling the largest land and sea force since the Vietnam war, and killing tens of thousands of Iraqis. That Iraq's Saddam Hussein had been one of America's favorite despots before he issued the order to invade Kuwait did not alter our determination to prevent him from threatening our supply of oil.

Here again, however, the external threat has served as a means of psychological escape. The real responsibility is to be found on the home front: Were the United States to invest in conservation and in alternative sources of energy, the nation would become less vulnerable to the ambitions of small tyrants in foreign deserts. One of the most efficient means of encouraging conservation and spurring the search for alternative, and environmentally sustainable, energy supplies would be to raise the tax on gasoline. Such a move requires obvious sacrifice, however. It has been easier to fulminate against foreign aggressors, and to pretend that the cause of our energy insecurity lies beyond our borders.

The American public must accept responsibility for illegal drugs in our midst, for uncompetitive products produced in our factories, for our dependence on foreign oil and for other problems of our own making. The enemy is not "out there." Democrats should lead the conversion of America from a Cold War culture that spends vast sums of money defending itself from evil forces beyond its borders, to a post–Cold War culture that employs its resources to rebuild itself—physically and morally.

The third form of contemporary escapism—the secession from the national community—is perhaps the most insidious, for it threatens America's core understanding of nationhood. Many of the more fortunate and economically successful members of American society have been quietly seceding from the rest. Thus

the third great challenge of Democratic leadership in American society: to reengage the wealthy in the common good.

It is by now well established that the growth of the American economy during the 1980s did not benefit all Americans equally. In fact, families whose income placed them in the top fifth—incomes of at least $78,000 a year—received more than 100 percent of the growth in average family income. Families in the lower two-fifths actually lost ground. This trend would be less alarming had these beneficiaries continued to function as full participants in the rest of American society, but they have not.

Their escape has taken several forms. In many cities and towns, wealthier residents have in effect withdrawn their dollars from the support of public spaces and institutions shared by all and dedicated the savings to their own private services. As public parks and playgrounds have deteriorated, there has been a proliferation of private health clubs, golf clubs, tennis clubs and every other type of recreational association in which costs and benefits are shared exclusively among members. Condominiums and the omnipresent residential communities dun their members to undertake work that financially strapped local governments can no longer afford to do well—maintaining roads, mending sidewalks, pruning trees, repairing street lights, cleaning swimming pools and protecting life and property. The number of private security guards in the United States now exceeds the number of public police officers.

Most of America's large urban centers have splintered, in effect, into two separate cities: the first composed of professional, managerial and technical workers whose services are linked to the world economy; the second composed of custodians, security guards, taxi drivers, clerical aides, parking attendants, salespeople, restaurant workers and others whose services are provided in person. The wage gap between the two cities has grown. Meanwhile, the cities have created two school systems—a private one for the children of the first group and a public one for the children of the second.

People with high incomes live, shop and work within areas of cities that, if not beautiful, are at least aesthetically tolerable and reasonably safe. Precincts not meeting these minimum standards of charm and security have been left to the less fortunate. Public funds have been spent on downtown "revitalization" projects, entailing the construction of post-modern office buildings, multilevel parking garages, hotels with glass-enclosed atriums, upscale shopping plazas and galleries, theaters, convention centers and luxury condominiums. The wealthy are thus able to shop, work and attend the theater without risking direct contact with the outside world—that is, the other city.

When not living in urban enclaves, the fortunate fifth have been congregating in the suburbs or exurbs where corporate headquarters have been relocated, research parks have been created, and where bucolic universities have spawned entrepreneurial ventures. By the 1990s, real estate developers had even invented what they called "gated communities," surrounded by walls and security guards, whose inhabitants could quite literally escape from the problems besetting the remaining society. And the fortunate fifth were investing substantial sums in other forms of security: State governments' major capital expenditure was the building of new prisons; the fastest growing public-sector occupation was prison guard; and the second fastest growing public-sector occupation was security guard.

Wealthier Americans have been escaping into their own neighborhoods and clubs for generations, of course. But the new escapism is more complete because the highest earners now occupy a different economy from other Americans. Today's elite is linked by jet, modem, fax, satellite and fiber-optic cable to the great commercial and recreational centers of the world. Requests for their software designs, financial advice, management consulting services, legal insights or engineering blueprints may come from anywhere in the nation or on the globe. Meanwhile, their connections to the rest of the American economy have grown more attenuated.

This escapism has been encouraged by Federal policy. Between 1981 and 1992, Washington in effect shifted responsibility for many public services to local governments. At their peak in the late 1970s, Federal grants had made up 25 percent of state and local spending; by 1992, the Federal share had dwindled to 17 percent. Direct aid to local governments, in the form of programs introduced in the Johnson and Nixon administrations, has been the hardest hit by budget cuts. Federal dollars for clean water, job training, transfers, low-income housing, sewage treatment

and garbage disposal shrank by some $50 billion a year, and Washington's share of spending on local transit declined by 50 percent. In 1990, for example, New York city received only 1.6 percent of all its revenue from the Federal Government, compared with 16 percent in 1981.

The states, in turn, have transferred many of these new expenses to fiscally strapped cities and towns, with the result that by the start of the 1990s, localities were bearing more than half of the costs of water and sewage, roads, parks and public schools. Cities and towns with affluent inhabitants have been able to bear these burdens with relative ease. Poorer ones, faced with the twin problems of lower incomes and greater demand for social services, have had far more difficulty. And as the gap between America's richest and poorest communities has widened, the shift in responsibility for public services to cities and towns has functioned as another means of relieving wealthier Americans of the cost of aiding the less fortunate citizens. The result: A growing inequality in basic social and community services.

Many financially successful Americans continue to make charitable contributions, to be sure. In his speech accepting the presidential nomination in 1988, George Bush likened the magnanimity of Americans to "a thousand points of light." Studies reveal, however, that benevolence does not flow mainly to social services for the poor—to better schools, health clinics or recreational centers. Instead, most voluntary contributions of wealthy Americans go to the places and institutions that entertain, cure or educate wealthy Americans, such as art museums, opera houses, theaters, orchestras, ballet companies, private hospitals and elite universities. And even these contributions have become relatively skimpy. In 1990, American households with incomes of less than $10,000 gave an average of 5.5 percent of their earnings to charity or to a religious organization; those making more than $100,000 a year gave only 2.9 percent. After the 1988 tax-code overhaul reduced the benefits of charitable giving, the very rich became even stingier. According to Internal Revenue Service data, taxpayers earning $500,000 or more slashed their average donations from $47,432 in 1980 to $16,062 in 1988.

The third challenge facing Democrats and the nation will be to stop this secession, and to reclaim the energies and resources of America's fortunate citizens for the benefit of all. The goal should not be to redistribute their wealth to their less fortunate compatriots. Rather, it should be to invest the resources of the more fortunate members of society in the future productivity of their compatriots—in their education, training, child nutrition, roads and bridges, clean air and water—so that all Americans may gain ground together.

The combined effect of the three forms of escape chronicled here is large-scale denial: denial that the nation faces large problems, denial that the nation has the capacity to deal with large problems. The problems are not discussed—public discourse replaced by gossip and pageantry. Or the problems are blamed on other nations. Or fortunate Americans simply turn their backs on the problems, and erect walls to protect themselves from them.

It is in this respect that presidential leadership has been particularly disappointing in recent years. Rarely can an individual in American society command and focus the nation's attention as can the President of the United States. The President is, more than anything else, a teacher, whose words and deeds serve to remind the society of its goals and educate the society about how its goals can be achieved. Presidents of recent vintage have accomplished some important and useful things, but they have also done one terribly bad thing: They have convinced the American public that escapism is acceptable. They have encouraged the trivialization of public discourse, the externalization of public responsibility and the secession of that portion of the population most able to lend its hand.

The essential challenge of Democratic leadership in the future is to overcome this dangerous legacy of escapism. Nothing else can be done until this is accomplished. Then, almost everything is possible.

# PHOTO CREDITS

Page placement is denoted by: Top(T), Bottom(B), Left(L), and Right(R)

All photos courtesy of the Library of Congress except the following:

143(B), 153, 154 courtesy of AP/Wide World Photos

22-23, 27, 168(B), 170(T) courtesy of Architect of the Capitol

144, courtesy of the Jimmy Carter Presidential Center Library and Museum

200, Designed by Steven C. Carter and photographed by Robert M. Nash, Worcester, MA. All materials courtesy of The Museum of American Political Life, University of Hartford, Hartford, CT

70, courtesy of the Illinois State Historical Society

19, 25(T,R), 25(B,L), 46, 168(T), 180, 182, 184 courtesy of the Independence National Historical Park Collection

198, courtesy the Lyndon Baines Johnson Library

196, courtesy of the John Fitzgerald Kennedy Library

112, 118, 119, 120, 124(B), 125, 126, 127, 130, 131(T&B), 132(T&B), 133, 134, 135, 137, 139, 150, 163, 164, 166, 174(T&B), 175, 176, 177 courtesy of National Archives

2-3, courtesy National Graphics, Inc.

68-69, courtesy of the R.W. Norton Art Gallery, Shreveport, Louisiana

192, courtesy of the Franklin D. Roosevelt Library

55(B), 67(B), 75, 78, 83, 86, 92, 101(T), 114(B), 138, 142 courtesy of the Smithsonian Institution

194, courtesy of Greta Kempton, Harry S. Truman Library

128, 136, 143(T), 147(B), 149, 152, 165 copyright Washington Post; Reprinted by permission of the D.C. Public Library

# INDEX

abortion rights, 146, 152.
Acheson, Dean, Ill. 134, 135, 141.
Adams, Abigail, 30.
Adams, John, 14, 21, Ill. 29, 30-31, 33.
Adams, John Quincy, as President, 15, 47, Ill. 47, 49-50.
Adams, Samuel, 30.
AIDS, 215.
Alamo, Ill. 59.
Alien and Sedition Acts, 29, 32-33, 160.
Altgeld, John Peter, 90-92, Ill. 91.
Americans for Democratic Action (ADA), 134.
Anderson, Marian, 159.
Anti-Federalist Party, 21.
Army-McCarthy hearings, Ill. 136.
Articles of the Confederation, 20.
Atlantic Charter, 125.
Atomic Test Ban Treaty, 141.

Baker, Howard, 148.
Bank of North America, 19.
Bank of the United States, 19, 26-27, Ill. 26.
Battle of New Orleans, 44, Ill. 45.
"Battle of Standards" in 1836, 92.
Bay of Pigs, 140, 176.
Beckley, John, 30.
Begin, Menachem, and Camp David Accords, 150-151, Ill. 150, Ill. 177.
Benton, Thomas Hart, 50, Ill. 51, 53.
Blaine, James G., 87.
Bland, Richard, 90.
Boren, David, 155.
Bork, Robert, 155.
Bradley, Bill, 155; biography, 202, Ill. 202.
Brandeis, Louis D., 106.
Breckinridge, John C., 71, Ill. 71.
Britain, 17-18, 21, 24, 27-28, 32, 35, 41-43, 124, 171; and War of 1812, 43-44, "Old Ironsides vs. Guer-riere", Ill. 44; Battle of Lake Erie, Ill. 45; Battle of New Orleans, Ill. 45, 167.
Britain's Stamp Act of 1766, 28.
Bryan, William Jennings, 91-92, Ill. 92, Ill. 94, 95-100, Ill. 96, Ill. 100, 105-106, Ill. 105, 159, Ill. 161, 171; and "Cross of Gold" speech, 91, Ill. 93; and woman suf-frage, 99, 101, 162; biography, Ill. 188, 189.
Buchanan, James, 64, Ill. 67; as President, 70.
Burr, Aaron, 30, Ill. 32, 33.
Bush, George, 11, 12, 154, 219.
Butler, William, Ill. 64.

Calhoun, John C., Ill. 50, 50.
Cambodia, 145.
Camp David Accords, 150-151, Ill. 150, 177, Ill 177.
Carter, Jimmy, 149; as President, Ill. 144, 150-151, 160, 164, 177; and Panama Canal, 150, 177; and Camp David Accords, 150-151, Ill. 150, 177, Ill. 177; biography, 203, Ill. 203.
Cass, Lewis, 61, Ill. 64, 64.
Castro, Fidel, 140, 141.
Chesapeake, 41.
Child Labor Act of 1916, 162.
China, 135-136.
Church, Frank, 145, 149.
Churchill, Winston, 125, Ill. 126, 127, Ill. 174, Ill. 175.
civil rights, Ill. 76, 77-78, 134, 139-140, 141-142, Ill. 142, 146, 153, 155, 160, 164.
Civil Rights Act of 1866, Ill. 76.
Civil Rights Act of 1964, 140, Ill. 140, 141, 142, 160, 164.
Civil War, Ill. 62, 71-73, Ill. 72, 159, 171.
Civilian Conservation Corps (CCC), 163.
Clark, Champ, 100, 103.
classical republicanism, 13, 14.
Clay, Henry, 49-51, Ill. 51, 54, 57-58, Ill. 59; "Ameri-can System", 47, 51.
Clayton Anti-Trust Act, 106.

Cleveland, Grover, Ill. 80, 81, 86-87; as President, 87-88, Ill. 87, Ill. 89, 90-91, 160, 162, 171.
Clinton, Bill, 155; biography, 204, Ill. 204.
Clinton, George, 14.
Cohen, Richard, 154.
Cold War, 141, 155, 175-177, 218; origins of, 130.
Common Sense, (Paine), 17.
Confederacy, 62, 71-79, 159.
Congressional Budget and Impoundment Act, 149.
Connally, Tom, 135.
Constitution, 14, 20-21, signing of, Ill. 22-23.
Constitutional Convention, Ill. 20, 21.
Constitutionalist Party, 18-19.
Continental Army, 21.
Continental Congress, 16, 30.
Coolidge, Calvin, 115; as President, 116.
Copperheads, 74, 159.
Cox, James M., Ill. 110, 111, 117.
Creel, George, 108.
Cross of Gold speech, 91, Ill. 93.
Cuba, 96-97; and Bay of Pigs, 140, 176.
Cuban Missile Crisis, 140-141, 176.
Cuomo, Mario, 153.

Davis, Henry, Ill. 98.
Davis, Jefferson, 74, 159.
Davis, John W., 115.
Declaration of Independence, 16, 17-18, Ill. 16 Ill. 18, 30.
Debs, Eugene V., 105, 108, 111.
Democratic Party, origins of, 13-15, 48, 50-51.
Democratic Republican Party, 15, 27, 33, 50-51.
Democratic-Republican societies, 28-29.
Dever, Paul, 137.
Dewey, Thomas E., 126, 133, 134.
Dickens, Charles, 95.
Douglas, Stephen, 64, Ill. 65, 71-72, 75, 159; and Kansas-Nebraska Act, 66-67, Ill, 66; and Lincoln-Douglas Debate, Ill. 70, 71.
Dred Scott decision, 71.
Dukakis, Michael, 154.
Dunne, Finley Peter, 145.

Egypt, and Camp David Accords, 150-151, Ill. 150; 177, Ill. 177.
Eisenhower, Dwight D., 134, 136, 137, 139.
Ervin, Sam, 148, Ill. 149.
escapism, 215-220.

factionalism, 13-14, 28.
Fair Deal, 134, 141, 164.
Farley, James A., 119, Ill. 124.
Federal Deposit Insurance Corporation, 122.
Federal Reserve Act, 106, 162.
Federalist Party (Federalists), origins of, 13-15, 17-33.
Ferraro, Geraldine, 153-154, Ill. 153; biography, 205, Ill. 205.
Fifteenth Amendment, 78.
Fillmore, Millard, 67.
Findley, William, 18-19, Ill. 19, 21.
Follette, Robert La, 116.
Ford, Gerald, 149.
Forrestal, James V., Ill. 131.
Founding Fathers, 13, 17.
Fourteen Points Speech, 107-108, Ill. 109, 172.
France, 27-28, 31-32, 36, 37, 41-43, 130, 167, Ill. 169, 177; Revolution, 27-28, 36.
Frank, Barney, 155.
Franklin, Benjamin, and Declaration of Indepen-dence, 16.
Free Soil Party, 61.
Freedman's Bureau, 78.
Freemont, John C., 67.
Fries Rebellion, 32.
Fulbright, J. William, 177.

Gallatin, Albert, 31, 37, Ill. 37, 39.
Garfield, James A., 85.
Garner, John Nance, Ill. 117, 119.
gay rights, 146, 152.
Germany, and World War One, 106-108, Ill. 108, 172; and World War Two, 124, 129, 133 173-175, Ill. 173, 177; and Berlin Wall, Ill. 139, 140, 176.
Gilded Age, 81-82, 88-89.
Godfrey, Arthur, 129.
Goldwater, Barry, 141.
Gore, Albert, biography, 206, Ill. 206.
Grand Old Party (GOP), 82, 84.
Grant, General Ulysses, 75-76; as President, 77, 81, 83.
Great Depression, 117, 119, 163.
Great Society, 141-142, 164-165.
Greece, 130, 175.
Greeley, Horace, 77, Ill. 79, 81.
Gromyko, Andrei, Ill. 176.

Halberstam, David, 142.
Haldeman, H.R., Ill. 149.
Haley, Alex, 160.
Halpin, Maria, 87.
Hamilton, Alexander, 13-14, 21, 24-28, Ill. 25, 30, 32-33, 37, 39, 157; as first secretary of the treasury, 35-36.
Hancock, General Winfield Scott, 85, Ill. 85.
Hanna, Mark, 96.
Harding, Warren G., 113.
Harrison, Benjamin, as President, 88.
Harrison, William Henry, 55; as President, 56-57, Ill. 56.
Hart, Gary, 153.
Hayes, Rutherford B., 83-84.
Hayne, Robert Y., 53.
Hearst, William Randolph, 96.
Hendricks, Thomas A., Ill. 80, Ill. 84.
Hickory Clubs, 51-52.
Hiroshima, Ill. 131.
Homestead Strike, Ill. 90.
Hoover, Herbert, 115, 119.
"Hooverton," Ill. 158.
Howe, Louis, 117.
Hughes, Charles Evans, 106.
Humphrey, Hubert H., 134, 142, 143 , Ill. 147, 160.
Hussein, Saddam, 218.

imperialism, 97, 171, Ill. 171, 172.
Indian Removal Act of 1830, 53.
Indians, 41, Ill. 43, 53, 159, 164, 169.
Inter-State Commerce Act of 1887, 90.
Iran, 130; and hostage crisis, 151, Ill. 151.
Israel, Ill. 132, 133; and Camp David Accords, 150-151, Ill. 150; 177, Ill. 177.
Italy, 130.

Jackson, Andrew, 15, Ill. 48, 49-52, 61, Ill. 61; as Presi-dent, 52-56, Ill. 52, 159, 160; and "bank war", 19, 53-54, Ill. 54, Ill. 55, 159; biography, Ill. 186, 187.
Jackson, Jesse L., 153, 154, Ill. 154; biography, 207, Ill. 207.
Japan, 217; and World War Two, 129-130, Ill. 131, 173.
Jay, John, 28.
Jefferson, Thomas, 13-14, 17-18, 21, 25-33, Ill. 27, Ill. 34, 155, 157; as President, 34-42, 160, 167, Ill. 168, 177; and Declaration of Independence, Ill. 16, 17-18, 165; biography, Ill. 180, 181.
Johnson, Andrew, as President, 76-77.
Johnson, Hugh, 163.
Johnson, Lyndon B., 141, Ill. 165; as President, 141-142, 155, 157, 160, 219; and Civil Rights Act of 1964, Ill. 140, 141, 142, 164-165; and Voting Rights Act of 1965, 141; and Great Society, 141-142, 164-165; and War on Poverty, 141, 164; and Vietnam War, 142, Ill. 143, 176; biography, Ill. 198, 199.

Jordan, Barbara, 148; biography, 208, Ill. 208.

Kai-shek, Chiang, 135.
Kansas-Nebraska Act, 66-67, Ill. 66.
Kearney, General Stephen, 60.
Kelly, John, 78.
Kennedy, Edward M., 151, 153, 155; biography, 209, Ill. 209.
Kennedy, John F., 137-139, Ill. 138; as President, Ill. 128, 139-141, Ill. 139, 155, 157, 160, 164, Ill. 165, 176, Ill. 176; and New Frontier, 139-140; and Cuban Missile Crisis, 140-141, 176; and Atomic Test Ban Treaty, 141, 176; and Vietnam, 141; biography, Ill. 196, 197.
Kennedy, Robert F., 142-143, Ill. 143.
Kerrey, Robert, 155.
Khomeini, Ayatollah, 151.
King, Dr. Martin Luther, Jr., 139, 142, 160.
Korean War, 135, Ill. 135, 175, 176.
Ku Klux Klan, 113, 115.

laissez-faire, 83, 86.
League of Nations, 107-111, 113.
Lenin, Vladimir Ilyich, 172.
Lewis & Clark, Ill. 39.
Lincoln, Abraham, Ill. 70; as President, 71, 73, Ill. 73, 75-76, 104, 159.
Lincoln-Douglas debate, Ill. 70, 71.
Lippmann, Walter, 119.
Livingston, Robert R., 40, Ill. 168.
Log Cabin Campaign, Ill. 55.
Louisiana Purchase, 39, Ill. 40, 167, Ill. 168.
Lovett, Robert, 133.
Lundestat, Gier, 133.
*Lusitania*, 106.

Mabus, Raymond, 155.
MacArthur, General Douglas, 135-136.
Maclay, William, 21.
Madison, James, 13-14, 25-31, Ill. 25, as President, Ill. 42, 43-47, 160, 167; biography, Ill. 182, 183.
Manifest Destiny, 57-58, Ill. 57, 59, 169-171, Ill. 170.
Marijuana, legalization of, 146.
Marshall, George C., Ill. 131, 133.
Marshall Plan, 130, 175.
Maurols, Andre, 163.
McAdoo, William Gibbs, 113-115, Ill. 114.
McCarthy, Eugene, 142.
McCarthy, Joseph, 136, and Army-McCarthy hearings, Ill. 136.
McClellan, General George, 72, Ill. 73, 74-76, Ill. 74.
McGovern, George, 145-147, Ill. 147; biography, 210, Ill. 210.
McKinley, William, 92; as President, 96-97, Ill. 171.
Medicaid, 141, 165.
Medicare, 141, 165.
Mexican War, 58-61, 171; and Alamo, Ill. 59; and Chapultepec, Ill. 170.
Mexico, 171.
Miller, Arthur, 164.
Missouri Compromise, 66-67.
Mitchell, George J., biography, 211, Ill. 211.
Mondale, Walter, 149, 153, Ill. 153.
Monroe, James, 15, 40, 167, Ill. 168; as President, Ill. 46, 47, 169; biography, Ill. 184, 185.
Monroe Doctrine, 46, 47, 169.
Montesquieu, 18.
Monticello, 30.
Morgan, J. Pierpont, 159.
Muskie, Edmund, 145.

Napoleon, 40, 168.
National Labor Relations Board (NLRB), 163.
National Youth Administration, 164.
Neutrality Acts, 173, Ill. 173.
New Deal, 119, 120, 121-123, Ill. 121, Ill. 122, Ill. 123, 126, 134, 135, 136, 160, Ill. 160, Ill. 164.
New Freedom, 104-106, 162.
New Frontier, 139-140, 141.
Nineteenth Amendment, 111, 162.

Nixon, Richard, 139, 143, 147, 164, 219; and Watergate, 147-149.
North Atlantic Treaty Organization (NATO), 133, Ill. 134, Ill. 166, 175.
Nunn, Sam, 155.

O'Neill, Thomas P. "Tip," 152, Ill. 152; biography, 212, Ill. 212.
O'Sullivan, John L., 57, 169, 170.

Paine, Thomas, 17.
Pakenham, Sir Edward, 45.
Palmer, A. Mitchell, 109.
Panama Canal, 97, 98, 150, 177.
Parker, Alton B., 97-98, Ill. 98, 99.
Peace Corps, 140.
Perry, Captain Oliver, 45.
Philippines, 97, 171.
Pierce, Franklin, 65-66, Ill. 65.
Pinckney, Charles Cotesworth, 31, 33, 39.
Polk, James Knox, 57, Ill. 58; as President, 58-61, 170-171.
Populist Party (also known as Populists and People's Party), 90, 92, Ill. 96.
Prohibition, 98-99, Ill. 101, 113, 115, 163.
Puerto Rico, 97.
Pulitzer, Joseph, 96.
Pullman Strike of 1894, 91.

Randall, Sam, 83, 86.
Randolph, Edmund, 21.
Reagan, Ronald, as President, 11, 12, 152-153, 216.
Reconstruction, 63, 76-78.
Reconstruction Finance Corporation (RFC), 162.
Red Scare, 105, 109, 111, 113 (see also Eugene V. Debs).
Republican Party of 1792 (later became modern Democratic Party; see also Democratic-Republican Party and Democratic Party), origins of, 13-15, 17-33.
Republican Party of 1856 (modern Republican Party), origins of, 13-15, 66(caption), 70.
Revolution, American, 18, 20-21, 28.
Richards, Ann, 155; biography, 213, Ill. 213.
Rockefeller, Jay, 155.
Roosevelt, Eleanor, 111, 117, Ill. 118, 121, 134, 159, 163.
Roosevelt, Franklin Delano, 9, 11, Ill. 105, Ill. 110, 111, 117, Ill. 118, 119; as President, Ill. 112, 119-127, Ill. 119, Ill. 120, Ill. 125, Ill. 127, 129, 155, 159, 163-164, 165, Ill. 174, 177; and New Deal, 119, 120, 121-123, 125-126,135, 159, 160, 162-164, Ill. 164; and World War Two, 124-126, Ill. 124, Ill. 126; 173-175, Ill. 173, Ill. 174; biography, Ill. 192, 193.
Roosevelt, Theodore, 97; as President, 97-98, Ill. 99, 100, Ill. 102, 102-105, 111, 117.
Rush, Benjamin, Dr., 33.

Sadat, Anwar, and Camp David Accords, 150-151, Ill. 150, Ill. 177.
Scott, General Winfield, 60, 66.
Sevareid, Eric, 148.
Seymour, Horatio, 77, Ill. 77.
Shelby, Richard, 155.
Sherman Anti-Trust Act, 90.
Sherman Silver Purchase Act, 90.
Sinclair, Upton, 98.
slavery, 61, 66-67, 71-72, 75, 76, 159, 169, 171; and the Declaration of Independence, 17-18.
Smith, Alfred, E., 113-116, Ill. 116.
Social Security Act of 1935, Ill. 119, 122, 164.
Sons of Liberty, 28.
Spanish-American War, 97, 171.
*Spirit of the Laws*, 18.
Stalin, Josef, Ill. 126, 127, Ill. 174, Ill. 175.
Steffens, Lincoln, 98.
Stevenson, Adlai, 136-137, Ill. 137, 157, Ill. 158.
Stimson, Henry L., Ill. 131.

Taft, William Howard, 98; as President,100, 102.

Tammany Hall, 78, Ill. 82, 83.
Taylor, John, 32.
Taylor, General Zachary, 60-61.
Tecumseh, 41, Ill. 43.
Thoreau, Henry D., 15.
Thurmond, Strom, 134.
Tilden, Samuel, 77, 83-84, Ill. 84.
Tillman, Ben, 90-91, Ill. 91.
Tocqueville, Alexis de, 15.
Trade Expansion Act of 1962, 139.
Treaty of Ghent, 47.
Treaty of Guadalupe Hidalgo, 60.
Treaty of Versailles, 172.
Truman, Harry S., 9, Ill. 125, 126; as President, 129-136, Ill. 130, Ill. 132, Ill. 133; 155, 159, 175-176, Ill. 175; and World War Two, 129-130, Ill. 131; and United Nations, 130, Ill. 132; and NATO, 133, Ill. 134, Ill. 166; and Fair Deal, 134, 164; and Korean War, 135-136; biography, Ill. 194, 195.
Truman Doctrine, 130, 175.
Turkey, 130, 175.
Twain, Mark, 81.
Tweed, William "Boss", 78, Ill. 82, 83.
Twelfth Amendment, 14, 33.
Twenty-Sixth Amendment, 146.
Tyler, John, 56, Ill. 56; as President, 57, 58.

Underwood, Oscar W., 102.
Underwood-Simmons tariff, 106.
Union, 61, 63, 71-79, 159.
United Nations, 125, 130, Ill. 132, 135, 173-175.
*USS Missouri*, 129.
U.S.S.R., 130, 133, 135, 140-141, 142, 151, 169, 175, 215, 216; and Cold War, 130(origin of), 141, 155, 175-177, 218.

Vallandigham, Clement C., 72-73.
Van Buren, Martin, 15, 50, Ill. 50; as President, 55-57.
Vietnam War, 141, 142, 145, 176-177; demonstrations against, Ill. 146.
Voting Rights Act of 1965, 141, 165.

Wagner Act of 1935 (also known as National Industrial Recovery Act), 122, 163.
Wallace, Henry, Ill. 125, 126, 134.
War of 1812, 43-44, 167; "Old Ironsides vs. Guerriere", Ill. 44; Battle of Lake Erie, Ill. 45; Battle of New Orleans, Ill. 45.
War on Poverty, 141, 164.
War Powers Act, 145.
Warner, Charles Dudley, 81.
Washington, George, 13-14; as President, 21, 24, Ill. 24, 28-29.
Watergate, 147-149, Ill. 148, Ill. 149.
Webster, Daniel, 52, Ill. 53.
Wechsler, James, 134.
Welch, Joseph, 136.
Whigs, 15, 55-57, 61, 64, 67, 70.
Wicker, Tom, 164.
Wilder, Douglas, 155.
Willkie, Wendell, 124.
Wilmot, David, 61.
Wilson, Woodrow, 102-105, Ill. 103; as President, 105-111, Ill. 104, Ill. 105, Ill. 109, 117, 159, 171-172, 177; and New Freedom, 104-106, 155, 162; and World War One, 106-109, Ill. 107, 171, 172, Ill. 172; and League of Nations, 107-111, 130, 172; biography, Ill. 190, 191.
woman suffrage, 99, Ill. 101, Ill. 162; and Nineteenth Amendment, 111, 162.
Wood, Fernando, 71.
Woodward, C. Vann, 146.
World War One, 106-109, Ill. 108, 113.
World War Two, 124-126, 129-130, Ill. 131, 173-175, Ill. 173.

XYZ Affair, 31-32.

Yalta Conference, Ill. 126, 127.